The Neurobiology of
Attachment-Focused Therapy

The Norton Series on Interpersonal Neurobiology
Louis Cozolino, PhD, Series Editor
Allan N. Schore, PhD, Series Editor, 2007–2014
Daniel J. Siegel, MD, Founding Editor

The field of mental health is in a tremendously exciting period of growth and conceptual reorganization. Independent findings from a variety of scientific endeavors are converging in an interdisciplinary view of the mind and mental well-being. An interpersonal neurobiology of human development enables us to understand that the structure and function of the mind and brain are shaped by experiences, especially those involving emotional relationships.

The Norton Series on Interpersonal Neurobiology provides cutting-edge, multidisciplinary views that further our understanding of the complex neurobiology of the human mind. By drawing on a wide range of traditionally independent fields of research—such as neurobiology, genetics, memory, attachment, complex systems, anthropology, and evolutionary psychology—these texts offer mental health professionals a review and synthesis of scientific findings often inaccessible to clinicians. The books advance our understanding of human experience by finding the unity of knowledge, or consilience, that emerges with the translation of findings from numerous domains of study into a common language and conceptual framework. The series integrates the best of modern science with the healing art of psychotherapy.

A Norton Professional Book

The Neurobiology of Attachment-Focused Therapy

Enhancing Connection and Trust
in the Treatment of Children and Adolescents

Jonathan Baylin and Daniel Hughes

W. W. Norton & Company
Independent Publishers Since 1923
New York • London

Note to Readers: Standards of clinical practice and protocol change over time, and no technique or recommendation is guaranteed to be safe or effective in all circumstances. This volume is intended as a general information resource for professionals practicing in the field of psychotherapy and mental health; it is not a substitute for appropriate training, peer review, and/or clinical supervision. Neither the publisher nor the author(s) can guarantee the complete accuracy, efficacy, or appropriateness of any particular recommendation in every respect.

For information about permission to reproduce selections from this book, write to Permissions, W. W. Norton & Company, Inc., 500 Fifth Avenue, New York, NY 10110

For information about special discounts for bulk purchases, please contact W.W.Norton Special Sales at specialsales@wwnorton.com or 800-233-4830

Manufacturing by LSC Harrisonburg
Production manager: Christine Critelli

Library of Congress Cataloging-in-Publication Data

Names: Baylin, Jonathan F., author. | Hughes, Daniel A., author.
Title: The neurobiology of attachment-focused therapy : enhancing connection
   and trust in the treatment of children and adolescents / Jonathan Baylin
   and Daniel A. Hughes.
Description: First edition. | New York : W.W. Norton & Company, [2016] |
   Series: The Norton series on interpersonal neurobiology | Series: A
Norton
   professional book | Includes bibliographical references and index.
Identifiers: LCCN 2016012930 | ISBN 9780393711042 (hardcover)
Subjects: LCSH: Attachment disorder in children—Treatment. | Parent and
   child.
Classification: LCC RJ507.A77 B39 2016 | DDC 618.92/8588—dc23 LC record
available at https://lccn.loc.gov/2016012930

W. W. Norton & Company, Inc., 500 Fifth Avenue, New York, N.Y. 10110
www.wwnorton.com

W. W. Norton & Company Ltd., 15 Carlisle Street, London W1D 3BS

3 4 5 6 7 8 9 0

For Youngblood and Tyree and the yet unborn to B. and A.,
the future —Jonathan Baylin

For the Members of the DDPI Community —Daniel Hughes

Contents

Contents

Preface

Three Layers of Transparency

The screen door is partially open
  to allow for the cat to come in
  and go out at his leisure
This space opens to the outside air
  and my arm could easily reach through
  to that freshness
The screen door, in a more reserved and veiled way,
  also allows the cool morning air
  to pass through to the inside
Further to the left of the screen is the glass sliding door
  a hard clear shell that, too, allows light to pass through
  but clearly defines inside and outside,
Three layers of transparency,
  three ways of being
There are times I am glass
  when I allow things in and peer out at the world
  but remain separate and distinctly myself
At times I am the screen
  permeable, allowing light and air to pass through from
  either side
  with only a skin of protection
when trust has begun to deepen with ones I love
And the open space, that's what I long to be
  when all barriers have dissolved

when the air inside is no different than the air outside
and I am free to roam fearlessly in all the spaces
When compassion for myself floods into the open space of
compassion for all
—Eric Baylin, August 2015

Stephanie and Chad were quite happy with their life together in a peaceful suburb on the outskirts of St. Louis. They had two remarkable teen girls who seemed to defy the rumors that the teen years would be rocky, good careers that were satisfying and provided for their needs and more, and strong extended families—what more could they ask for? They felt they had more to give and more room in their family for a child who needed a home. After many discussions with their daughters, friends, and a social worker, they chose to adopt, and within a year welcomed nine-year old Mark into their home. He had a very difficult history but seemed to be doing well in his latest foster home and they had confidence—supported by their social worker—that they could provide Mark with the home he needed.

Within four or five months, they began to have doubts. They had been patient with Mark's forgetfulness about the rules and few chores he was assigned. They knew he needed time to adjust, but after the first few weeks when he seemed to show a forced cheerfulness, he seemed chronically unhappy. He did not seem to enjoy things they did for him or with him. Nor did he ask for their help when he couldn't do something or when he made a mistake. Instead, he would lie about his mistakes and become irritated when they doubted him. Gradually his irritation became anger and his anger became severe, marked with threats and running to his room and refusing to talk.

Stephanie and Chad sought psychological treatment and spoke with a counselor while Mark saw his own therapist. After another four or five months, their doubts increased. The therapist said that

Mark needed time, but his behavior was only getting worse at home and at school. What bothered them the most was what Mark said to them. Often he said that he hated them, he didn't want to live with them, they weren't his parents and never would be. When they gave him consequences for his behavior, he would threaten to pay them back and then he did. Things in their home disappeared or were broken. The hardest was when Mark started to treat their daughters as badly as he treated them.

A year after Mark entered their home, they barely remembered the family they used to have, the family they wanted to share with him. They bickered with each other and spent more time away from home. They now experienced little laughter or joy. Stephanie and Chad were convinced that they had made a horrible mistake in adopting Mark. They felt trapped. They had long since stopped feeling love for him. He was a duty, a job. What had happened?

After receiving good care from Stephanie and Chad for a year, Mark still did not trust them. If anything, he trusted them less, finding more reasons each day to justify never trusting them. As the weeks and months passed and their irritation increased, he became more convinced that they were not trustworthy. What would it take for Mark to move from mistrust to trust? Whatever it was, it was now less likely to happen because Stephanie and Chad began to stop caring. If good care was not helping, poor care was not likely to do so. It was now a perfect storm. Mark came to his adoptive family with blocked trust, and nothing that his adoptive parents, social worker, or therapist could do enabled him to begin to trust. Stephanie and Chad were now in blocked care. Even if Mark were somehow able to take a tentative step toward beginning to trust, they were not likely to see it or respond to it. Their primary response was defensiveness. They were protecting their hearts from the pain of enduring his anger and rejection for months and months.

This book is written for people like Mark, Stephanie, and Chad. If trust is to develop and care is to be restored, we have to know what is preventing the development of trust in the first place when a child is living in an environment of good care for a long period of time. What do abuse and neglect do to the development of children's brains that makes it so difficult for them to trust adults who are so different from those who hurt them? We have to know what we—both parents and professionals—might do to encourage the development of such trust.

Acknowledgments

To Dan, my coauthor and friend, thanks for bringing me into the international world of attachment-focused treatment and connecting me with all of the wonderful therapists in the dyadic developmental psychotherapy network. Thanks for being receptive to early morning musings about the brain and therapy, even when your first reaction is sometimes "that dog won't hunt." Brothers Eric and Steve, thanks for continuing to inspire me as we move ever deeper into elderhood. To my young colleagues in practice, Brian, Christy, Liz, and Stacey, thanks for being such eager students of the brain and innovative therapists embracing the complex work of attachment therapy. Brain group, now many years together, thanks for the always stimulating monthly discussions when we "put the brain in therapy." To Jessica Sinarski, thanks for your enthusiasm and organizational skills in putting together the mental health counselors' brain study program. Zach, Kate, Ben, Abby, my "kids," the four of you give me hope for the future with your passion for life and your creativity. To Ben Yarling at Norton, thanks for being such a supportive, patient, and precise editor, for helping make this book much more readable. Thanks, too, to the rest of the able folks at Norton for helping give birth to this project. Finally, I give thanks to my wife, Sarah, known to some as Porgy, my partner in all things lo these many years since we met as teenagers, then only looking forward, now often looking back, with wonderful memories of 50 years of a good marriage, now, too, blessed with M and M.

—Jonathan Baylin

Acknowledgments

Thanks to you, Jon, for our lively discussions about all things psychological and neuropsychological and for those chats, too, that extended to the meaning of life, especially grandchildren and baseball. And thanks to the many therapists and professionals who were with me in the development and practice of dyadic developmental psychotherapy. There are too many to mention them all, but I would like to give a bit of recognition to Deb Shell and Robert Spottswood in the US, Sian Phillips in Canada, and Geraldine Casswell, Kim Golding, Edwina Grant, and Julie Hudson in the UK. Thanks to my kids, Megan, Kri, and Maddie and my grandkid, Alice Rose. Being with you four gives new meaning to the terms comfort and joy.

—Daniel Hughes

The Neurobiology of
Attachment-Focused Therapy

Introduction

If we are to protect young children from harm . . . we will have to value more and give response to what children bring to human life—the eager spirit of their joyful projects beyond their seeking to survive."
—Colwyn Trevarthen (2013, p. 203)

How can therapists and caregivers help maltreated children recover what they were born with: the potential to experience the safety, comfort, and joy of having trustworthy, loving adults in their lives? This is the topic of this book. The authors have been collaborating for a number of years now about the treatment of maltreated children and their caregivers. Both experienced psychologists, we're committed to helping these children learn to trust caregivers and helping caregivers be the "trust builders" these children need. Our shared project is developing a science-based model of attachment-focused therapy that links clinical interventions to the underlying biobehavioral processes of trust, mistrust, and trust-building.

Our approach is embedded in the growing field of interpersonal neurobiology (IPNB) (Siegel, 2012; Schore, 2013), a clinical model that seeks to inform psychotherapy with the exploding knowledge from social neuroscience. In particular, we draw from (1) research showing how early exposure to poor care tunes the child's brain for living defensively (Perry et al., 1995; Cushing & Kramer, 2005; Roth et al., 2006; Beach et al., 2010; Tottenham, 2012; Meaney, 2013) and (2) research showing that later in life, "enriched" social experiences can retune the brain and support a biobehavioral shift from mistrust to trust, reawakening and strengthening the child's capacity for social engagement (Branchi, Francia, & Alleva, 2004; Weaver, Meaney, & Szyf, 2006; Curley et al., 2009; Dozier, Meade, & Bernard, 2014; Humphreys et al., 2015; Moretti et al., 2015).

Our earlier work on the development of a brain-based model of caregiving led to the book *Brain-Based Parenting* (Hughes & Baylin, 2012), in which we focused mostly on the neurodynamics of parenting, introducing the concept of blocked parental care, or simply blocked care. In this book, we turn our attention to children who are forced by poor care to develop what we call blocked trust: the suppression of inherent relational needs for comfort and companionship to survive neglect and abuse. How do infants, who are not aware of learning anything, learn to trust and mistrust adults? Once young children develop blocked trust, is this learned defensiveness reversible? Can their blocked potential for trusting in the care of a trustworthy adult be reawakened after years of living defensively? Can these children learn to feel the social emotions—separation pain, remorse, empathy, joy of connection—that they had to suppress to be asocial earlier in life? If so, how do they make this journey from mistrust to trust, and what needs to happen in their relationships with caring adults to facilitate this shift? How do their caregivers avoid the risk of blocked care from repeated experiences of being mindlessly mistrusted and manage somehow to sustain their compassion for these complicated hurt children? How can caregivers, therapists, and other adults send strong, consistent messages of safety and approachability deep into those mistrusting brains where safety and danger are first detected?

Children develop blocked trust in response to frightening and painful relational experiences with adults. Neuroscientific research reveals that these experiences sensitize a neural "alarm system" (Liddell et al., 2005) called the mid-brain defense system, laying the foundation for chronic defensiveness, the core of blocked trust. At the same time, maltreatment suppresses the development of the child's "social engagement system" (Porges, 2011), the brain system that would normally be activated and strengthened by good care. Maltreatment triggers chemical reactions in children's brains that decrease subjective suffering from the pain of rejection and abuse (Lanius, Paulsen, & Corrigan, 2014) while enabling them to remain vigilant and defensive around uncaring caregivers. This combination of pain suppression and chronic, mindless defensiveness is at the heart of the deep emotional disengagement and mistrust we see in these children. Treatment for blocked trust has to target the mid-brain alarm system, disarm it, and remove the blockage that keeps the child from feeling the need for care and comfort from adults. To accomplish this, children need to have comforting, enjoyable experiences with adults, experiences that can awaken their brains to experience the safety they have never known. They need to hear the caring voices, see the shining eyes, and feel the loving touch of people who somehow manage to keep caring deeply about them in the face of their mistrust.

Dyadic Developmental Psychotherapy: A Brain-Based and Attachment-Focused Model

Dyadic developmental psychotherapy (DDP) is a model of treatment that is squarely focused on providing the kind of safe, trustworthy experiences with adults that can facilitate this brain-shifting process and help children with blocked trust move from chronic defensiveness toward open engagement (Hughes, 2006; 2007; 2011). DDP targets the heart of blocked trust: the social brain switch where the implicit process of appraising safety and danger begins. In this brain circuit, we use crude sensory information such as facial expressions to appraise trustworthiness at a preconscious level faster than we can be aware that we are appraising anything. This is where attachment-focused therapy needs to work; this, as Sebern Fisher (2014) so powerfully puts it, is the "epicenter" of the chronic defensiveness at the heart of blocked trust and developmental trauma. Crucially, the DDP therapist embraces the child's defensiveness, putting connection before correction, knowing that the child had to develop this core relational strategy to survive poor care. This radical acceptance of the child's mistrust (which can feel like hugging a porcupine) is essential to the process of helping a mistrusting child begin to trust.

Maltreated children who have never felt safe with caregivers need to experience safety on at least three basic levels: (1) safety to feel the pain of disconnection and to seek comfort from a trustworthy adult; (2) safety to engage a caregiver in positive, playful, rewarding interactions; and (3) safety to share inner experiences and enter an intersubjective relationship with a trusted adult. These are the three levels of safety children need to recover from blocked trust and the suppression of attachment needs.

In DDP, change is driven by relational and emotion-focused processes that work from the bottom up, creating new positive experiences with caregivers, and from the top down, promoting new meaning making and the development of more coherent narratives as the child awakens to the reality of being in a safe, trustworthy environment. The relational processes used in DDP are similar to the trust-building processes parents use with young children to develop secure attachments, processes that are now known to buffer the child's defense system and foster healthy brain development (Tottenham, Hare, & Casey, 2009). The DDP therapist uses relational skills to help caregivers and mistrusting children revive the suppressed reciprocal processes of attachment and caregiving that were absent in the child's earlier relationships with adults. DDP helps caregivers and therapists function as trust builders by being in the "right" mind to send safety messages deep into that hypersensitized defense circuit and switch on the social engagement system.

When a child's alarm system is off, and the social engagement system is switched on, the child can begin to use the higher brain regions, especially the prefrontal cortex, that have to be activated to support the new learning to make the journey from mistrust to trust. We link the processes of DDP to the neurobiological processes of reversal learning, fear extinction, memory reconsolidation, reflection, and reappraisal, which depend on the awakening of the prefrontal regions. These processes enable mistrusting children to start learning from experiences with adults and gradually change their minds and their behavior based on new experiences, something they are not able to do as long as their brains remain in the shut-down state of blocked trust. Using such processes as PACE (playfulness, acceptance, curiosity, empathy), follow-lead-follow, co-regulation of affect, storytelling, co-creation of meaning, emotional state induction, affective/reflective dialogue, and relational repair, the DDP therapist establishes a rhythm of reciprocal nonverbal communication with the child. Then she blends this nonverbal engagement with words congruent with the traumatic events of the past, while remaining socially engaged with PACE, enabling the child to participate in this dialogue without defensiveness. This allows the child to experience care differently and start creating new meanings for past traumatic events, moving toward developing a coherent autobiographical narrative. PACE constitutes a therapeutic mind-set or "attitude" that helps ensure adults will send messages of approachability and trustworthiness into the child's brain, helping prevent the mutual mistrust scenario that often develops between mistrusting children and adults. The attitude of PACE is the opposite of an adult's frequently defensive approach toward these children.

By concentrating on the main agenda of creating a safe connection with the mistrusting child, the therapist learns in real time, constantly monitoring the child's feedback, how to engage the child. Once some level of engagement is attained—what we call engagement light—the therapist concentrates on extending and deepening this dyadic connection while modeling the engagement process for caregivers and coaching them in becoming messengers of safety and trustability for the child. The therapist uses the engagement to help the child travel emotionally from a shut-down state to a state perhaps of light playfulness, toward a state of sadness, with the goal of helping the child safely remove the neurobiological block from the separation distress system that is a core component of attachment.

This in turn enables the child to start feeling the need for care and seeking comfort from an adult who is ready, willing, and able to provide it—an adult who is not in blocked care.

DDP includes intensive work with caregivers to enhance their capacity to sustain a caring state of mind toward the child. In brain terms, this involves helping caregivers strengthen the brain circuitry that enables them to "keep their lids on" and regulate their emotions and actions when faced with oppositional behavior and defensiveness. By helping the adults learn to rise above their "low-road" instinctive feelings of rejection, DDP helps caregivers provide the enriched kind of care that is needed to undo the damaging effects of earlier exposure to adults who didn't (for whatever reason) rise above their own defensive needs to be trustworthy caregivers for these children.

Here is what lies ahead. In Chapter 1, we discuss the new science of attachment and caregiving and how children learn to trust sensitive caregivers and experience the comfort and joy of deep connections. In Chapter 2, we present the concept of blocked trust, developing a brain-based model of how poor care forces children to adopt a style of living that combines heightened defenses with suppression of "social emotions." In Chapter 3, we turn to the caregiver side of the dyad, revisiting the concept of blocked care we introduced in *Brain-Based Parenting* to emphasize the importance of working with parents on an emotional level to help them become trust builders for their children.

In Chapter 4, we introduce the four R's of change—reversal, reconsolidation, reflection, and reappraisal—tying the neuroscience of change to attachment-focused treatment. We describe how enriched care facilitates the learning process by disarming the child's defense system and awakening the higher regions of the child's brain suppressed by chronic mistrust. Beginning in Chapter 5, we describe specific processes used in DDP to promote positive change in parent–child relationships. Here we introduce PACE, follow-lead-follow, affective-reflective dialogue, co-regulation of affect and co-creation of meaning, interactive repair, and emotional state induction processes as core brain-based change-promoting processes in DDP.

Chapter 6 presents the concepts of awakenings and engagement practice, the twin processes of helping children start to recover their suppressed, underdeveloped capacity for feeling the need for care and helping them "do the reps" of social engagement with therapists and parents. We describe in detail the process involving the co-regulation of affect and introduce the important process of state induction as the therapist helps the child reenter forbidden emotional states, especially sadness, to activate the all-important experience of the need for comfort from a caregiver. This discussion emphasizes the crucial process of helping the parent/child dyad revive the call and response process that got derailed when the child had to learn to suppress his attachment needs earlier in life.

In Chapter 7, we further define the process of affective-reflective dialogue presented in Chapter 5 and describe the healing power of storytelling and story voice to promote change. We present the neuroscience behind the power of stories to move us and the importance of the emotional tone or prosody in the voice of the story teller to promote engagement with hard-to-engage children. From this engagement the child is able to begin to co-create with the therapist and caregiver new meanings of his life story, including the previous rigid or dissociated segments involving terror and shame that emerged within the context of abuse or neglect.

Chapter 8 explains why playfulness is essential in attachment-focused treatment. We give a brain-based explanation of how reciprocal play between parents and children is part of the trust-building process, helping deactivate the self-defense system in the child and the parent. Mistrusting children seldom experienced spontaneous self- and life-affirming delight, laughter, and joy that deepen the attachment relationship and provide a background of unconditional love and confidence that help sustain the relationship through the hard times.

Chapter 9 focuses on the essential parent work that is key to helping children make the shift from mistrust to trust. This work begins with assisting the parent in feeling safe and experiencing trust in the therapist and the therapeutic process itself. With trust established and reestablished as often as necessary, the parents explore their history as parents and their own attachment histories that are fundamental in providing them with the caregiving schemas from which they habitually engage their children. More specific, day-to-day interventions and strategies that are consistent with the brain-based model of trust-building will also be presented.

In Chapter 10 we focus on the therapist and the importance of therapists strengthening their capacity for being in the right state of mind in relation to both parents and children in this work. We focus on the need for therapists to understand and know how to respond to the child's or parent's defensive behavior to remain safe themselves. We also stress the need for therapists to be able to acknowledge their slips into defensiveness and then repair relationships with their clients. The importance of both intrapsychic work, such as mindfulness, and interpsychic work, such as the therapist's own attachment schemas, are emphasized.

Finally, in Chapter 11, we discuss ways that the DDP model can be expanded to include more processes that are being shown to decrease chronic stress and defensiveness, including mindfulness practices, bilateral stimulation, neurofeedback, pet therapy, sensory integration processes, music therapy, and other processes that could augment the core relational work of attachment-focused treatment.

Throughout the book we present clinical vignettes from our own work to illustrate the clinical processes and show how they promote change. All vignettes are composites of several cases rather than literal versions of single cases. Although not a substitute for evidence-based research regarding the efficacy of DDP, we hope that this brain-based model of change will lead to research that explores the biobehavioral impact of this treatment model in addition to helping therapists be more effective in treating children who live in a state of generalized mistrust.

CHAPTER 1

Good Care and Poor Care: The Neurodynamics of Attachment and Caregiving

Unlike reptiles, the mammalian nervous system did not evolve solely to survive in dangerous and life-threatening contexts, but it evolved to promote social interactions and social bonds in safe environments.
—Porges and Lewis (2009, p. 256)

Experiential factors shape the neural circuitry underlying social and emotional behavior from the prenatal period to the end of life.
—Davidson and McEwen (2013, p. 689)

Infants are born social, ready to engage with their world. They don't have to learn to seek close connections with caregivers. They are ready to shine in their parents' eyes, be a source of immeasurable delight even as they are also inevitably a source of stress, even for the most loving parents. Having already learned their mother's voice before birth, they enter the world searching for her face, being especially attentive to her eyes. Their brains get excited when they find those eyes, especially when they widen and brighten when receiving this magical gaze (Guastella, Mitchell, & Dadds, 2008). It's not an accident that human babies, along with other mammalian young, have big eyes and the ability to mimic the facial expressions of their caregivers from birth. Cuteness and sociability are all part of nature's plan for ensuring that the brains of parents will be responsive to the infant's signals and become obsessed in the loveliest way with taking care of them (Noriuchi, KiKuchi, & Senoo, 2008; Carter & Porges, 2013). (The authors can both attest that similar experiences await lucky grandparents, who also find it easy to fall in love with their new grandchildren.)

Infants bring energy and excitement to their interactions with receptive caregivers, expressing what Dan Stern (1985) calls the "vitality affects": the capacities for feeling the pains and pleasures of being social, of needing comfort and companionship. When children are well cared for, they develop a deep, abiding trust in their caregivers, getting the benefits of a safe environment in which to play, express all of their emotions, and be exuberant, passionate, and curious.

What can suppress this natural vitality, this inherent readiness for social engagement? Fear of engagement. Children exposed to very poor care early in life learn to fear expressing the very needs for comfort and pleasurable companionship that normally lead to enduring emotional bonds with trustworthy caregivers. Poor care in the form of neglect, abuse, or lack of an attachment figure can force children to suppress their attachment-based needs, making them shrink from engagement with adults whom they would otherwise approach to get comfort, be playful, and share their thoughts and feelings. Instead of fully engaging with untrustworthy caregivers, they stifle their relational needs while learning to be as self-sufficient as they can be, keeping caregivers at a safe-enough distance. This process of living defensively results in what we call blocked trust, a complex developmental adaptation forced on children who cannot depend on caregivers to meet their emotional and social needs. Let's meet Mavis and Danny, two inherently social beings who find themselves in radically different social environments early in their lives.

A Tale of Two Cooks

Mavis is 15 months old, and her mom is holding her in one arm while making scrambled eggs with the other. "That's it, girl. Stir it some more and then we'll add a little pepper." Mom gives Mavis the pepper shaker as she says, "Shake shake shake. You're the best helper ever." Mavis smiles as she seasons those golden eggs she just helped mom beat. This is the beautiful dance of one-arm cooking as mother and child stay in connection to start another day together in this lucky girl's young life.

Danny is two. His mother is asleep on the sofa after a night of drug use and fighting with Danny's father. Danny is opening a jar of peanut butter to make himself a sandwich for breakfast. He tries to rouse his mom, but she just moans and turns over to sleep some more. At age seven, Danny is in the care of his grandparents. He tells them, "I'll live with you long enough for you to teach me how to cook dinner and then I can go home and be with Mom." His grandfather holds him tight and says, "You miss her so much. You did your best to take care of yourself and your mom. You're such a smart, brave boy." Danny smiles and pulls away. He doesn't want any comfort from his grandfather. That would make him feel little and needy. He needs to be strong and take care of himself.

Mavis and Danny are on different developmental trajectories, preparing for very different lives based on what they are learning early on about the nature of people, including themselves. Now we know from neuroscience that their brains are developing differently in response to the radically different kind of care they are experiencing. The nurturing care that Mavis is experiencing is promoting a pattern of brain development that will support a leisurely childhood during which she can immerse herself in the loving care of her parents, spending years learning from and delighting them, while teaching them how to care for her well. She can roam to explore, using them as a safe base, and then share the excitement over her discoveries. Securely attached to her trustworthy caregivers, she cares about these relationships and is greatly invested in keeping them going. She loves to look into her parents' faces, especially their eyes, and hear the musical sounds of their voices as they express their utter delight in being with her.

Danny is not so fortunate. He has already lost his innocence and much of his childhood, forced to start fending for himself as an infant. Having to be ever vigilant in the presence of his caregivers, on the lookout for signs that they were about to fight, hurt him, or just be dangerously unaware of his existence, he has already become more like a little man than a boy, with little opportunity to play, cry, or be curious about his world. Danny is not delighting anyone; instead, he is doing his best to keep himself safe in a world where he doesn't expect big people to care for him, much less delight in his presence. While Mavis is looking into loving eyes and feeling precious, Danny avoids the eyes of his caregivers, having spent his early years seeing eyes that were variably blank, angry, or terrified, eyes that frightened him and made him feel unloved, devalued, either unseen or too seen.

While Mavis can take her time with some aspects of her development, Danny actually has to accelerate his, getting on with the business of living in a world of scarcity and little comfort. As neuroscientist Nim Tottenham describes it, "If the environment is enriched and favorable, neurobiology will optimize for growth and development. If the environment is harsh, then neurobiology will optimize for thrift and adversity" (Tottenham, 2014, p. 2).

Experience-Adaptive Brain Development

Neuroscientists have learned that early in life, good care and poor care affect brain development by activating and silencing genes in brain systems or circuits that are under development (Weaver, Meaney, and Szyf, 2006; Champagne and Curley, 2011). This interplay between genes and environment is called epigenetics, a process earlier brought to light in the field of cancer research (Baylin and Ohm, 2006) and more recently taking center stage in the field of developmental neuroscience. This fast-growing research reveals how experiences with caregivers affect the way genes "behave" in the child's brain, genes that are involved in building all of the key neurotransmitter systems, the dopamine, serotonin, opioid, and oxytocin systems that support the formation of secure attachments. Epigenetically, good care and poor care can either wake up or silence genes to orchestrate the structural development of the child's brain in accordance with the nature of care the child is sensing. These epigenetic processes help build the key brain systems that make up the social brain (Callaghan et al., 2014).

The young infant's brain, primarily the right hemisphere (Chiron et al., 1997), awaits input from experiences with caregivers to start adapting its structure and functioning for relating to the kind of care being offered (Belsky, 2005, 2013). Does the quality of early care presage a life of milk and honey where resources are plentiful and others delight in your being? Or is life going to be constantly stressful, a world in which everyone is looking out for number one, competing every moment for scarce resources, a world where no one can really be trusted, where no eyes are safe? Or will life be somewhere in between, with degrees of trust that gradually decrease from the world of family to neighborhood, school, and community to more distant social settings inhabited by strangers? Answering these fundamental questions about the nature of the social world and adapting accordingly is exactly what the child's preverbal brain is doing, even though the infant has no conscious awareness of this social learning process. This is implicit, emotion-driven learning, perhaps the most powerful kind of learning humans experience in life, learning that sticks with us, literally embedded epigenetically in our brains and bodies. What kinds of messages from caregivers trigger epigenetic effects in a baby's brain, and what brain systems are sensitive to these effects? Primarily nonverbal signals from facial expressions, tones of voice, and different kinds of touch, multisensory inputs to the baby's brain that affect the construction of several brain systems which together make up the social brain.

Face, Voice, Touch:
How Caregivers Get Inside a Child's Brain

Infants are equipped to pay attention to those aspects of a caregiver's presence that have immediate relevance to survival. From birth, the infant responds differently to sensory experiences that cause pleasure and those that cause pain. This ability to differentiate between pleasurable and painful experiences drives the approach and avoidance learning that lies at the heart of social development (Berridge & Kringelbach, 2008). All external sensory information—the gleam in a mother's eyes, the tone of a father's voice, the warmth of a parent's touch—gets shunted to a region of the baby's brain that can rapidly appraise this sensory information for its relevance to survival, whether it is safe to approach or harmful, threatening, or something to avoid.

This is the job of a now famous part of the brain, the amygdala. This part is already working in humans before birth and is quite ready to help the baby learn what is safe and what is not in relation to a caregiver. Indeed, this is the way all baby mammals learn how to deal with their mothers to stay alive. For the infant to feel safe being close to a caregiver, that adult has to convince the baby's amygdala that this closeness is a good thing. Parents need to be amygdala whisperers (Cozolino, 2016) or, in the parlance of recent neuroscience, "social buffers" (Tottenham, 2014), someone whose very presence signals safety and calms the part of the amygdala that would otherwise sound the alarm and trigger defensive reactions. The amygdala orchestrates early approach and avoidance learning in a way that is fundamental to learning to trust or mistrust caregivers.

Neuroception:
Rapid, Unconscious Detection of Threat and Safety

The fastest way to send safety messages into another's brain is through nonverbal communication, which is generated and processed mostly in the right hemisphere (Corrigan, 2014). Nonverbal signals get to the emotion-generating right brain limbic system, rapidly shunted to the amygdala for quick assessment of safety or threat. Stephen Porges (2011) calls this ultra-fast appraisal process "neuroception" to distinguish it from the slower, more conscious process of perception. The neuroceptive process takes less than 50 milliseconds, whereas it takes about 300 milliseconds for the brain to form a clear image of someone's face. Through this process, nonverbal signals from other people can move us toward and away from each other faster than the meaning of spoken words can register. Because of this difference in the speed of brain processing, nonverbal communication trumps verbal communication when it comes to engendering feelings of safety or threat between a parent and child. Therapists see this all the time when working with highly defensive, rejection-sensitive people for whom a subtle shift in eye movements or tone of voice can trigger instant disengagement or even dissociation.

When infants are in good care, they absorb the sights, sounds, and tactile experiences of safety, biasing their sensory systems toward detecting safety over danger. When babies experience poor care, the opposite occurs. The child's neuroceptive system develops a bias for detecting threats to help the child stay safe enough in the presence of untrustworthy adults. This negativity bias creates "safety blindness," making it hard for the child to see, hear, and feel the signs of safety in their relationships with caregivers. In the process of assessing sensory experiences for safety and threat, the infant's senses get tuned for processing the range of information that is relevant for survival in their particular environments. This sensory appraisal process is similar to how the infant's auditory cortex starts to specialize in processing the sounds of the child's native language, a trade-off that makes it harder for the child literally to hear spoken sounds that aren't part of the native language sound system. Prior to committing the young brain to the sounds of the native language, the child has the capacity to hear the sounds of all languages; after this tuning process, hearing those non-native sounds becomes more difficult. Regarding attachment-based learning, the newborn arrives with the capacity to see, hear, and feel the signs of safety and danger, and over time, his or her brain devotes itself to processing the specific kinds of social experiences that are available in this first environment of care. The young brain starts to dedicate its development to living in the kind of sensory world that it first encounters.

A good example of this sensory tuning process is in the way the brain responds to different tones of voice, to the prosody or musical quality of human speech. Certain prosodic patterns are inherently detected as safe, whereas other vocal sounds are inherently threatening. The child's brain tunes this listening system to be adept at picking out the sounds first caregivers use with them and with each other. Very specifically, as elegantly described by Porges and Lewis (2009), beginning with the responsiveness of muscles in the middle ear to the sounds of safety and danger, the auditory system channels the process of responding to other people's vocalizations toward safe engagement or self-defense.

When filtering for safe vocal sounds, these inner ear muscles prioritize higher pitched sounds, facilitating the ability to hear the sounds of friendliness and approachability, the sounds of "motherese" or child-directed speech. When filtering for danger, these muscles prioritize the lower frequency sounds that generally are more predatory and threatening in nature. This includes the lower pitched sounds of anger or annoyance in other people's voices as well as the flat monotone of a depressed parent. By focusing the middle ear muscles on the intensity of sounds, it is easier to detect these lower pitched sounds of potential threat, such as the shift in a parent's voice from a higher pitched, friendly tone to a lower pitched tone that begins to sound like anger.

Children growing up in threatening homes tune their auditory system to hearing the sounds of threat while tending to ignore or suppress the higher pitched, more prosodic, more musical sounds of safety. Once this kind of sensory tuning takes hold, these systems would need to be retrained, like learning a second language, when the environment changes from threatening to safer. In attachment-focused treatment when therapists use the higher pitched vocal tones, children almost invariably respond more positively and become more engaged. These are the sounds of safety that quickly reach the limbic system, triggering the release of oxytocin in the amygdala to calm the threat-sensitive region and enable the child to feel somewhat safer. If the therapist shifts into a lower register to discuss a problem, the child is likely to perceive this as a threatening tone and shift immediately back into self-defense. Empathic words of comfort may actually be a bridge that brings safety to the experience of threat and distress whereby the therapist or caregiver's words tend toward the lower register but are expressed with rhythm and light intensity, not at all like the monosyllabic high intensity of a stern lecture.

So we can see how infants start to learn to trust or mistrust caregivers based on the quality of care they receive. Now let's go deeper into the process of how good care and poor care affect the developing brain. To do so, it's useful to consider the brain systems that are under development early in life that contribute to attachment and the development of social engagement and self-defense, trust and mistrust. Here we turn to the neuroscience of how life experiences get turned into brain matter and sculpt or "program" the developing social brain. To understand this complex subject, we draw from the field of social developmental neuroscience, the study of how early relational experiences with caregivers affect the way the child's brain adapts its structure and functioning (deHaan & Gunnar, 2009). To wrap our minds around this process, it's useful to consider several core brain systems that are under construction within the first year and half of life, how each is affected by good care and poor care, and how the interplay of these systems differs in the brains of trusting and mistrusting children.

Five Core Brain Systems:
Social Engagement, Self-Defense,
Social Switching, Social Pain, and Stress Reactivity

The interplay of the social engagement, self-defense, social switching, social pain, and the stress reaction systems differs in the brains of well-cared-for, securely attached children and the brains of poorly cared-for, insecurely attached children. Early in the first year of life, these are primarily subcortical systems that are sensitive to early experience and targets for epigenetic effects. As the brain grows and matures, these systems get connected to higher brain regions in what is called the ventromedial prefrontal cortex or VMPFC. (The VMPFC combines parts of the anterior cingulate cortex [ACC] and parts of the orbitofrontal cortex [OFC].) Once these so-called fronto-limbic connections are strong enough in a child's brain, typically around the age of 18 months, the VMPFC functions as the executive system for the social brain, orchestrating the interplay of these five core systems in a top-down manner, replacing the primarily bottom-up process that governs earlier brain functioning. In effect, this helps a child (and a parent) keep their lid on during emotionally "hot" interactions, the key to staying in connection rather than shifting into mutual defensiveness and losing this good connection.

This healthy maturation of the child's brain supports the emergence of exclusive attachments to caregivers beginning around seven months and progressing toward the end of the first year. This process supports heightened self-awareness, including the ability to distinguish between different people and between self and others. This becomes the neural basis for stranger anxiety and the process in which the primary attachment figure becomes a secure base, a co-regulator of the child's emotions and a soother of the child's distress. A key aspect of this story is that good care fosters the shift from bottom-up to top-down functioning, whereas poor care tends to keep the child's brain in a less developed, less connected state that prolongs the kind of bottom-up, survival-based reactivity that is only really adaptive to living in a dangerous environment. When the premium is on "better safe than sorry," it is adaptive to keep using the mostly subcortical circuits that favor the self-defense system over the social engagement system. The problem is that this becomes a habitual pattern, making it hard for the child to adapt to living in a safer environment.

Attachment-focused treatment has to zero in on this chronic use of the self-defense system, provide the buffering co-regulation the child needs to disarm this system, and provide ample opportunities for the child to experience what it's like to use the social engagement system. This is why it is so important that the caregivers have a well-developed, top-down self-regulatory system themselves to stay engaged when the child is disengaged. Fortunately for therapists, caregivers, and maltreated children, epigenetic changes in gene expression in response to new experiences can occur throughout the life span, providing a neurobiological mechanism for changing our brains and our minds if life presents us with radically different conditions from those that prevailed during the sensitive period for learning to trust or mistrust caregivers.

Differences in the development and interplay of these core brain systems underlie all of the different attachment styles, from secure, to avoidant, to ambivalent, to disorganized. In the context of a good care scenario, the child's brain develops in a resilient way that enables him or her to spend a lot time in social engagement, relatively little time in self-defense, while being able to feel the natural social pain of separation and to seek and benefit from the comfort caregivers provide. In a securely attached brain, the child can regulate the process of shifting between engagement and self-defense in a more mindful way using the top-down VMPFC to regulate the reactivity of the amygdala. This helps the child shift flexibly between open engagement and self-defense and provides more capacity to stay engaged with a caregiver without becoming defensive. Finally, the secure child's stress response system, the hypothalamic-pituitary-adrenal (HPA) axis, turns on and off efficiently to help the child mobilize to meet positive and negative challenges, rather than staying on all the time to keep the child in a state of constant readiness like the poorly treated child must do.

We look at each of the five core brain systems and how each is affected by good and poor care.

The Social Engagement System

The capacity for social engagement is a mammalian trait that became highly developed in primates, reaching new heights in human evolution. The uniquely human ability to sustain social engagement even when interactions become tense rests on a newer part of the parasympathetic nervous system, an upper region of the vagus nerve above the diaphragm that is highly developed in humans (Porges, 2011). This so-called smart vagus circuit (technically the ventral vagal, as opposed to the dorsal vagal circuit) evolved to enable mammals (especially primates) to form close social bonds, undergirding the processes of caregiving and attachment to help ensure the survival of the young (and thus the species). The smart vagal circuitry functionally connects the muscles of the face, the vocal cords, and a muscle in the middle ear that regulates the listening process to the workings of the heart and lungs. This functional circuit supports our unique capacity for sustained sociality, for getting and staying very close without shifting into defensiveness. This higher vagal system, Porges explains, acts as a braking mechanism on the heart, helping regulate changes in heart rate (or more precisely, heart rate variability), in a manner that is adaptive to changing energy demands of different social situations. The smart vagus enables people to stay engaged and open with each other, rather than shifting into a full-blown defensive state when social interactions become challenging but don't really require a defensive response.

In effect, having good vagal tone—the effective functioning of this upper vagal system—is the neurobiological key to being socially competent. While genes contribute to vagal tone, this smart vagal system is under construction early in life and is responsive to the quality of care a child receives. In short, the smart vagal system supporting social engagement develops more effectively in a safe environment of care than in a harsh, threatening environment. Maltreated children are likely to have poor vagal tone due to their chronic defensiveness; helping improve their vagal tone is a major goal of treatment.

The Default Mode Network and Development of Reflective Functioning

Tied to the social engagement system is the development of the brain circuitry that supports self-awareness and the ability to think about self and others by looking "inside" instead of "outside." Neuroscientists have found that we use two different brain systems for looking outward and looking inward—one when we are focusing on the external environment, being vigilant toward the outer world, and the other when we are focusing on our own inner life, thinking about ourselves and our relationships (Raichle & Snyder, 2007). This second brain state is called the default mode network (DMN). In healthy development, the DMN eventually becomes the brain system that supports reflective functioning and "relational thinking" (Mitchell, Banaji, & Macrae, 2005; Broyd et al., 2009). The DMN is connected to the social engagement system, while being suppressed when the self-defense system is on. We require safety in our external environment to go inside and spend time in the DMN being introspective and reflective. Using the DMN for self-reflection is a process unavailable to a person who is chronically defensive. In effect, the DMN is the thinking part of the relational brain, the place we go when we're safe to do so to reflect on our experiences with other people and make better sense of these experiences than we can when stuck in our lower, defensive brain system. The DMN supports what Dan Siegel (2012) calls "mindsight" and what neuroscientists call "mentalization"—the process of thinking about other people's inner life and understanding how their thoughts and feelings may differ from one's own. When the DMN is fully functional, we can use it to attune to another person, to combine empathy and mentalization to develop a compassionate state of mind toward ourselves and others. This makes the DMN a very important brain system for caregivers—essential for being able to think about one's child and rise above simpler, lower reactions to that child's behavior.

The DMN starts to develop quite early in life, during the later stages of infancy. When children receive good care as this system is developing, they are building a default network that can support the development of reflective functioning and the process of reappraising old, self-referential learning in the light of new experiences (Chen & Miller, 2012). Poor care, meanwhile, can suppress the development of this system, making it hard to be reflective and spend time thinking about and making sense of self–other relational experiences. When we don't feel safe with our inner life, hanging out with our thoughts and reflections while not occupied with something outside ourselves, the DMN is not a safe place to be; our inner world is a space to be avoided because it is full of terror and shame, not a pleasant place to dwell, and it isn't safe to shift attention away from the immediate environment. Maltreated children are often doubly unsafe: unsafe with the outside world and with their own inside world (van IJzendoorn, 1995; Daniels et al., 2010). Furthermore, staying vigilant for signs of impending harm in the external environment suppresses the development of the DMN. In this sense, one of the important goals of helping a child develop a secure attachment is helping make the child's default system a safe place, making the child's inner life rich and generative, not a state of mind to be avoided by constantly staying too busy with threat detection to "go there" (Sripada et al., 2014). Related to attachment-focused treatment, helping the mistrusting child be safe enough to go inside using the DMN to start making new sense of past experiences is one of the keys to change, a process that helps with the reversal learning the child needs to do to make the brain journey from mistrust to trust.

The Self-Defense System

Everyone needs to have a capacity for defending the self against physical and emotional threats. The self-defense system is present in healthy, securely attached, well-cared-for children, but it can often stand down because good care promotes safety and lessens the need for using the self-defense system—in effect, saving this system for later in life when the child moves out into the world and encounters new challenges that may require self-defense. Self-defense is rooted in what neuroscientists call the mid-brain defense system, a set of brain regions involved in the process of early appraisal of safety and threat and the activation of self-defensive actions, including fight, flight, and freeze reactions. Good care keeps this system relatively quiet, whereas poor care keeps it active and promotes the growth and strengthening of connections among the regions of the brain that together make up the mid-brain defense system.

This system consists of regions of the brain that receive sensory input from the external environment and internal input from the body early in the sequential processing of sensory information. One of the key regions that make up this system is the superior colliculus, a small, powerful region atop the brain stem, just below the back of the thalamus, that receives input from the eyes, ears, and somatosensory cortex, triggers the "obligatory orienting" response to bring attention to bear on salient information, and then shunts this package of sensory input to the amygdala for rapid assessment of relevance for survival (Field et al., 2008; Lanius, Paulsen, & Corrigan, 2014). The amygdala can then trigger defensive reactions from a part of the mid-brain or upper brain stem called the periaqueductal gray (PAG) and can also trigger the stress response system, the HPA axis, to produce stress hormones from the adrenal gland. This defense circuit can do its work in less than 50 milliseconds to shift the brain into self-defense mode if threats are detected by the amygdala.

The amygdala has particularly strong connections with the PAG, the region that is hardwired in the mammalian brain to release both defensive behaviors when signaled to do so from the amygdala and prosocial approach behaviors when the amygdala detects safety. Good care channels safety messages into this system, keeping defensive reactions at bay while promoting social engagement. Poor care sends threat messages into this system, keeping the defensive reactions quite busy while sensitizing the pathways from the amygdala to the PAG to make it very easy to "get defensive" (Caldji, Diorio, & Meaney, 2003). This streamlined circuit releases the big, unmodulated defensive reactions in maltreated children, reactions

Figure 1.1 The mid-brain defense system

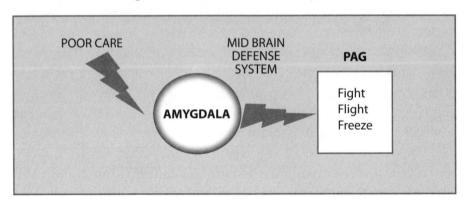

that effectively shut down higher brain systems to keep the brain in this quick-response, survival-driven mode without the distraction of more complex information processing or thinking. This makes the amygdala–PAG circuit a major target for treatment in attachment-disordered children. Treatment has to calm this hypersensitized mid-brain defense circuit so children with blocked trust can begin the journey toward a trusting relationship with a safe caregiver. See Figure 1.1 for an illustration of the mid-brain defense system.

Oxytocin: Disarming the Social Defense System
Good care triggers the release of oxytocin in the brains of the child and the parent. Oxytocin helps promote trust in a parent–child dyad, essentially by inhibiting the self-defense system. There are many oxytocin receptors throughout the subcortical brain regions, including the amygdala and the PAG, and this makes it possible for oxytocin, released from the hypothalamus, to inhibit or calm the defense system (Gimpl & Fahrenholz, 2001). Oxytocin plays a major role in helping people feel safe enough to remain open and nondefensive during close encounters with social partners (Domes et al., 2007; Neuman, 2008). The release of oxytocin into the mid-brain defense system, which has many receptors, can effectively disarm this system, turning off defensive reactions and promoting a shift into social engagement.

Oxytocin also seems to transport people empathically into each other's worlds, attuning them to each other's inner experiences, particularly experiences of suffering, both physically and emotionally. For example, listening to dramatic stories about people experiencing extreme stress and then having to overcome it, the emotional arc of many powerful stories, has now been shown (Zak, 2012) to trigger a chemical cocktail of stress hormones, like cortisol and oxytocin. This combination apparently promotes the process of projecting ourselves into the story, with both concern—a sense of drama—and empathy. In brain terms, early suppression of the oxytocin system by the need to be defensive is part of the adaptation to poor care that needs to be addressed and hopefully reversed by good care and good treatment. Zak's research suggests that storytelling may be one of the ways to prime the oxytocin system in children with blocked trust, along with friendly eyes, a kind voice, and soothing touch. Here is an example of the use of storytelling and story voice in treatment.

> Lance was 15, a loner, unmotivated at school, with frequent aggressive outbursts directed toward his peers (when he thought they were making fun of him) or his teachers (when he thought that they were being unfair to him). His foster mother, Betty, told his DDP therapist before the start of the session that he had seen a frightened nine-year-old boy being bullied by some of his classmates. Lance pushed the bullies away and then walked the boy two blocks to his home. When the therapist asked him about it, he dismissed what he had done, saying that the little boy didn't deserve what they were doing to him. The therapist paused, looked out the window, and became animated. He said rapidly, with a sense of urgency and need to understand:
>
> **Therapist:** I don't get it! I don't get it! People have said that you're just like your father! You've even told me! You've said, "I'm just like my father!"
> **Lance** stared at the therapist: So . . .

Therapist: So your father used to hit you and slap you when you were nine! And you didn't deserve it! If you had joined in and hit or teased that little boy you would have been like your father! But you didn't! What's that mean?! What's that mean?!

Lance: I don't know!

Therapist: We have to figure it out! What does it mean?!

Lance: It means I'm not like my father! (*Lance stopped, confused and shocked by what he said. Then he said it again, slower and quieter this time.*) I'm not like my father!

Therapist: (*now matching his softer and more rhythmic tone*) You're not like your father. You're not your father.

Lance: (*Looking stunned*) I'm not my father.

Therapist: (*With the same gentle tone*) Then who are you?

Lance: (*whispering*) I don't know.

Therapist: I guess that's something that we have to figure out, don't we. Who are you? (*turning to Betty, still speaking quietly*) Betty, I think that Lance is so confused now. His father hurt him badly, very badly, and at some level Lance knew that wasn't right. He deserved better. Yet he wasn't sure and he also thought that maybe he was a bad kid and did deserve it. The whole thing is very hard for him and he's been very angry about it. Very angry. Every time he has shown his anger, like at you sometimes, he has thought that maybe he's like his father. And now he does something like this—helping the boy being bullied by bigger kids—and he's all mixed up. He showed such caring and protectiveness toward that little boy. Things that his father seldom, if ever, showed him. Do you see those parts of Lance, Betty, that are nothing like what his father did to him, nothing like his father?

Betty: I do. I often see wonderful qualities about Lance.

Therapist: But he does get angry.

Betty: Oh, yes, he does. At me more than others sometimes.

But I know what that's about and I don't think it's about being like his father.

Lance: What does it mean then, when I swear at you and scream at you?

Betty: It means that I've done something that frustrates you and you think maybe that I did it because I don't care about you. That I'm being mean to you. Maybe it even seems that I'm almost being as mean to you as your father was when he would swear at you and beat you.

Lance: But you're not. I know you're not. (*with trembling voice and watering eyes*)

Betty: I'm glad that you know that, Lance. I'm glad. Though at times I think you just forget it and it doesn't seem like it does now. We'll keep working at it. Ok?

Lance: Yes. (*Betty reaches over to touch him, he leans toward her and she gives him a hug*)

Therapist: You both . . . you both . . . work so hard. You're going to make it happen and Lance will figure out who he really is. Who he was born to be.

From there, Lance continued the difficult process of change and developing a new identity based on trust in Betty. In this session, the therapist's storytelling voice evoked Lance's intersubjective engagement with the event where he protected the boy from the bullies and enabled him to use that event to begin to develop a new narrative, a narrative that would radically change the meaning of his father's abuse of him.

The Social Switching System

In addition to the social engagement and self-defense systems, we need a brain system that orchestrates the process of shifting or switching back and forth between social engagement and self-defense, depending on how our brains appraise threat and safety during interactions with other people. We call this the social switching system. This is an extremely important brain system in relation to good care and poor care. Good care biases the development of this system toward social engagement, and poor care biases the development of this system toward self-defense. Treatment must target the social switching system and shift this bias from the self-defense system toward the social engagement system to make it easier for the child to engage rather than avoid and disengage (Lanius, 2014).

In early infancy, the process of switching back and forth between social engagement and self-defense is orchestrated subcortically, primarily by the amygdala and its connections with other subcortical regions that support social approach and social avoidance. This amygdala-driven, bottom-up state shifting is the first stage in the development of the state regulation system. As the brain grows and matures in a good care situation, this subcortical, more primitive system of shifting gets connected to those higher prefrontal regions of the brain, the VMPFC, connecting parts of the ACC and OFC to the amygdala and other subcortical regions to form the fronto-limbic system (Johnston et al., 2006). Along the way, the hippo-campus comes online to partner with the amygdala and the VMPFC in the creation of a more mature, flexible state regulation system. In healthy brain development, the VMPFC ultimately becomes the executive system for regulating the process of shifting between the social engagement system and the self-defense system, orchestrating this process in a top-down fashion based on the ability of inhibiting the amygdala and, with input from the hippocampal complex, bringing more highly processed information to bear when deciding whether to stay engaged or shift into defense. In a well-developed self-regulatory system, the VMPFC and hippocampus automatically activate when the amygdala detects a threat, enabling top-down processing to kick in quickly to modulate amygdala reactivity.

Bottom-Up State Shifting: The Job of the Amygdala
While changing our internal states of mind and body is a process eventually orchestrated by prefrontal brain regions in healthy development, in infants and maltreated children, rapid switching opera-

tions are orchestrated by the amygdala. One neuroscientist describes the amygdala as follows:

> If one looks at a connectivity map of the brain, the amygdala looks something like Grand Central Station. It gets signals from throughout the brain and sends signals throughout the brain. This places the amygdala in a prime position to incorporate information concerning the emotional significance of events we encounter, in order to ensure that our cognitive functions, such as perception, attention, memory, and decisions, are modified to give priority to these events. (Phelps, 2009, p. 216)

The amygdala is working from birth, and it takes its cues from the quality of early care, adapting its structure and functioning according to the sensory input it gets from interacting with these first "programmers" of brain development (Tottenham, Hare, and Casey, 2009). In the developing brain during this period, the activity of the amygdala actually helps guide the development of the social engagement and self-defense systems, helping channel the growth and development of connections between regions within these two systems in accordance with how the amygdala reacts to the presence of the caregivers (Barr et al., 2009; Whalen & Phelps, 2009).

This rapid appraisal system relies heavily on detecting and assessing the immediate emotional "valence"—positive (safe) or negative (threat)—of another person's nonverbal behavior: facial expressions, emotional tones of voice (prosody), body language. Clearly, infants learn to trust or mistrust caregivers by relying on brain circuitry that does not yet involve higher cognitive processes or language. Even later in life when we do have higher cognitive powers, we continue to appraise trustworthiness and approachability of other people, at least initially, using this same nonverbal processing system. The difference between the infant and the adult is that the infant does not yet have the brain resources to rise above this rapid, automatic appraisal system. The young child is strictly a sensorimotor-based learner, wedded to processing the immediate facial expressions, tones of voice, and tactile sensations encountered while interacting with caregivers along with the visceral and proprioceptive messages coming up from the body during these encounters. The child's brain forms strong associations between these external social signals from the caregiver and those internal signals from the body to build a social memory system that attachment theorists call "an internal working model" of relationships, an implicit brain model the child uses unconsciously to navigate the social world and predict how other people will behave.

While this rapid appraisal system with the amygdala at its epicenter reacts to both positive and negative experiences, it has what neuroscientists call a "negativity bias." When we encounter something especially frightening or painful, when we get hurt, be it physically or emotionally, our amygdalas tend to react strongly. Research shows that there is a very strong correlation between the level of activation of the amygdala to something that has emotional significance and how well we remember that "something" later in life (Öhman, 2009).

This is why we have such strong memories of times in our lives when we were hurt, physically and emotionally, when bad things happened to us or to those we love. Importantly, the strength of these fear- and pain-driven memories has a lot to do with why it isn't easy to feel safe in situations that remind our brains of the times we were hurt or frightened. The amygdala links the feelings of pain and fear to the things or people who cause those feelings and then tends to generalize these conditioned emotional reactions to categories of things or people without making careful distinctions that could provide vital "news of a difference" and turn off the alarm system. This may explain why mistrustful children who have been traumatized by a caregiver later overgeneralize and react defensively to safe caregivers. This may also help one understand why some children make a distinction between broad categories of adults, avoiding "caregivers" but approaching strangers.

The negativity bias appears to have evolved to make sure we take a "better safe than sorry" approach to life, a process that inevitably generates many false alarms in safe environments. Because human interactions are complex and often ambiguous regarding people's intentions and real feelings, the amygdala tends to be biased toward a negative meaning of the event. It is important that adults work at reducing ambiguity in the way they relate to mistrustful children. Better to be very clear—nonverbally and verbally—that the child is safe with us. This is why attachment-focused treatment, and specifically DDP, places so much emphasis on helping caregivers be in a state of mind that sends consistent safety messages into those mistrusting brains, specifically targeting the child's hyperactive amygdala. This is why a DDP therapist takes a clear, nonverbally expressive stance in communicating her interest in and experience of the child in therapy, as opposed to the neutral stance that is often taken by the more traditional therapist.

The younger the child, the more dominant the role of the amygdala in orchestrating responses to emotionally salient experiences, especially interactions with caregivers. In this sense, young children are much more amygdaloid creatures than older people, more likely to be captured by their emotions and to experience life through their emotions. When the amygdala orchestrates reactions, feeling is believing; strong emotions drive the process of meaning making. Only when we get above the amygdala's quick appraisal of events to use the slower brain process of reflective functioning can we make richer, more complex, and often better sense of experiences with other people. Helping children with blocked trust get above their amygdaloid way of making sense to engage in "affective/reflective functioning" (Hughes, 2007) is a major goal of attachment-focused treatment.

The Hippocampus: Contextualizing Experiences to Detect Differences between Past and Present
A second stage in the development of the social switching system occurs when the hippocampus gets in on the act, joining the amygdala in processing sensory information to help the child decide whether it's

safe to approach a caregiver. The hippocampus, which is located next to the amygdala in the middle of the temporal lobe on both sides of our brains, is a region essential for putting experiences in the context of time and place and helping differentiate among different people in one's life. Good care promotes healthy hippocampal development epigenetically, programming gene expression in this brain region in ways that make the hippocampus functional and help it connect with the amygdala and the prefrontal regions. The development of these connections between the VMPFC, amygdala, and hippocampus is an essential aspect of acquiring the ability to regulate emotions and state switching in a more mindful, resilient, adaptive way. Poor care suppresses the development of this connectivity, keeping the VMPFC, amygdala, and hippocampus from working well together in an integrated way.

The process of developing a selective attachment to an adult that typically emerges between 7 and 12 months is now thought to depend in part on the onset of hippocampal functioning that enables the child to start differentiating more between people, the basis for the onset of "stranger anxiety." The hippocampus continues to mature and get more connected with other brain regions, including the prefrontal cortex, as life goes on and probably continues to develop throughout life in a healthy brain (Benes, 1998). Prior to the hippocampus coming online, especially in the first six months of life, intensely emotional experiences with caregivers are primarily processed in an amygdaloid manner, without the input from the hippocampus to help put these experiences in time and place, to do what neuroscientists call contextualizing the memory before it is stored in the brain.

The hippocampus is a part of the child's brain that is vulnerable to toxic effects of high levels of stress and excitatory chemicals, especially if these chemicals are released in a chronic fashion to support the need for ongoing hypervigilance and self-defense. Over time, the hippocampus can start to incur structural changes: loss of dendritic branching on neurons that eventually cause hippocampal shrinkage and loss of synaptic connections with other regions of the brain.

Also, over time, the neurobiology of chronic stress can suppress the very important process of neurogenesis, the production of new brain cells in the hippocampus. Some of these neuronal stem cells survive and take their place in the hippocampal system to help support new learning, so the suppression of neurogenesis in the hippocampus degrades the ability to learn new things from new experiences. This could be a part of what is going on in the brains of children exposed to maltreatment early in life, making it more difficult for them to learn from their new experiences with new caregivers and literally change their minds about the trustworthiness of adults.

When the child's hippocampus is not working well or is being suppressed by an overactive amygdala, it is very hard for the child to see, hear, and feel how a caregiver who is with them now is different from the ones who hurt them earlier. Helping the hippocampus work is one of the reasons that treatment has to target the hyperactivity of the amygdala and calm the pattern of firing in this brain region. Treatment and good care have to calm the amygdala to restore better functioning of the hippocampus so the child can effectively compare the present to the past, sense the disparities, and learn from the difference.

Through the VMPFC–amygdala–hippocampal connections, the child's brain stores attachment-based memories of what it feels like to interact with a caregiver, making them available later as a guide to what to expect from a caregiver. In this way, the amygdala, orbital region, anterior cingulate, and hippocampus work together to help the child use these early experiences as the basis for learning and storing knowledge about what to do when confronted in the future with similar experiences. The VMPFC–amygdala–hippocampal circuit is also key to the process of making adaptive changes in social functioning in response to changes in a child's social environment, a process that neuroscientists call "reversal learning" (Schoenbaum, Saddoris, and Stalnaker, 2007). Attachment-focused treatment has to address this fronto-limbic circuit and teach it to embrace the "news" that the child is now living in safety, not danger. Given the fact that chronic stress can impair the functioning of the VMPFC and the hippocampus while intensifying the reactivity of the amygdala–PAG defense system, these parts of the brain that are so important for reversal learning may not be working very well in maltreated children. This would make the reversal learning required to shift from mistrust to trust slower and more difficult. The VMPFC receives output from the hippocampus that it uses to help a mistrustful child become aware of differences between old and new caregivers, making it essential that treatment somehow "awaken" both the hippocampus and the prefrontal regions in the brains of children with blocked trust.

> Two experienced foster parents told their social worker that they had wanted to give their foster child, Jake, a special day and they had a series of activities and treats arranged for him. At the end of the day, they asked him how it went. They were surprised, disappointed, and frustrated when Jake, in all seriousness complained about the one frustration that happened that day, seemingly having forgotten all of the good times.
>
> **Social Worker:** Was Jake angry when he said that? Did something just happen that he was upset about?
> **Anne:** No, he seemed relaxed. I was just chatting with him about the day. Hoping maybe that since it had gone well, that he might remember it when he gets upset about something. He usually has so many reasons to complain, I thought that maybe this might help him to see that living with us is not as bad as he often thinks.
> **Social Worker:** So right after the fun and enjoyment with you was over, he didn't seem to remember it! No wonder it's hard for him to trust you. He remembers all of the frustrations when you say "no" to him, but none of the enjoyment that comes from you saying "yes" to him.

Actually, Jake had not even experienced the good times while they were happening, leaving his foster parents feeling confused and ineffectual. His perceptual and experiential bias, his habitual vigilance regarding what might cause him unhappiness, leaves little openings for experiencing what his foster parents are doing for him that might create a sense of safety and enjoyment. The danger then, with more days like that, is that Anne would begin to experience Jake as being ungrateful, "never satisfied," and then she would start to experience herself as being ineffectual as a parent. This places her at risk for experiencing blocked care.

The Social Pain System and Social Buffering

Nature ensured that infants would feel distressed when they are separated from their mothers, their lifeline for mammalian survival. Social pain caused by separation leads to the call-and-response dyadic relationship between infant and mother, causing the infant to cry and seek comfort and the mother to respond to the infant's distress in a caring way. The capacity of a child to feel this natural distress and of a parent to respond empathically to the child's distress vocalizations is one of the most powerful processes promoting deep, enduring emotional bonds between children and parents (Panksepp et al., 1978; Craig, 2003; Christianson et al., 2008). Part of good care, then, is the healthy development of this call-and-response system, providing the infant with trust-building experiences of needing, seeking, and receiving comfort when distressed (Eisenberger et al., 2011). Children who are poorly cared for, on the other hand, have to learn to deal with their separation pain differently, without depending on the comfort of others.

Naomi Eisenberger and Matthew Lieberman (Eisenberger & Lieberman, 2004), neuroscientists who helped develop a field of study dealing with social pain, have shown that in brain terms, "pain is pain," whether it's physical, like a broken toe, or emotional or social, like being dumped or just ignored, especially when rejection is unexpected or sudden (Eisenberger, 2011, 2012; Lieberman, 2013). This social pain research is very helpful for understanding the effects on children's brains of being neglected or just harshly judged, of not being a source of delight to their first caregivers. Research by Martin Teicher et al. (2006) showed that mean words and verbal abuse can cause long-term changes in our brains, sticking to us like scars from childhood bullying (also see Teicher et al., 2003). The amygdala and the rest of our emotional brain respond to physical and social pain—when we hurt our bodies and when our whole being is hurt when someone treats us badly. So we are talking about pain and the pain management system that we use for both physical and emotional hurts. This is why we emphasize that blocked trust is largely a pain management strategy for suppressing the pain of rejection and the fear of abandonment.

Research by Jim Coan intriguingly showed with brain scans of adults that having a trusted, caring partner close by, literally holding their hand, makes a painful experience more bearable by dampening the pain system in the brain (Coan, Schaefer, & Davidson, 2006). Their research also showed that the caring partner has an empathic brain response to one's expectation of pain. This social buffering process that Coan studied in adults is the same process that occurs when parents effectively buffer their children's stress system (Tottenham, 2014). Helping caregivers become effective social buffers for maltreated children is a major goal of attachment-focused treatment.

A recent line of research led by neuroscientist Nim Tottenham revealed the probable neuromechanism by which sensitive maternal care co-regulates the child's emotions. The key finding was that good care deactivates the child's amygdala in the caregiver's presence and activates the child's VMPFC (see Figure 1.2). This dramatically shows the depth of safety that a parent's presence can generate in a good care setting, enabling the child to be open and engaged with the world, leaving the task of being alert for any possible dangers to the parents. Insecure children who report higher levels of separation anxiety do not show this suppression of amygdala reactivity in their mother's presence. Tottenham's group summarized these findings as follows:

Our findings provide a neuromechanistic framework for how caregivers regulate children's emotional reactivity. Specifically, maternal presence appears to buffer against amygdala reactivity and induce plastic modulation of amygdala-mPFC connectivity, reflecting positive attachment and reduced anxiety. Moreover, for children who experience neural regulatory effects of their mother, maternal presence enables enhanced regulatory behavior. Thus, caregivers may serve an external regulatory function while circuitry supporting emotion regulation develops in childhood. (Gee et al., 2014, p. 10)

If no one is available to be a social bufferer, it is not adaptive for the infant to keep crying and calling for help. More important, perhaps, it is not adaptive for the infant to stay in a chronic state of pain due to the lack of a pain-relieving caregiver. To manage the pain of being left alone in states of need, the infant has to block the pain somehow to avoid chronic suffering. Also, crying is one of the most powerful triggers for child abuse, and maltreated children may need to learn to stifle their crying to avoid triggering intense anger in stressed out adults. So learning to suppress the pain of being left alone and the behavior that neuroscientists endearingly call "emitting distress

Figure 1.2 Social buffering

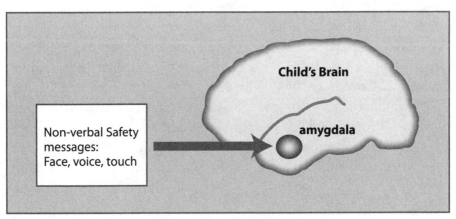

37

vocalizations" (i.e., crying) are both undoubtedly important for learning to survive without comfort.

Opioids: Comfort, Joy, and Suppression of Social Pain
Opioids play a crucial complex role in the dynamics of social pain and social pleasure (Curley, 2011). Opioids are released when a child receives comfort and also when a child and parent play together, especially when they both laugh out loud. So opioids do double duty in good relationships. They are an important player in (1) the pain relief and comfort that children experience when their parents heed their distress calls by providing soothing, "analgesic" care (Kalin, Shelton, and Lynn, 1995; Graves, Wallen, and Maestripieri, 2002; Panksepp, 2013) and (2) when children experience the pleasure of companionship. An intriguing line of recent research dedicated to the study of the opioid system is clarifying how important these substances are to the subjective experiences of comfort and joy in good relationships, helping orchestrate the dyadic dance of parent–child relationships (Barr et al., 2008; Way, Taylor, & Eisenberger, 2009). On the other hand, opioids play a key role in the development of defenses in response to poor care. Opioids are central to the process of pain suppression and the onset of dissociative defenses when infants are exposed to painful kinds of experiences with caregivers, including neglect and abuse (see Lanius, Paulsen, & Corrigan, 2014). Opioids are known to be released in response to all kinds of pain, including perinatal procedures in neonatal intensive care units (LaPrairie & Murphy, 2009). Furthermore, the early activation of the opioid system in response to pain leads to an increase in thresholds for feeling pain later in life (LaPrairie & Murphy, 2009; Lanius, Paulsen, & Corrigan, 2014). This line of research is extremely relevant to understanding the neurobiology of blocked trust and blocked care, conditions in which social pain leads to a suppression of feelings, especially feelings related to subjective pain, including the pain of separation. In all likelihood, opioids play a central role in the young child's response to poor care and in the development of the chronic suppression of social emotions, including empathy. We see one of

the primary goals of attachment-focused therapy as the removal of this chronic opioid block to enable children to feel what they need to feel to seek comfort and experience the joy of connections. Restoring the opioid system to its typical functional role in the attachment-caregiving dyadic system is a key dynamic in the neurobiology of attachment-focused treatment.

Opioids have a similar role for the parent in managing the stress and joys of caregiving. When parents are experiencing what we call blocked care following experiences of rejection by their children, their brains may release opioids to numb them from the pain. Just as treatment needs to address the effects of opioids in children, treatment needs to address this chemical blockage in parents to enable them to recover their ability to feel caring again toward the child.

The Stress System

One of the most compelling lines of social developmental neuroscience has to do with the early epigenetic programming of a child's stress response system (Moriceau et al., 2009; Conrad, 2011). This brain–body system is activated when we encounter some kind of challenge and need to mobilize our resources—cognitive, physical, and emotional—to deal with it. We couldn't survive long, or at least well, without the stress response system because we wouldn't be able to cope with challenges effectively enough.

Importantly, stress reactivity is not a bad thing. We activate our stress response system and produce hormones like cortisol in response to good challenges, too, like seizing an opportunity to get something great to eat or to meet a wonderful new person, just as we produce stress hormones to meet negative challenges, like fending off an attack from a mugger. The word *stress* has a bad reputation, so it's important to emphasize that the stress response system supports the ability to react and mobilize responses to all kinds of challenges in life and that cortisol, at moderate levels, helps us learn and remember new things associated with the challenging situation. The problem comes when there is a pattern of chronic activation of the stress system, when this system is too easily triggered and hard to turn off (McEwen and Morrison, 2013). There is a high risk of creating this kind of chronic reactivity in children who are exposed to unmanageable levels of stress early in life, especially stress caused by caregivers.

The stress response system is the brain–body circuitry that triggers stress hormones like cortisol and shunts these chemicals all over the body and back to the brain to mobilize for dealing with a stressor. The anatomy of this system runs from deep in the middle of the brain, from part of the hypothalamus, down to the bottom of the brain to the pituitary gland, and then down into the body through the bloodstream to the adrenal glands, where the stress hormones are produced and released back into the bloodstream and transported back to the brain. Using the first letters of these three regions (hypothalamus, pituitary, adrenal), this is called the HPA axis.

A key triggering mechanism for the HPA axis is the activation of the emotional brain system, the limbic system, which assesses and orchestrates responses to things that have emotional value, positive or negative. The key region of the limbic system that can trigger the HPA axis is the amygdala, which we mentioned as having the job of being the first filter in the brain for appraising the level of safety and danger in the environment, including the safety and danger presented by another person. When the amygdala detects a threat or an opportunity, one of its many outputs is to the hypothalamus, setting off the HPA axis to launch the stress response. Some neuroscientists, emphasizing the triggering role of the amygdala, refer to the A-HPA system or the L-HPA system, the L standing for "limbic" (Yehuda & McEwen, 2004).

Neuroscientists have found that the quality of early care received by young rodents and primates programs patterns of gene expression in the infant brain, including gene expression in regions such as the amygdala, hippocampus, and lower and middle prefrontal regions that have everything to do with a child's social and emotional learning and development (Meaney, 2013). Recently, there has been growing evidence that these epigenetic effects on the developing stress response system occur in humans as well. The amygdala and hippocampus are involved in the workings of the stress response system, and the ventromedial (lower and middle) prefrontal regions (VMPFC), specifically the orbital region and the ACC, eventually become the executive system for regulating emotions, stress reactions, the autonomic nervous system (including both sympathetic and parasympathetic systems), and social behavior. The amygdala is a main source of "go" signals that keep the HPA axis "on" when stress hormones are detected there; the hippocampus is a main source of "stop" signals that automatically turn the HPA system off.

The Trust-Building Cycle

In all relationships, including parent–child relationships, misattunement is inevitable and normal. Researcher Ed Tronick (2007) emphasized that what builds trust in the parent–child relationship is the parent's ability to repair connections rapidly and effectively after misattunements occur. It's the recurring cycle of attunement, misattunement, and repair that eventually promotes the development of a trust-based relationship in which the child learns that misattunement is not rejection or abandonment, that times when the parent and child are out of sync with each other will be followed by reparative interactions that bring them back into sync. Regular repair after a break for whatever reason, including a conflict, shows the child that the relationship is more important than any conflict, now or in the future, thus deepening trust. The key is that the caregiver has to be attentive to the signs of misattunement and has to be in an open enough, nondefensive state of mind to initiate repair rather than exacerbate the misattunement either by being inattentive to the signs that repair is needed or by having a negative emotional reaction to the child that promotes mutual defensiveness rather than reconnection or reparation.

During moments of attunement, parent and child are in their social engagement systems with the self-defense system off. When misattunement occurs, the child may tend to shift into defensiveness, especially if he or she is mistrustful. This is when it is vital for the parent to stay in social engagement or make a quick recovery from having a defensive reaction so that parent is in the right state of mind to help the child shift from defensiveness to openness. These moments of misattunements are actually good opportunities for the parent to practice being a social bufferer, the amygdala-whispering partner the child needs to learn how to trust that times of misattunement can be weathered without losing the connective bond with the parent. Repeated practice going through the attunement, misattunement, and repair cycle promotes the child's capacity to regulate social pain, while increasing the ability to control unnecessary shifts into defensiveness. Over time, these interactive reps should help the growth of the child's top-down regulatory system, the VMPFC–amygdala–hippocampal circuit.

Mavis, the partner in one-arm cooking, is learning to trust her parents because they are attentive to the quality of their connections with her and quick to initiate repair of these connections when inevitable misattunements occur. Danny, on the other hand, has no experience with repair, but has to contend with chronic misattunement in his relationships with his biological parents, who do not attend to this misattunement and do not initiate repair. In short, the adults who are initially responsible for Danny's care do not provide the virtuous circle of attunement, misattunement, and repair that would make them trust builders for Danny. At some point, Danny will have to experience this trust-building cycle with a sensitive caregiver if he is going to have a chance to learn to depend on an adult for comfort, guidance, and companionship and make the journey from blocked trust to trust.

Summary

Good care and poor care send different messages deep into the developing brains of young children, and these messages have different effects on patterns of gene expression in five core brain systems: the social engagement system, the self-defense system, the state switching system, the social pain system, and the stress response system. Depending on these epigenetic effects, well-cared-for children and poorly cared-for children emerge from early childhood with different brains, brains that have different patterns of connectivity and communication among the core systems. A big part of this story is how good care promotes the development of connections between the largely subcortical systems and the ventromedial regions of the prefrontal cortex to support a more mature, top-down way of regulating changes in states, those shifts between engagement and defensiveness. Good care promotes the development of this top-down capacity, literally triggering the growth of connective pathways that enable the child to be more intentional and mindful about approaching and avoiding other people. In addition, good care promotes the development of the DMN, the brain system needed for reflective functioning and reappraisal of old beliefs about self and relationships. The interplay among these systems, including the degree of maturation of the fronto-limbic connections, determines attachment styles, potential for change, and capacity for forming trust-based relationships with others. When caregivers are trust builders, sending consistent safety messages into the developing brains of their children, their children build brains that are well suited for living in connection with trustworthy others. When caregivers fail to be such trust builders, children are at risk for developing what we describe in the next chapter as blocked trust, a habitual way of relating to caregivers that reflects the suppression of the social engagement system in favor of chronic activation of the self-defense system using the bottom-up, more primitive circuit for orchestrating social and emotional functions.

We hope to show our readers how the relationship between good or bad care and the complex development of the structure and functioning of a child's brain is crucial to understanding whether the child will trust the caregiver (and teacher or therapist). This will give us a more complete understanding of why children who were initially raised in bad care have such difficulty responding differently to good care. This in turn helps us understand why trying to manage the mistrustful child's behavior through external reward and punishment is often insufficient. Knowing the neurobiological reasons for behavior is likely to lead to interventions that are brain-informed and realistic and thus likely to facilitate the process of building trust and preventing blocked care.

CHAPTER 2

Blocked Trust: Stress and Early Brain Development

The retreat into isolation can sometimes feel more controllable than being flooded with a sense of needing another person for comfort and connection.
—Siegel (2012, p. 385)

When we begin to understand the nature of the separation distress system at the neurobiological level, we may learn how to disentangle the damage wrought by emotional misfortunes.
—Panksepp (2003, p. 237)

To survive very poor care, children learn to fend for themselves by developing a strategy to meet their physical needs for food, warmth, and protection from the elements (self-provisioning); protect themselves from untrustworthy caregivers (self-defense); and manage the emotional pain of being on their own in a dangerous world without a comforting other (self-regulation of social pain). In the process, the child must heighten those aspects of brain functioning that support chronic defensiveness while suppressing those emotions that normally support social engagement and attachment, including separation pain, pleasure of companionship, empathy, and remorse—emotions that would prompt the child to move toward an untrustworthy caregiver and get hurt even more. In the process of heightening defensiveness and suppressing social emotions, the child also has to suppress the development of his inner life, that inward-looking default mode system that eventually enables reflective functioning to emerge in typical development. Poorly cared-for children don't feel safe enough in the presence of a caregiver to look inside; instead they are compelled to constantly monitor the external environment for threats. Blocked trust is the combination of these different processes that constitute the child's survival strategy, his or her tool kit for getting by largely through self care, for maintaining a "me" orientation to life in the absence of a healthy "we" (Siegel, 2012).

Let's look at how this developmental trajectory affects the five core brain systems we discussed in Chapter 1. Then we consider the processes of heightening self-defensiveness and suppressing social emotions and reflective functioning. Last, we describe three types of blocked trust strategies commonly seen in a clinical setting.

Blocked Trust and the Five Core Brain Systems

In terms of the core brain systems discussed in Chapter 1, the maltreated child has to suppress the social engagement system and the social pain system while activating and strengthening the self-defense system. To do this as an infant, the child has to rely on the bottom-up, primarily subcortical brain systems in which the amygdala takes the lead. The child has to use the amygdala-driven neuroception system to rapidly detect threats and keep the self-defense and the stress systems up and running, basically on 24/7 duty. The child also uses the ability to release pain-suppressing chemicals, mostly opioids, into the amygdala and the anterior cingulate cortex (ACC) to dampen the subjective pain of having to deal with poor care. This requires the child to use the social pain management system for self-defense rather than experiencing the co-regulation of separation distress by a trusted caregiver. This forces the child prematurely to develop a self-regulation strategy at a time in brain development when there is no other option besides the automatic, unconscious use of the opioid-driven pain suppression system, an emotion regulation strategy that promotes chronic disengagement and dissociation. Meanwhile, the need to stay hypervigilant toward the outer world interferes greatly with the development of the child's inner life, making the child doubly unsafe: unsafe looking outside and unsafe being inside. This lack of external and internal safety underlies the disorganized style of attachment most of these children develop and goes to the heart of blocked trust. Understanding these dynamics informs us, as therapists and caregivers, that we need to target both levels of safety to help these children recover from this developmental trauma.

Heightening Self-Defense Processes
Hypervigilance

Defensive living requires the ability to rivet attention on the signs of impending threats to safety in the behavior of other people. This includes the art of reading other people's intentions, of "minding their minds" to see harm on the rise, catching threats emerging before they actually materialize in various forms of abuse, neglect, invalidation, or rejection. Chronic mistrust requires a strong negativity bias, a constant hyperfocusing on the subtlest shifts in other people's faces, voices, body language, and interactions that reveal anger, disgust, or apathy. This early threat detection process is sufficient in highly defensive children to trigger defensive action: evasion, preemptive aggression, a charm offensive, or some form of frantic excitement that distracts everyone, including themselves. Based on this quick appraisal of impending harm, some kids become tigers, others opossums, other chameleons, different styles of blocked trust all serving the function of keeping others at a physical and emotional distance.

Implicit Memories, False Alarms, and Over-the-top Reactions

Understanding how the amygdala helps create implicit, preverbal memories of exposure to maltreatment helps us understand why children with blocked trust react the way they do when caregivers (and therapists) try to engage them. When these preverbal memories are triggered later in life, they have the quality of coming up out of the blue, out of context to the realities of the new environment and triggering emotional reactions that are way out of proportion to what is actually occurring during an interaction with a caregiver. This is how those big feelings that we often see in mistrusting children get triggered and take over a child's (and often a parent's) brain while this brain storm is going on. This is the neurodynamic explanation for the many false alarms that mistrusting children get in their brains during their interactions with adults and peers, those moments when the children's brains jump to the conclusion that the other person is having a negative reaction, getting ready to reject, abandon, or physically abuse them.

Early life experiences with being rejected, with experiencing, as one child expressed it, being "set aside," are certain to trigger the amygdala–periaqueductal gray (PAG) defense system, that deep-brain primitive alarm system that can activate big defensive reactions in the blink of an eye. This is how rage, running away, or freezing in fear happen out of the blue in these children, the result of having their mid-brain defense system triggered in the absence of top-down regulation from the ventromedial prefrontal cortex (VMPFC) regions as we described in Chapter 1. Repeated experiences with being uncomforted, unseen, neglected, and/or abused sensitized the child's quick emotional appraisal system in such a way that any future experiences that even hint at rejection, abandonment, or physical abuse can trigger these over-the-top defensive reactions. Think, for example, about the way adults with a diagnosis of borderline personality disorder react so dramatically to seemingly innocuous, subtle shifts in a therapist's facial expression or tone of voice, as if these were the early warning signs that the therapist is abandoning them. Think about the still face experiment when mothers are asked to put on a blank face and their babies decompensate within seconds, only coming back to life when the mother starts smiling and cooing again. In both instances, we are witnessing the power of perceived loss of safe connections to another person to make us "flip our lids" and fall into a dark, terrifying place, a black hole of disconnection that can even rob us of the will to live.

It is telling that wild animals who live in environments with much more uncertainty than their tamer relatives have larger amygdalas, particularly in the region that orchestrates the release of defensive behaviors (Kagan, 1994). Maltreated children are forced, in a way, to shift into a trajectory of brain development more suited for life in the wild than for living in very safe environments. Knowing this can help therapists and caregivers better understand the seemingly wild, over-the-top emotional reactions and behavior exhibited at times by maltreated children living in tame environments.

> Carl was a four-year-old boy who had experienced considerable neglect and periodic physical abuse during the first three and a half years of his life. According to Catherine, his foster mother, he reacted instantly to situations of distress with rage outbursts, and these tended to be as unpredictable as they were frequent. For example, Carl was running through the doorway from the dining room to the kitchen and, as was common, he banged against the wall hard with his shoulder and head. He screamed at Catherine, "You hurt me!" as he tried to hit and kick her. Another time Catherine was on the couch reading the paper when Carl screamed at her, "You hate me!" and then hit her leg. She had no idea why he hit her until she realized that she probably had a sad look on her face because she was reading an article about a local family being injured in a car accident. It was not uncommon for Carl to confuse her looks of distress as well as the source of her distress.

> **Therapist:** (with much animation, since Carl tended to be intense with a short attention span and the therapist had to relate with heightened affect, ranging from animation to very soft and gentle) Oh my, Carl! How confusing is that! Sometimes you get upset and you're not sure if Catherine was being mean to you or not! You're not sure if she hates you or not! How hard is that! How confusing! Can I trust Catherine . . . or not!

A few months later Catherine mentioned in therapy that Carl seemed to be changing his perception of her and of how to handle his stress. Instead of hitting her or screaming at her when he was upset, he would run away from her. The therapist wondered if she thought he might be afraid of her. She said that she first thought he might be, but now she was puzzled. He would often run toward her first, and then turn and run away from her. She thought he might be ambivalent about wanting her to cuddle him. The therapist thought she might well be right, that Carl was becoming aware of attachment behaviors toward Catherine and was afraid of wanting her comfort. The therapist suggested that Catherine accept Carl's ambivalence about getting a hug when he is upset. She might "cuddle him with her voice and face," so that he could hear and see her caring for him from a safe distance, until he was ready to come closer.

Catherine was right. A few weeks later, Carl did not run, but timidly approached her and allowed her to pick him up and cradle him in her arms. A few days after that, he ran to her without any hesitation when upset. Catherine laughed when recalling how desperate she had been to comfort him, and now Carl seemed to find countless, seemingly tiny reasons for a cuddle. She smiled as she said, "But I'm not complaining. He's making up for lost time!" She felt so wonderful that her caring for Carl was being received so freely and fully by this little boy who needed it so desperately.

Safety Blindness

Studies show that abused children detect anger in other people's faces and voices faster than typical children do and then have a harder time withdrawing their attention from what they perceive as expressions of anger to move on to paying attention to other things (Pollak, 2003). This hyperfocusing on threat-related facial expressions (and tones of voice) makes it hard for maltreated children to detect signs of safety in a newer, safer environment. In a sense, deeply mistrustful children have "safety blindness," a strong tendency to miss signs of safety in their environment because they are hyperfocused on signs of threat. Attachment-focused treatment has to address this strong negativity bias in maltreated children to help them learn to perceive signs of safety and trustworthiness in a caregiver when their brains are good at detecting the opposite in other people and locking on to these negative aspects. This is why attachment-focused therapy focuses so strongly on nonverbal communication. From a brain-based perspective, the core goal of attachment-focused treatment is to disarm the child's overdeveloped threat-sensitive system and awaken the suppressed attachment system by getting the child to see, hear, and feel signs of safety in their current environment of care.

Human communication is inherently fraught with potential for misunderstandings and misreadings of intentions, partly because we use the dual systems of ultra-fast nonverbal and slower language-based communication, whereas simpler mammals rely on the nonverbal, nonsymbolic forms of social communication, which are inherently less ambiguous. This is why we find it much easier to feel safe with our pets, such as dogs and cats, who convey their intentions toward us in easily deciphered ways as they move toward us, seeking contact, or away, trying to avoid us. They don't give us the kind of mixed signals that keep us wondering how they really feel about us. This is no trivial phenomenon; pets can play an extremely helpful role in attachment-focused treatment precisely because a mistrustful child is much more likely to feel safe with a nonjudgmental, easy-to-read animal than with a complicated human.

Tiny Allison was six months of age when she was placed with her foster mother, Darlene. She had already established patterns of mistrust quite well. She avoided all eye contact with Darlene, and she would react strongly by arching her back and pulling her head away whenever Darlene would pick her up. She was silent—a baby who did not cry or babble! She had stopped asking for help. She did not even seem to want to be seen. She wanted to be invisible. Her efforts to avoid Darlene were intense. She tolerated contact with her foster father and two adolescents in the home, but she became completely frozen when Darlene approached her. It was hard to give her a bottle. When she saw or smelled it, she would become frantic, thrashing around. It was harder to hold her than it usually was and even harder to get the bottle in her mouth.

The therapist asked Darlene if she was able and willing to have Allison with her continuously, never out of eyesight, often holding her in a baby carrier where she was tight against her chest. Darlene was to keep a steady sing-song voice with many lullabies going throughout the day, talking to herself about whatever she was thinking or doing, with an inviting and engaging voice. She could hold the bottle under her chin while holding Allison in her arms, facing her to encourage eye contact. When Allison glanced at her for a split second, Darlene was to respond with a smile and a warm, cooing voice, with no pressure to maintain eye contact. Darlene did all the therapist asked and more. It took 13 months of such consistent maternal care for Allison to begin to show that she wanted to be with Darlene and to show a fear of separation and strangers.

At 19 months, Allison was mobile and still wanted to be with Darlene. But it was very hard on Allison when Darlene would mildly correct her, take something away from her, or not let her do something. Allison would wail and fall on the floor. She would resist comfort. It was as if Darlene had rejected her, abandoned her, when she said "no" to her. This went on for 12 months, during which time Darlene had child-proofed her home and developed a very soft, gentle manner of discipline that still did not seem to provide Allison with much sense of safety. Each "no" seemed to activate her mistrust. Then one day, Darlene called the therapist and with great excitement, said: "I took a small gadget from Allison that she should not have and I turned to put it on the counter. I then heard a strange sound and did not know what it was. I turned back to look and there was Allison with her hands on her hips, staring straight at me, stomping her foot! I didn't know what to say. Then Allison yelled, 'I'm mad at you! And I'm going to my room and I'm going to be mad at you there, too!' Then she marched down the hall, entered her bedroom, and slammed the door! Isn't that amazing?!"

It was amazing and it was also the first day of many such days, increasing in intensity! Allison discovered defiance. From 31 months to 45 months Allison invented her own super-charged version of "the terrible twos"! Allison was learning that she was safe with Darlene, even safe enough to argue, defy, be angry at her. She would not be hurt or rejected. She would not be abandoned! She could discover her inner self, going safely inside, and still have a secure relationship with Darlene. This relationship was stronger than any conflict, any difference, any emotion. She had learned to trust Darlene.

When Allison was brought to Darlene's foster home, she was described as a "quiet, good baby," not as a child with blocked trust. Being quiet, good, and invisible was her uncon-scious plan to create her own safety as she tried in the best way that a six month old could, to meet her own needs. She was failing at it but she had no alternative. Her life, based on just six months of mistrust and rigid self-reliance, had trained her brain to be rigidly defensive, making it hard for her to change when exposed to exceptionally good care. It took almost three years of incredibly good care from Darlene before Allison was consistently able to trust her and start to live a life of safety, where she could develop her inner self and her relational self without having to sacrifice one or the other.

Deer in the Headlights: The Automatic Orienting Response

One of the most important connections the amygdala makes is to a small part of the brain called the superior colliculus, just under the thalamus that controls the automatic or "obligatory" orienting response (Öhman, 2009). This amygdala–superior colliculus circuit is the system that makes us suddenly shift our attention to a loud, unexpected noise or to sudden movements at the periphery of our vision. This is the "deer in the headlights" response that can lock attention on to something that is detected as potentially threatening. This system is probably highly sensitized in maltreated children who tend to lock their attention on to perceived threats while ignoring other aspects of their immediate environment in the process. This is how a hyperresponsive amygdala can create that safety blindness we described already.

Heightened Need for Control

For maltreated children, one of the ways to reduce uncertainty is to control other people's emotions and actions as much as possible. This includes getting other people to show clear emotional reactions like anger rather than having to guess what an adult is feeling behind an ambiguous face or look of surprise. Better to see an angry face or hear an angry voice and know what's coming than having to decipher the meaning of hard-to-read nonverbal expressions. This is probably why many maltreated children seem to "like" making caregivers upset. These children are probably unknowingly trying to reduce the uncertainty and ambiguity in their world by reflexively mistrusting caregivers rather than giving them the benefit of the doubt. In short, being controlling helps these children feel safer.

Resisting "Authority": Saying No!

Since mistrust requires resisting the influence of untrustworthy parental figures, the child has to make the process of mindlessly resisting authority a part of the strategy of blocked trust. Mistrust has to become a no-brainer, an automated, "mindless" reflexive process that at least buys the child time, gives him a chance to further assess whether it is safe to let an adult be in charge. It would feel dangerous to the child to give the parent the benefit of the doubt regarding their intentions in trying to get the child to do something or just to listen to the parent. The child's mantra has to be "mistrust, then verify." Behaviorally, this often takes the form of children reflexively saying "no!", either verbally or nonverbally. It's easy to see how many of these kids often end up with a diagnosis of oppositional defiant disorder. They earn it the hard way, by experiencing poor, untrustworthy care earlier in life.

How early in life can children start to learn to mistrust the intentions of caregivers and resist authority? Even infants have their ways of resisting the influence of adults. They can look away and avoid those scary eyes. They can flail their arms, kick their legs, and reject food by spitting it out. They can also learn to inhibit approach behaviors by automatically activating the parts of their brains that suppress actions to avoid harm, including the outer regions of the lower prefrontal cortex that can put the brakes on approach behaviors (Gee et al., 2013). Through these various strategies, deployed without any awareness of learning the art of mistrust, very young children can start to erect a "good enough" defense against parental influence to enable them to stay physically close enough to get basic care without really being nurtured, without being a source of delight. Many of these children learn "connection light": the art of engaging just enough to keep a lifeline to the stuff they need to get by while quickly shifting into resistance mode when the caregiver tries to exert some benign authority. In the process, the child is using that bottom-up state shifting system to make these kinds of rapid changes that turn their social engagement system on and off, as if they have a switch in their brains. The triggering mechanism for this switching is often a subtle shift in the parent's voice from the higher pitched prosody of playful engagement to the businesslike tone of needing to stop the play to get ready for bed or do homework.

Provisioning: Seeking and Seizing Opportunities to Meet Basic Needs

While the well-cared-for child can trust the caregiver to provide, poorly cared-for children have to be self-provisioners. These children have to learn to seize opportunities to get what they need and want in life. "Seeking" behavior (Panksepp, 1998) is supported by the dopamine system in the brain—the chemistry of motivation, movement, and learning. In effect, poor care promotes epigenetic sculpting of the dopamine system to support an opportunistic approach to life whereby the child stays vigilant for opportunities to get food and other things that help him survive. This experience-dependent programming of the child's dopamine system biases this system toward immediate gratification over the development of the capacity to wait for an adult to provide. This involves epigenetic effects on genes that code for different types of dopamine receptors. Dopamine supports social learning and motivated behavior, whether the motivation is to approach a trustworthy caregiver or to avoid an untrustworthy one and fend for oneself. Successful avoidance of harm is a trigger for the release of dopamine to help the child remember how he or she managed to stay clear of danger. Meanwhile, another trigger for the release of dopamine is acquiring stuff that makes the child feel better in the moment. While good care entrains the dopamine system to be a social reward system that helps to support the maintenance of pleasurable connections, poor care effectively hijacks the dopamine system for the purpose of helping the child survive without depending on good care.

The Boy Who Loved Watches. Jimmy was adopted at age six months from a Russian orphanage by two loving people. After crying inconsolably for two months, he didn't cry again in the presence of his parents for years. Meanwhile, he developed an intense need for immediate gratification from acquiring expensive goods, particularly high-end watches at one stage. He would steal his parents' credit cards and order $500 gold watches, which he then wore to school and showed everyone, as if this would make people like and admire him. Only after a year of attachment-focused treatment was Jimmy able to start experiencing his relationships with his parents as more rewarding than the acquisition of a shiny new watch. Shifting his dopamine system from favoring stuff over relationships was quite an undertaking and took great patience and compassion.

Suppressing Social Emotions and Reflective Functioning

While the nurtured child can afford to feel all of the pain and joy of being fully engaged with a responsive caregiver, the unnurtured child has to learn to suppress these social emotions. Why? Because these are the feelings associated with attachment needs, the feelings that propel the infant toward the caregiver, not away. When coming close triggers pain, the child has to have a different emotional strategy for relating to the caregiver, one that enables him or her to be in proximity to receive basic care while not feeling the pain of being devalued, unseen, or too seen. The need to disengage emotionally while being physically close to a caregiver presents an early life dilemma to an infant, who is born ready to approach, engage, and connect with a caregiver who is wired to do the same. The process of learning to emotionally disengage channels development down a very different trajectory than the process of engagement.

One of the most important things for therapists and caregivers to understand about the process of disengagement and the development of blocked trust is this emotional component, the necessity for the child to suppress the pain of being too alone in the world way before he or she has the resources to escape to a better place. Instead, the child has to escape chemically, by releasing the same chemical in his brain and body that would normally be released when an infant in distress receives comfort from a parent: opioids. Understanding the role of this pain suppression process is vitally important for understanding the habitual disengagement and all of the behavioral traits these children exhibit later in life when they are in a safer environment. The suppression of the pain of rejection, abandonment, and abuse goes to the heart of blocked trust because when the young child has to use this strategy to comfort him- or herself, he or she is starting down a developmental pathway that inherently involves the suppression of the very social emotions that would normally help a child bond with and sustain a loving connection with a nurturing caregiver: empathy, remorse, and eventually guilt, the "secondary emotions" that are essential to the maintenance of trust-based relationships.

This is the beginning step in blocking the development of social emotions—empathy, remorse, and guilt—the emotions that are adaptive to being in a bonded, trustworthy relationship with another human being.

Suppression of Social Pain and Empathy

Even very young infants tend to cry when they hear other babies crying. This early responsiveness to the distress sounds of others is thought by developmental scientists to be a precursor to the kind of empathy seen in older children, who are affected by the distress of another person (Decety, Michalska, & Kinzler, 2012). When poorly cared-for infants start to suppress their crying and stop calling out for a responsive, comforting other, they may also suppress the development of empathy. Empathy, feeling another person's pain, is connected to feeling one's own pain, so when a child blocks his or her own suffering to avoid the chronic pain of being neglected, the child may be blocking the capacity to respond to the distress of others. Suppression of empathy is often seen clinically in these children and is one of the most distressing traits they exhibit to their caregivers.

This is precisely what John Bowlby (1982) and others observed in babies who were in institutions where they were not given contingent care, where there was no call-and-response relationship with an attachment figure. The babies had learned to stop calling, and they appeared to be having little (if any) emotion. In short, they had learned to block their felt need for care, to stifle their cries by not feeling the pain of their chronically neglectful care. They were physically there, but not emotionally there. They had disengaged to survive the lack of an engaging partner, a warm, responsive, go-to adult. Of great relevance to attachment-focused treatment, introducing warm, responsive caregivers to these shut-down children reportedly reawakened the children's capacity for engagement, rescuing them from chronic blocked trust (Cassidy & Shaver, 2008).

Lack of empathy in children with blocked trust is one of the most troubling traits for caregivers and creates one of the greatest risk factors for developing blocked care and rejecting these children. It's vital that therapists and caregivers understand that empathy suppression is part of the child's defense system for surviving poor care, and recovering the capacity for empathy is inextricably linked to the process of recovering the capacity to feel the need for care rather than blocking attachment-related emotions.

Empathy is related to the pain-processing circuitry in the brain and body (Masten, Morelli, & Eisenberger, 2011). Brain imaging studies of people experiencing empathic pain show brain activity in a connected subset of regions that ultimately leads to activation in part of the ACC and in the insula, a region that is now known to be a vital player in our emotional life, especially our "gut feelings" ranging from love, to hate, to disgust (see below). Connections between the ACC and the anterior part of the insula support the capacity for empathy (Craig, 2011). Other mammals who display high levels of empathy, such as elephants, some whales, and some great apes, also have a well-developed ACC–insula circuit (Allman et al., 2011). Meanwhile, sociopathic people show low levels of activity in this circuit in response to other people's pain, as do people who are alexithymic (don't feel their own emotions much) (Vogt and Lane, 2009).

The parts of the ACC and insula that are active in these studies are known to be on when a person is having the subjective experience of suffering. You may have heard the saying "pain is unavoidable, but suffering is optional." Brain studies now show that indeed, the sensation of pain and the process of suffering from that pain are separable, or "dissociable," to use the scientific jargon. In other words, we can actually separate the process of suffering, of being in a state of anguish from a physical or emotionally painful thing, and the objective awareness of hurting, the physical sensation, intensity, and location of pain. In fact, this is a goal of Buddhist meditation and most forms of meditative and mindfulness practices. The emotional component of pain and the somatic sensation of pain are different and engage the brain differently.

This ability to separate emotional suffering from sensing pain enables us to blunt or suppress the subjective experience of "hurting." Intriguingly, the part of the ACC active during the suffering component of pain is close to the part that controls both distress vocalizations (crying)and other sounds of suffering plus the facial expressions of suffering. This is a two-way system in the sense that we can decrease subjective suffering by relaxing our facial muscles and our vocal cords (maybe by humming, chanting, or singing) and by using thoughts or images of safety or pleasant things to send positive messages down from the ACC all the way to the spinal cord, where pain messages originate, quieting the whole pain system from the top down. (Neuroscientists call the process of sensing pain "nociception" and the pain suppression process antinociception. The technical name for the brain–body pain inhibition system that originates in the cingulate is the descending nociceptive inhibitory system, or DNIS). (See Vogt, 2009 for the details).

Even young infants have some capacity to suppress the suffering system when they have to. They use this capability when they learn to stop crying and stop showing pain from not having a responsive attachment figure. All pain processing involves the opioid system, and this system can be used to suppress pain by triggering the release of opioids into the ACC and sending messages downstream that activate opioid receptors all the way down into the brain stem to turn off the pain messages. (This is the workings of the DNIS.) This opioi-dergic system also seems to be involved in the process of dissociation as well as playing a role in placebo effects, hypnosis, and the use of positive imagery to reframe potentially hurtful experiences (Vogt and Vogt, 2009; for an extended discussion of the role of opioids in dissociation, see Vogt, 2009; Lanius, Paulsen, & Corrigan, 2014).

The Insula:
The Visceral Cortex Involved in Social Feelings

The insula is an old, hidden part of the cortex that is now considered to be the visceral cortex, the place in the brain where information is received from the body (Craig, 2009). The insula is active when we feel social emotions—positive ones, such as loving feelings, and neg-ative ones, such as envy, hate, and jealousy. Disgust is also mediated by the insula. People who are very aware of their feelings and bodily sensations have active insulas, especially on the right side of the brain (Craig, 2009). Figure 2.1 illustrates the location of the insula, made visible only by pulling back the temporal lobe and the outermost layer of the lower frontal lobe.

The part of the insula closest to the front of the brain, the anterior insula, becomes especially active in people who exhibit and report high levels of empathy. In contrast, people who are alexithymic, who

Figure 2.1 The insula

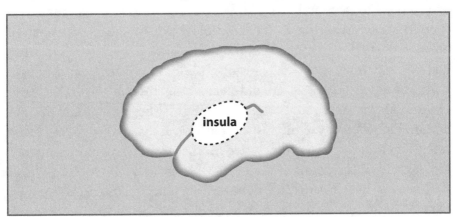

generally don't tune in well to their own or other people's feelings, do not activate their anterior insula nearly as much as the highly empathic, "feeling" people. Intriguingly, people who practice forms of mindfulness that involve tuning into their own bodies and feelings appear to experience growth in their insulas. Clearly there is a brain system that supports the capacity for empathy and when this system isn't activating, for whatever reason, a person does not feel as much and has a lower awareness of their own bodily states (Craig, 2009).

Is it possible that maltreated children who show low empathy somehow learned to blunt the activity of their anterior insulas and ACCs as part of the process of dulling their pain to decrease their suffering? Very likely. The front part of the insula and the ACC regions are rich in opioid receptors. This would facilitate the suppression of the visceral social pain of being left without comfort. Once this pain suppression mechanism starts operating in the insula–ACC network, it would suppress the development of the empathy brain system, leading to what later appears to be an empathy deficit disorder.

It is very important to distinguish between the kind of empathy deficit that is a part of blocked care and those seen in people diagnosed as sociopathic or psychopathic. Most maltreated children have a form of environmentally induced empathy deficit that is part of their adaptive defense against the pain of being poorly treated. The difference in these scenarios is critical because there is strong reason to believe that environmentally induced empathy suppression is more treatable than the kind of cold-blooded, low-heart-rate form of empathy deficit seen in true psychopathy. Indeed, brain research that compares people with histories of childhood adversity and people with consistent histories of cold-hearted aggression show that early childhood trauma is more often associated with high states of arousal and limbic reactivity, while psychopathy is associated with low heart rates, low arousal, and underactive limbic systems, including smaller and less active amygdalas (Vogt, 2009; Vogt & Lane, 2009).

There is reason to think that a child who has blocked his own pain of being neglected as a defense can be helped to recover the capacity to feel that pain, to feel the need for care; this will also help the child start to recover the capacity for empathy. In brain terms, empathy is clearly connected to the capacity to feel one's pain. When a child is helped to do this as part of the recovery from blocked trust, this should also facilitate the recovery from blocked empathy.

You might wonder what would activate the capacity to feel one's pain and thus facilitate the recovery from blocked empathy. Experiencing empathy, of course. We like to say to the therapists we supervise, "Empathy is like aspirin, it works for anything, except when it doesn't!" The problem is that the instant the child experiences empathy, he or she is likely to feel a slight tendency to want comfort for the pain that has been suppressed for so long. He is drawn to feel vulnerable. So this child may react with anger: "Don't talk to me like that, I'm not a baby!" Or might challenge the therapist: "You just want me to cry!" As if the therapist were engaged in a horrible act of manipulation. It was a sad day early in our learning to treat children and teens experiencing blocked trust, when we had to go slow—sometimes very slow—in expressing the empathy we felt for these children. They did not feel safe enough to feel it. Thus we need to continue to experience empathy for them and be sensitive and flexible in our expression of it.

> Dwayne was a seven-year-old boy about whom it was said, "Nothing bothers him." Nor did it seem was he bothered when someone else was bothered. He frightened his adoptive parents when he would simply walk away if another child was crying or upset about something. Dwayne did not seem to experience much empathy for others. In fact, his emotional expressions generally seem constricted, and it was hard to know what he felt about something—except anger. His parents and the neighborhood knew when he was angry. He screamed loud and long in reaction to all sorts of frustrations. The therapist had a hint of this in the second session. After hearing the adoptive father, Ed, talk about how difficult it had been for Dwayne to have to come to the therapy ses-

sion because he had wanted to ride his bike, the therapist turned to Dwayne.

> **Therapist:** (*with a gentle, supportive voice*) That must have been hard, Dwayne, that you had to come here when you really wanted to ride your bike. Yeah, it must have been very hard, I can understand that.
>
> **Dwayne:** (*screaming, with an intense look of rage at the therapist*) Don't talk to me like that! I'm not a baby! Don't talk to me like that!
>
> **Therapist:** (*with more animation, stronger, more matter-of-fact, sensing that Dwayne did not want to experience the therapist's empathy for him*) Of course, Dwayne, of course you're not a baby and if I talked in a way to make you think that I thought that you were, I'm sorry! You're quite a boy! And you can ride a bike really well is my guess! (*turning to Ed*) Dwayne is very clear with me. I can understand why he'd get angry with me because he thought that I thought that he was a baby. And he's seven! I know that! Sometimes I talk quietly and Dwayne thinks that means that I think that he's a baby. I'll have to be careful about that.

For a number of sessions, the therapist related with Dwayne in a more reflective, relaxed manner, being careful not to convey empathy through emotion in his voice. When he did express empathy for something that seemed to be challenging for Dwayne, he did it by talking to Ed rather than talking to Dwayne directly. Ed responded similarly to the therapist about Dwayne. During one such exchange, Dwayne joined in.

> **Therapist:** I wonder, Ed, if your son sometimes is not sure why you won't let him watch TV. I wonder if he thinks

that you don't like him then and if he thought that, I'd think that it would be hard for him.

Ed: Yes, it would, and I do think that he thinks that sometimes. He's even said something like that. He's said, "I don't think you like me very much." And I felt sad then because that would be hard to think that about your dad.

Dwayne: I don't think that you like me.

Ed: I'm sorry, son, if you don't think that I like you. I need to find a way to show it better, I really do. You're not likely to trust me if you don't think I like you.

Dwayne: Why do you like me?

Ed: *(with a few tears)* Oh, Dwayne, because you're my son. Because you are you. Because I've been happy from the first time you said "hi" to me. I could give you a new reason for why I like you every day until you're 21! *(more tears, staring at his son, who was staring back at his father)*

Dwayne's face softened, and he looked sad. Seeing the vulnerability in his son's face, Ed moved over on the couch and pulled Dwayne to him and Dwayne cried for the first time in 15 months of living with his adoptive parents. Ed whispered to his son as he rocked him in his arms and stroked his hair. He seemed to be talking to Dwayne as if he were a baby and Dwayne did not mind.

Dwayne was beginning to trust. This change was not consistently present every day. But within a few weeks, signs of trusting and discovering the full range of his emotional life were more evident. Over the next several months, Dwayne was able to become comfortable accepting comfort from his parents. He could accept empathy from them and from the therapist. Then his parents reported that he was showing empathy for other children. He no longer turned away from their distress or his own.

Suppression of Guilt and Remorse: Shame

Poorly treated children often experience chronic shame. Shame, as Alan Schore explains (1994, 2013), is a natural emotion for very young children to experience, but when shame states are not effectively co-regulated by a caring adult who helps the child recover quickly and restore the connection with the caregiver, shame can start to become a toxic emotion that is extremely dysregulating. Children left by insensitive caregivers to linger in a state of shame cannot regulate this emotion well on their own. Rather than experiencing brief moments of shame that are followed by reconnection with a caring adult, a process that actually is a precursor to the development of the capacity for remorse and eventually a healthy guilt or a superego, poorly cared-for children get stuck in shame states, hiding from caregivers without knowing how to repair the connection and regain their good standing with the adult. In this scenario, shame is a blocking emotion that suppresses the child's potential for feeling safe with a caregiver.

Clinically, we find that unregulated shame is associated with the child's anger and tendency to go into rage rather than into more vulnerable emotional states that can help heal the broken connection. Shame is a very painful emotion, and rage can be a powerful means of suppressing it. Children in chronic shame also have other effective means to avoid that experience, including lying, minimizing, blaming others, and making excuses for their behaviors.

This kind of toxic shame blocks remorse, sadness, and empathy, making it very difficult for caregivers to understand how their children can be so lacking in these softer, prosocial emotions that are typically an essential component of trusting relationships. As we discuss when we get to the treatment process, it is essential that therapy addresses the dysregulating, blocking effects of shame and helps the child and caregiver repair their connections, most importantly by helping caregivers learn to be good co-regulators of the child's negative emotions, including shame.

Suppression of Curiosity and Wonderment

Even before young children learn the word *why*, they appear to wonder at things that are somewhat novel or unexpected, at least when they feel safe enough to indulge in the inner state of curiosity. Mavis, the little girl who was helping her mother cook breakfast in Chapter 1, looks quizzically at her dad when he makes a face she hasn't seen before, as if she's asking, "Why are you making that face, Daddy? What does that expression mean?" Then she may try to copy his expression, trying to move her facial muscles to reproduce that funny look.

Danny, however, with his eyes and ears alert for external threats, doesn't look with wonder on strange things in his environment. Instead, he looks with concern or outright fear, an emotion that constricts his vision and his thinking, forcing him to forgo the process of being curious and certainly forgo the act of asking his stressed-out parents any questions, especially ones beginning with *why*. Being curious is the safe child's way of engaging with the world and then making new sense of the nature of his world, himself, and other people. This early wondering is the forerunner of reflection or reflective functioning, the capacity to step back from immediate ways of seeing things to think about one's experiences, knit together the remains of the day, shed new light on old beliefs, and reappraise.

Suppression of "Reality Testing": Telling Tall Tales and Believing Them

Relevant to our model, blocked trust may originate in an early dissociative process that enables maltreated children to remove themselves mentally from their situation even while they have to stay physically present. Eventually this dissociative process enables a child to construct alternative realities using imaginative processes to comfort them from the harsh realities of their outer and inner worlds. They learn what we call the art of "sweat-free lying"—the ability to make things up to suit their defensive needs without triggering their own stress system and creating the normal discomfort most people feel when we tell untruths. Maltreated children learn to construct their own reality to keep themselves safe or get some of the attention they need by creating a different world to live in than the real world they were forced to inhabit. Because this imaginative process is disconnected from feelings through the pain suppression process, this kind of storytelling is disconnected from the need for "reality testing," freeing the child's mind to create stories that help them survive the harshness they experience in their defensive state. This kind of free-floating reality creates thoughts and mental scenarios that are just as real to these children as the kind of reality safe children live with. The mental scenarios created in this free-floating state of mind seem just as or even more real to them than the real world. This process that begins very early in life with tuning out the harsh realities of their uncaring world lays the foundations for the process of confabulation so often exhibited by maltreated children, to the consternation of most adults in their lives. As one young girl said about her time in an orphanage, "I made up a family for myself just in case I never really got one." Now this brave kid is often in trouble for telling tall tales!

Suppression of Complexity: Black and White Thinking

Uncertainty is the biggest trigger for human anxiety. Our brains work hard at making life more predictable, at making quick sense of what is going on so we can decide what action we need to take. We see every day that fear tends to turn us all into either/or thinkers, for us or against us, us versus them. Neuroscientists have shown that the amygdala is highly reactive to ambiguity, triggering increases in arousal and attentiveness to rapidly disambiguate the immediate sensory experience (Whalen and Phelps, 2009). This process is very heightened in maltreated children, who need to complete this assessment process as quickly as possible to stay safe enough in a world they constantly experience as threatening. Reducing ambiguity and going into defensive action is the priority, not taking ample time to study things in their environment or wonder about their own or other people's feelings and actions. This need for rapid decision making suppresses complexity and interferes with the development of higher brain systems that use slower, deeper processes to make richer, more nuanced sense of experiences (the VMPFC that provides top-down self-regulation and the MPFC, the brain's "self-reflection" zone, a key part of the default mode network) (Raichle and Snyder, 2007). The ultra-rapid processing of the defensive brain channels the meaning-making process into simple categories of black and white, good and bad, for me or against me, good me, bad me.

Three Survival Strategies:
Tigers, Opossums, and Chameleons

Anyone who works with children who were exposed early in life to poor care knows that there are several types of kids with blocked trust. Let's look at three common variations on the theme of blocked trust: tigers, opossums, and chameleons. Jimmy is a tiger, ever ready to actively resist any perceived attempts of caregivers to exert their authority over him. He is an expert at detecting the slightest signs that one of his parents is about to tell him what to do and to defend himself from being controlled, actively pushing back against anything he perceives as restricting his freedom of movement. Jimmy's form of blocked trust is based primarily on the sympathetic nervous system, the defense system that supports active forms of self-defense (fight or flight). In this fighter mode of blocked trust, the Jimmies of the world stay in a chronic state of readiness to do battle with anyone who tries to boss them, deeply mistrusting authority figures based on earlier experiences with bad bosses.

Maria's style of blocked trust looks totally different from Jimmy's. She learned to use her parasympathetic nervous system to keep an extremely low profile, in essence, playing opossum, like feigning death. When Maria is around other people, her go-to, mindless, habitual strategy of blocked trust is to make herself as small and invisible as possible. To help her do this, her brain suppresses her vocal cords so she won't make a peep. Also, by keeping her vegetative vagal system on (Porges, 2011), she is able to be present without moving around much. She can be present without feeling present.

Maria's "opossum" strategy of blocked trust is to stay out of sight and out of mind to others so she can live under the radar of their attention. Jimmy, in habitual fight mode, cannot avoid the radar, but Maria constantly suppresses all forms of expansiveness, shrinking herself to avoid drawing attention. Whereas Jimmy is likely to acquire a diagnosis of oppositional defiant disorder (ODD), Maria is likely to be diagnosed as dissociative or at least depressed.

Carrie, in contrast to Jimmy and Maria, relies on a style of blocked trust in which she constantly adapts her affect and behavior to the moods of those around her. Her chameleon-like style probably relies heavily on her innate ability to read adult emotions and make quick changes internally that enable her to stay in superficial connection with caregivers by suppressing her own needs and feelings and accommodating to the needs and moods of the adults. Her style is often seen in children living with substance-abusing adults where the child adapts by learning to be good and go along to get along to the nth degree. Carrie defends herself by being superficially social while having to suppress her real needs for the comfort and joy of deep, trustworthy connections with adults.

How different children respond to poor care early in life likely depends on temperament or genetic predispositions and also to some extent on gender. Children with the different styles of blocked trust described here tend to elicit different reactions from parents. Fighters are most at risk of triggering negative, aggressive reactions from caregivers and initiating the cycle of mutual defensiveness that can lead to chronic mutual mistrust. Children who have adopted the hiding strategy, the opossums, are less likely to elicit aggressively negative care from adults. Instead, these children can promote feelings of rejection or failure in parents who try to engage them and get little response from them in return for parental investment. Caregivers for hiders are at risk of suppressing the feelings of rejection and failure and, in so doing, tend to feel less caring. As it becomes a job, they are also likely to enter the cycle of mutual defensiveness that leads to chronic mutual mistrust.

Chameleons may mask their blocked trust the best and may be perceived by others as friendly and happier than the tigers and opossums. These kids are less likely than the other two types to trigger blocked care in the caregivers. The risk is still present, however, as the chameleons' caregivers are likely to experience their child as being engaged in chronic manipulation, and in being not real or fake. Over time, the connection with such a child may begin to feel not real.

In terms of parenting and therapy, it is important to realize that all three styles are rooted in early childhood experiences with inadequate parenting and all three groups of children have significant trust issues that need to be addressed. The tigers are the squeaky wheels of blocked trust, are most likely to be brought to treatment, and are most at risk for being harshly treated or rejected by adults. It is important that adults who work with kids be attentive to the opossums and chameleons to help ensure that these children receive help with feeling genuinely safe with trustworthy others.

Summary

Children exposed to poor care early in life have to channel their brain development toward self-defense while suppressing the development of their potential for social engagement. In the process, they develop what we call blocked trust, a complex, multifaceted strategy for surviving life in a harsh, unnurturing environment by depending mostly on themselves rather putting their trust in caregivers. Blocked trust emerges through the epigenetic effects of neglect and abuse on five core brain systems: the social engagement, self-defense, social switching, social pain, and stress systems. To live defensively, maltreated children develop a highly sensitive self-defense system and use the amygdala-driven social switching system to suppress their social engagement system in favor of spending most of their time in a defensive state of mind and body. Along with this negatively biased state regulation system, these children suppress the pain of rejection by activating their opioid system to inhibit the social pain that would normally play a key role in the development of a secure attachment to a responsive, comforting adult. This pain suppression also inhibits the development of the prosocial emotions, including empathy and remorse. Finally, poor care programs the development of the stress response system, the HPA axis, to be on high alert, combining with the self-defense system to create chronic hypervigilance and readiness to deal with perceived threats. Understanding these combined processes of heightening brain systems to stay on guard and hypervigilant for threats and suppressing attachment-related emotions can help therapists and caregivers understand the challenges these children face when adults want them to shift from mistrust to trust. We believe that this brain-based understanding of these children can help inform treatment and facilitate a more integrated and effective approach to helping them recover from the damaging effects of poor care.

CHAPTER 3

Blocked Care: The Parenting Brain and the Role of the Caregiver

Children who experience early adversity, such as neglect, abuse, exposure to domestic violence, and separations from caregivers, are at increased risk for developing disorganized attachments. These children's caregivers need to provide nurturing, sensitive care, indeed even therapeutic care, if such children are to develop organized attachments.
—Bernard et al. (2012, p. 623)

Young children are at the mercy of their caregivers' states of mind toward them and have to adapt accordingly to survive. The ability of a parent to develop and sustain a compassionate state of mind or attitude toward the child—embracing the whole child—is, in our clinical experience, the most important factor contributing to a child's recovery from blocked trust. Parents who can resist the natural tendency to respond defensively to a child's defensiveness and can recover effectively from inevitable moments of losing empathy with a mistrusting child are the trust builders these children need to have.

Developing and sustaining this kind of resilient compassion is no easy task—far from a no-brainer. One parent described it as "hugging a cactus." Indeed, parenting a chronically defensive child takes all of the brain power an adult can muster, demanding the use of instinctual aspects of caregiving we share with other mammalian parents and the highest executive powers we access by turning on our most uniquely human brain regions in our prefrontal cortex. To make it even more challenging, these higher brain regions are the very ones most likely to shut down when a parent is experiencing great stress.

In brain terms, the ability to be a nurturing parent over time depends heavily on the social engagement system (that smart vagal circuit we described in Chapter 1) (Porges, 2012), the brain–body system that enables people to stay open and engaged with each other even when there is tension or misattunement in the relationship. Parents who stay open, mindful, and engaged with their children over time in spite of the stresses and strains of parenthood are relying on their good vagal tone to stay parental in an enriched way that supports a child's healthy brain development. Parents with good vagal tone can keep defensive reactions at bay and recover more quickly from lapses into defensiveness than can parents with poor vagal tone. Fortunately, a growing body of research shows that parents can strengthen their capacity to be open and engaged in their relationships with their children (Tang et al., 2010). (We discuss this in Chapters 8 and 11.)

As we discussed in our previous book, *Brain-Based Parenting* (Hughes & Baylin, 2012), parenting well actually calls on at least five different brain systems that enable us to (1) feel safe being very close to our children; (2) derive pleasure and joy from taking care of and interacting with our kids; (3) attune to our kids' inner lives using our powers of empathy and "mindsight"; (4) construct positive, affirming stories or narratives about being parents; and (5) control our negative, uncaring reactions sufficiently to stay parental most of the time, to be the adult in the room. We call these systems the Approach, Reward, Child Reading, Meaning Making, and Executive Systems. When a parent can access all five systems and keep them up and running over time, a child gets to interact with an open-minded, empathic, attuning other in ways that we now know enhance a child's brain development and build strong bonds of trust between parent and child. A parent's ability to access and sustain this open state of engagement depends on the parent's visceral sense of safety, physically and emotionally, in the relationship with the child. Having supportive, secure relationships with other adults and freedom from chronic stress over issues of daily survival are also essential for a parent to interact in an open, engaged way.

Normally, when parents go through the experience of pregnancy and then are present to be trust builders in a child's first year of life, there is a mix of joy and stress in which the joy outweighs the stress, enabling the parents to hold on to their loving feelings and compassion for their child and gain the child's deep trust in their care. The hormonal changes during pregnancy, especially the rise in oxytocin and prolactin levels around the time of birth, prime the caregiving system in the mother, while expectations of fatherhood may have similar priming effects on the father-to-be, including the suppression of testosterone and other hormones that would normally inhibit a dad's more nurturing, empathic potential (Bridges, 2008). With the birth of the child and the beginnings of face-to-face, voice-to-voice, touch-to-touch interactions, oxytocin and dopamine are triggered in parents and children, helping create strong emotional bonds that pave the way toward secure attachment and sustained caregiving (Fleming & Li, 2002).

This emotional bonding process helps build a strong foundation of trust that enables parents and children to weather the inevitable tensions that accompany the next stage of development when the child is mobile and the parents have to engage in more socializing functions, including saying "no" and helping the child learn to accept limits and rules. Once children deeply trust their parents' intentions in setting limits and directing behaviors, the children are free to turn their attention to what is really important to them—play, discovery, delight, adventure, learning interesting things. The parents can do the heavy lifting regarding basic issues of safety and the child is free to be a child.

One of us has a friend with a three-year-old child. This child, Erika, had already had much experience with her mother saying "no" to her when she wanted something badly, as well as saying "no" when her mother wanted her to do something. It didn't quite seem fair to Erika that her mother's "no" might be followed by behavior that tended to make it more compelling while she had no such behavior available to her. Erika decided to see what power she did have. When her mother told her to do something that she did not want to do, she would stop, glance at her mother, and calmly, yet forcefully say, "I don't love you!" At other times, when she had done something she was not supposed to do, she would use the same stare and voice and say, "I'm not sorry." She was discovering whether her mother would accept—would even cherish and protect—her inner life of thoughts, feelings, and wishes, when her mother was still exerting control over her behaviors. Erika was lucky. She was able to trust her mother with her inner life, and her inner life was able to thrive! She was able to not worry about the possibility of losing her special relationship with her mother while she was involved in the process of organizing her sense of self.

How did her mother respond to Erika's clear communications of "I don't love you!" or "I'm not sorry!"? She responded in various ways, each way communicating acceptance of what Erika said. Sometimes she replied with empathy, "My goodness, sweetie, you must really be angry with me if you don't love me because I won't let you play that game now." Sometimes this was joined with curiosity, "Could you help me understand? What makes it so important to you that you're saying that you don't love me anymore because I won't let you do that? That is really important to you I guess." Sometimes she responded with playfulness, "I wonder if you're aware of not liking me now because I won't let you play your game. I wonder if there is still some love for me somewhere inside of you. I can tell if there is by checking behind your ear. If there is a little red circle there, that means you still love me but don't like me now." With various responses like this, Erika felt safe to communicate her inner life to her mother, and discovered that she and her mother could disagree and still have a close, trusting, relationship. You might remember these types of responses—playful, accepting, curious, and empathic—as they will take a front row seat when we explore how to help mistrusting children in the difficult journey of learning to trust.

Mutual Defense Societies: When Blocked Trust Meets Blocked Care

Having to be a socializer without the benefit of first being a comforter and trust builder has much to do with why foster and adoptive parents of older children experience great challenges as they try to combine trust-building with socialization, "connection with correction." Under the inevitable stress of parenting hurt children, parents are at risk for blocked care (Hughes and Baylin, 2012). The concept of blocked care refers to a scenario in which too much stress suppresses the higher brain functions needed for caregiving, engendering a self-defensive stance toward a child. In blocked care, the parent's nurturing capacities are suppressed, temporarily out of commission. Caregiving is supported by the social engagement system, not the defense system; defensive states of mind inhibit the caring process. When a parent gets stuck in a defensive state of mind, this puts the parent–child relationship in jeopardy because, in effect, there is no caring mind "in the room."

We readily understand how an adult is likely to begin to experience "blocked care" when an adult partner does not respond to expressions of interest and care for a period of time. Rejection by our child is likely to trigger the same social pain system activated by adult rejection. Although we may be able to see the difference between our child's and our partner's hurtful actions, it is still challenging to manage feelings of rejection and sustain caring feelings for our child. The risk that our care will weaken and may even become blocked, is still present.

Common Characteristics of Blocked Care

Shifting between states of social engagement and self-defense is normal in the give-and-take of parent-child relationships. Blocked care sets in when the parent gets stuck in defensiveness and cannot shift out of this negative state of mind towards the child. In this scenario, the parent's brain is using the defense system to protect the parent from the pain of perceived rejection.

Rejection Sensitivity and the Brain: It Feels Personal

Because parenting is such a demanding, emotionally meaningful process, parents have a strong tendency to take their children's reactions to them personally. In brain terms, taking things personally is related to the activation of the limbic system, which is tightly connected to our hearts and the rest of our bodies. When we react to anything that moves us strongly, this system is turned on; when this system is on, we experience what is happening as highly personal, as happening to us, as being about us. This is why it is often difficult for us to deal with signs of rejection or invalidation when we interact with another person. Our first appraisal in these situations comes from our limbic brain, including our amygdala, not from our higher, more reflective regions of the brain, particularly the middle prefrontal regions, that can help us to step back from our immediate experience and gain a better perspective. We can easily get captured in this egocentric, personalizing part of our brain's reaction, especially if we are interacting with someone whose reactions to us really matter. For parents, reactions from their children matter a lot and are very likely to stir up the limbic system, for better or for worse.

In many ways, the parents of children with blocked trust face the same dilemma that the children faced earlier in life when they had to protect themselves from the chronic pain of being neglected and/or abused. Just as the children turned to the pain suppression process, the parents are likely to use the same process to buffer themselves from having to experience the constant pain of feeling rejected by their children. This is how blocked care can set in—initially as an adaptive response that protects the parent from the pain of caring when it hurts to care. The risk here is that this process may suppress the caring process because the two are interlinked in the brain. That is, feeling caring and empathic toward a child and feeling the pain of being rejected by the child activate a very similar region of the brain, parts of the anterior cingulate cortex (ACC) (Eisenberger, Lieberman, & Williams, 2003). To suppress the pain of rejection, the parent uses the ACC to inhibit the pain system in a top-down way, using opioid receptors all along the way to the brain stem from where pain messages get relayed upward into the cingulate (Vogt & Sikes, 2009). Suppressing the pain of rejection, then, also suppresses the capacity for empathy, for subjectively caring about the child.

In short, the brain processes that underlie the development of blocked trust in maltreated children operate in the adult brain, as well, creating the potential for getting stuck in the same kind of limbic reactivity that is at the heart of chronic defensiveness in children with blocked trust. While adults have more brain power than do young children (increased prefrontal powers are associated with the transition from adolescence to adulthood), this does not guarantee that adults faced with intense stress will be able to access these higher powers and regulate negative, self-protective reactions toward a defensive child.

> Two years ago, Sharon came for her first appointment to speak about her concerns regarding her adopted 11-year-old son, Tim, to ask what she could do to be more successful in raising him. After hearing about his history before he was adopted at age seven and his significant challenges since then, the therapist indicated that Tim had been hurt so badly for so many years that most likely he did not trust her and

her partner to provide him with the safety and guidance that he needed. Most likely he also may have felt that he did not deserve their love. This led to the following exchange.

Sharon: Well, if that's true, what am I supposed to do?

Therapist: I really cannot suggest anything to do. He needs to trust you, and if he doesn't trust you, he is not likely to trust any one thing that you do. We will discuss ways that might help him learn to trust you.

Sharon: So your saying it is my fault! If he doesn't trust me, it must be me!

Therapist: I'm sorry that what I said caused you to think that I'm blaming you! I'm not saying that you caused him not to trust you. He came to live with you not trusting anyone, including you. You did not create his not trusting you!

Sharon: How do you know?

Therapist: I've treated many adopted kids and their families, and over and over I've seen how many of them have great difficulty trusting their adoptive parents because of how badly they had been hurt by their first parents. They weren't hurt by their adoptive parents.

Sharon: (*sitting silently, staring out the window. Tears appear in her eyes*) You don't know. Sometimes I hate him. (*crying now*) Sometimes I wish that I had never seen him . . . Sometimes I even wish . . . that he had never been born.

Therapist: (*after sitting silently for a while with Sharon's tears*) Oh, Sharon, that must be so painful for you. So painful. After being filled with such joy when you first met Tim, having such wonderful hopes and dreams . . . to now be aware that sometimes you hate him, sometimes you wish that you had never met him . . . so painful.

Sharon: Why . . . why doesn't he want my love?

Therapist: (*responding as if Sharon was requesting information*) Sharon, Tim wanted the love of his first parents and

> did not get it. So he stopped trusting that he would ever get it. Then he began . . .
>
> **Sharon:** Why? Why?! Doesn't he want my love?
>
> **Therapist:** (*Now guessing what Sharon might have really been wanting to hear*) I don't know, Sharon. I don't know. I just know that you're in a great deal of pain. I know that you want my help so we can figure it out together. You don't want to be alone with this anymore.
>
> **Sharon:** Will you help me?
>
> **Therapist:** Yes I will.

This dialogue is common when a competent and committed adoptive or foster parent first seeks help to understand and care for a child who has been rejecting their care. At first it might seem that the parent wants specifics about providing effective care. The danger is that the therapist will be content with that and provide specifics. Often, though, the parent is asking for help—sometimes without knowing at first what they are asking for—to be able to care again. Not what consequences will work, but how to feel love, compassion, understanding, and worry again for their child. It is breaking their heart, and they can't turn their heart on again. We have come to know that reality and we have come to call it blocked care.

When professionals speak with a parent who expresses her despair and lack of love for her child as Sharon did, it is important to ask about other factors in the parent's life that might be contributing to the lack of felt care for their child. Is there a crisis involving the relationship with the partner, a job, medical problem, or another loss? Also it is important to understand the parent's own childhood and their relationships—past and present—with their parents. The adopted child might well be activating something from the parent's own history. However, the current lack of care for the child does not prove that there are other issues. Caring for a child who does not accept, value, or seem to benefit from the parent's ongoing caring places *any* parent at risk for blocked care. Our brains are designed for reciprocity, and in our most intimate forms of relationships—attachment, caregiving, and our relationship with our partner—ongoing, reciprocal initiatives and responses are especially important if our neurobiological processes are to remain active and not become blocked.

Blindsided by a Child's Blocked Trust

Adults who are used to being trusted and to making people feel safe in their presence may experience being deeply mistrusted for the first time when they try to get close to a child with blocked trust. If these caregivers don't see this coming, if they are blindsided by the child's intensely negative reactions to their offerings of love, they may experience the intense pain of perceived rejection and recoil to protect themselves from this awful feeling. This can be the beginnings of a process in which a caregiver takes the child's defensiveness personally, not understanding that this habitual defensiveness is really not at all personal but an overgeneralized, nondiscriminating response that lumps this adult together with all past adults who have mistreated the child.

When a child's blocked trust meets a parent's blocked care, the parent–child relationship becomes a mutual defense society that keeps reinforcing defensiveness in both parent and child. In blocked care, the parent tends to be in survival mode, parenting reactively rather than proactively. In brain terms, survival-based, defensive parenting is generated from the more primitive limbic and self-defense circuitry, without much use of higher brain functions that support the processes of reflection, mentalization, flexibility, and self-regulation. When the parent is in a "narrow-minded" self-protective state, the child and the relationship are at risk for chronic misattunement. Parents in this stressed-out state of mind do not respond empathically to the child's distress, do not engage in repair operations, and do not reflect on their parenting to make changes and do a better job. Parents who enter parenthood with high levels of stress are more at risk for developing blocked care than are parents who embark on parenthood with emotional resilience, a secure adult attachment style, and a well-developed capacity for self-regulation and self-reflection.

Preventing blocked care, whenever possible, is a primary task in attachment-focused treatment. Addressing blocked care when it has already set in is also an essential component of treatment, because there is little possibility of helping a mistrusting child learn to trust if the adults trying to care for him are not able to approach him nondefensively, indeed, with compassion. Helping caregivers recover from blocked care and then strengthen their capacity for sustaining a compassionate state of mind toward their mistrustful child is a major part of the therapeutic process in attachment-focused treatment.

It behooves therapists to understand the dynamics of parental rejection sensitivity and to be prepared to work empathically with parents like Carol who are experiencing this distressing conflict between their personal reaction to their child's mistrust and their goal of being a loving parent.

> **Missed Innocence:** Carol is the legal guardian for her nephew, Bobby, who spent the first seven years of his life with his biological mother. His parents had addiction problems, and Bobby was often left on his own to take care of himself. He also witnessed domestic violence and lived in a violence-prone neighborhood.
>
> Carol feels that God has given her the task of loving and raising Bobby. While she is doing all of the basic caring, she is struggling with the loving part. In a session where she meets alone with the therapist, she cries some when she talks about her guilty feelings about not feeling loving toward Bobby.
>
> Carol says, "I missed his innocence." When the therapist asks her to elaborate, she says, "I missed learning to love him when he was just completely lovable, like I learned to love my own biological children."
>
> The therapist said, "Bobby isn't innocent anymore and he's not easy to love in that natural, endearing way. That makes so

much sense, Carol. No wonder you're finding it hard to feel those feelings you want to feel so badly."

Mother Blame: Why Is It Typically the Mothers Who Get the Brunt of the Child's Mistrust?

Neuroscientists have now clearly established that infants get to know their birth mothers before they are born, during fetal development. They learn their mother's voice, her smell, and her heart rhythms. When they are born, they are looking for what is familiar and start immediately connecting the voice and smell to the face and touch. Being separated from all that is familiar about this particular mother inevitably produces some degree of distress, even if this separation is very early and adoptive care begins very soon after birth (Callaghan & Richardson, 2011). In studies with other primates such as rhesus monkeys, separation from the birth mother at one week has different effects on brain development than separation at one month (Sabatini et al., 2007). At both times, the loss of the birth mother triggers the infant's stress response system, setting off the HPA system we described in Chapter 1 and causing stress hormones to circulate throughout the child's brain and body. With father figures, no prior associations are likely to be competing with the cues that child gets from a new father because the child did not learn strong associations with the biological fathers smell, voice, and so on. Even in children adopted very early, the infant is losing associative cues when separated from the birth mother that probably cause a competitive process in the child's brain when he or she encounters a new mother figure. Inevitably, at some sensory level, the question is always "Are you my mother? You don't smell like or sound like my mother, so . . . what's going on here?" There is an inherent conflict in the child's brain between the sensory experiences of interacting with a new mother figure and the old sensory memories of the birth mother, a competition between the old and the new that makes the process of learning to feel safe with a new mother figure more complicated than the process of learning to feel safe with a father figure.

Mistrusting children's suppression of separation pain and the desire for comfort is another closely related reason for their stronger defensive resistance to having a closer relationship with their mother than with their father. Mothers tend to evoke the desire to be babied, to be cuddled and comforted, more than do fathers. (Even big strong soldiers are likely to call for their mothers when they are frightened, as seen in movies like *Saving Private Ryan*.) A strong way to prevent feeling the need for mothering is to keep your mother angry with you and to keep yourself angry with her.

How Stress Can Affect the Parent's Ability to Be a Social Bufferer for a Mistrusting Child

As we described earlier, caregivers need to send clear, unambiguous, and consistent safety messages, mostly in the form of their nonverbal behavior, to the child's limbic system, the rapid appraisal circuit the child uses to assess the level of safety in the presence of a caregiver. When a parent is experiencing negative feelings toward the child, in a state of blocked care, their nonverbal communication is unlikely to have the desired calming, social buffering effect that is needed.

For example, one of the most intriguing discoveries from the field of affective neuroscience concerns the process of fleeting facial expressions that are masked by the slower, consciously perceived facial expressions that we are aware of seeing in each other as we interact (Vuilleumier, 2005; Hurley, 2012). These so-called micro-expressions can be either congruent with or incongruent with the slower, consciously perceived expressions. When a caregiver has unresolved trauma or chronic anxiety or chronic anger, he or she is very likely to generate negative microexpressions that are then masked by more positive expressions when the parent is trying to connect with the child. Research using microanalysis of filmed interactions between infants and mothers shows vividly that when mothers make fleeting negative facial expressions, their four-month-old babies react negatively to these expressions, creating unintended misattunement in the dyad and dysregulation in the child (Beebe et al., 2010).

Researchers who study this microexpression phenomenon believe this "invisible" relational process may contribute to the intergenerational transmission of unresolved trauma and insecure attachment styles. In other words, the capacity of our brains to detect and respond automatically and unconsciously to each other's microexpressions could undermine the otherwise positive messages we think we are sending to each other and create chronic cycles of misattunement that get passed on from one generation to the next.

In therapy sessions, we frequently see very well-meaning parents having a dysregulating impact rather than a comforting, co-regulating effect on their children as they interact with them due to these fleeting facial signals. When we watch closely, we can detect at least the late stage of these microexpressions as a very brief but disconcerting look of disgust, annoyance, or fear on a parent's face, followed by subtle looks of doubt, misgiving or mistrust on the child's face and in the child's body language.

Because microexpressions are generated below the level of conscious awareness, we cannot simply inhibit them with conscious effort. The most effective way to clear away negative microexpressions is to let go of the defensive reaction that inhibits an open state of engagement. This may require some work on past unresolved wounds to achieve enough internal security to be in a state of mind conducive to being a calming presence for a defensive child. Adult attachment status is known to be a strong predictor of a child's attachment style, and part of the work in attachment-focused treatment for maltreated children is helping their caregivers resolve their own attachment issues if necessary. Research clearly shows that adults with a secure or autonomous style of attachment spend more time in a state of mind and body conducive to sending clear, unambiguous messages of safety and approachability to a child.

Interventions and Learning Processes

Maltreated children need to have emotional, embodied, visceral experiences with caregivers that can awaken their mistrusting brains to the news that these caregivers are fundamentally different from the ones who caused them harm. To provide these brain-changing experiences, caregivers have to learn to engage with the child across the spectrum of emotional states the child exhibits. The goal is to help the child to experience being unconditionally accepted and safe enough to be close to the caregiver while feeling the full range of emotions, from joy, to sadness, to anger, to fear.

Social Synchrony: When Parent and Child Are In Sync

Neuroscientists have found that parents show a particular pattern of brain activity when they are in sync with their children (Feldman, Greenbaum, & Yirmiya, 1999). There is a region in the cingulate, which lies above the corpus callosum and underneath the prefrontal cortex, that appears to be activated by "social synchrony" (Dumas et al., 2010). This is the upper or dorsal anterior cingulate cortex (dACC), in connection with the middle prefrontal cortex (MPFC). Intriguingly, these adjoining regions in the parenting brain combine mindsight or mentalization with the ability to (1) pay attention to, (2) empathize with, and (3) monitor the moment-to-moment quality of attunement to a child. The dACC is where those error signals we told you about earlier appear to originate, those electrical patterns that signal a need for corrective action. These error signals are like internal "uh ohs" that alert the parent to pay more attention to what is going on to reattune to the child and get back in sync after inevitable moments of misattunement. The dACC is part of the "executive attention system" (Posner et al., 2007), the process we use to stay focused on what's important, resist distractions, and shift our attention in an adaptive, flexible way when the situation demands it. Not surprisingly, research shows that parents who do well at controlling their attention tend to do well at attuning and reattuning in a sensitive way to their children during times of unstructured interactions (Atkinson et al., 2005; Fleming et al., 2008). In fact, research by Fleming's group showed that giving parents attention training using a computer-based format improved their ability to attune to their children during free play (Fleming et al., 2008).

We can reasonably posit that a brain-based goal of attachment-focused treatment is to help parents activate this dACC–MPFC cir-

Figure 3.1 Parent's compassion for child primes child's compassion for self

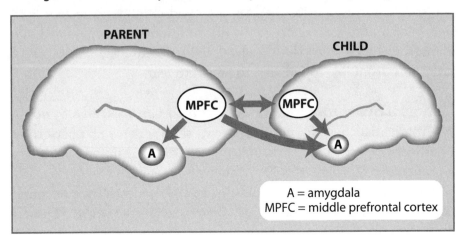

cuit and strengthen it to support their ability to attune in a sensitive, timely way to their children's affective states, needs, and intentions. When a parent is in this brain state, it is likely that the child will move toward this state and out of defensiveness, creating a dyadic state of mutual engagement that is the opposite of the state of mutual defensiveness. There is actually a reciprocal relationship between the MPFC and the amygdala: when the MPFC is on, the amygdala gets quieter through a process of top-down inhibition (Vogt, 2009; Kim et al., 2009). Figure 3.1 depicts this brain-to-brain interaction when the parent and child activate this dACC–MPFC circuit as they get in connection with each other.

Reflective Functioning: Slowing Down and Valuing Connection over Correction

If any notion turns immediately into an action without reflection, we are living our lives all gas pedal and no brakes.
—Siegel (2014, pp. 67–68)

A crucial aspect of good parenting is the ability to step back from stressful, amygdala-driven emotional interactions with a child to engage in the slower and deeper mental process called reflection.

Reflective functioning enables a parent to take a look at her own reactions, her relationship with her child, and her child's needs. This is a higher mental process requiring the use of the most uniquely human regions of the mammalian brain in connection with the amygdala (Ochsner et al., 2004). Reflective functioning enables parents to focus on the state of their relationships with their children rather than just focusing on how they can make their children behave. In a very important sense, reflective functioning is the key to parents being able to put connection before correction (Siegel & Bryson, 2011) in their overall approach to parenting.

Parenting that mostly focuses on correcting children's behavior does not foster the development of emotional and social intelligence and reflective functioning (National Scientific Council on the Developing Child, 2009). Studies show that correction-based parenting usually involves giving children a lot of directives, often in the form of "don'ts," as in "don't do this and don't do that." This style of parenting values a child's obedience over teaching the child to be aware of his own and other people's feelings and helping the child to develop his innate potential for self regulation, mentalizing, and empathy. The need to have children comply quickly with parental demands is typically associated with high levels of stress, with a more survival-based approach to parenting as opposed to a proactive, mindful approach (Golding & Hughes, 2012).

Reflective functioning depends on brain circuitry that develops with age and isn't fully mature until somewhere in our twenties, so children and younger teens have less reflective capacity than adults. This is why parents must use reflective functioning on a regular basis as an integral and vital part of parenting. Reflection isn't possible in the midst of a brain storm, when you have flipped your lid, literally lost the use (temporarily) of your prefrontal cortex. Reflection is part of what Kanneman (2011) calls "slow thinking." It's a prefrontal function that requires good connections among brain regions that have to connect in the moment, forming a circuit that brings together different processing streams. The integration of these streams in the MPFC enables reflection to occur.

The MPFC is a rich convergence zone that pulls together emotional and cognitive processes, empathy and insight, bringing both to bear on the task of deepening one's awareness and understanding of self and others. This brain region is part of the default mode network (DMN), part of that place we go inside to reflect on personal and interpersonal aspects of our lives when we aren't preoccupied with other tasks. This is the brain region that is most often associated with what researchers call mentalization or theory of mind and what Siegel (2012) calls "mindsight." In essence, these terms all refer to a uniquely human function that enables us, more than other primates, to get above our quick reaction system rooted more in basic survival to achieve a meta-perspective on ourselves and our relationships, a higher relational perspective that we need to build and sustain nurturing, trusting, enduring relationships.

Chronically mistrustful children challenge a caregiver's ability to tune in to their inner world rather than just react to often negative behavior. Reflection is only possible when one is not in defensive, survival mode. It requires at least a modicum of felt safety because you have to take your eyes and ears off your surroundings for a while to go inside and engage in a reflective process. You can see how important this ability to take the high road in the brain is to parenting and how essential this process is to parenting difficult, challenging children who so easily trigger a parent's low-road reactions (Siegel & Hartzell, 2003; Siegel & Bryson, 2011). In relation to attachment-focused therapy, the MPFC is the brain region that supports what is called "affective/reflective dialogue" in the DDP model of treatment (see Chapter 5).

Minding the Whole Child

We believe that the most powerful intervention for helping mistrusting children learn to trust trustworthy caregivers is to help caregivers embrace the child's mistrust. Rather than trying to redirect the child and eliminate mistrust, the caregiver who can approach and welcome the child's mistrustfulness, greeting this part of the child with empathy and compassion, can create a window of new learning for the child, an opportunity to experience the crucial difference between past experiences with caregivers and the experience of being with a truly safe caregiver. If a parent can shift from a corrective stance toward the child's mistrust to embracing the mistrust, change becomes possible, whereas before, in a mutually defensive relationship, no change could occur.

By using reflection, the parent can get her mind around seemingly opposite parts of the child, including the sweet part and the angry, oppositional, defensive part. When the parent can construct an integrated working model of the child that embraces all of the child rather than taking a polarizing stance, they construct an internal representation of the child that can promote the same process in the child. In other words, when the parent can build in her or his mind this integrative, coherent model of the child, the model becomes the basis for relating to the child in a more empathic, holistic, integrated, coherent way, in a way that the child will feel, will sense, and will mirror. This mirroring of the parent's holistic way of relating can promote psychological integration in the child, a key aspect of helping a child develop emotional resilience and a capacity to love herself, all of herself, not just her "nice" part.

Reflecting about your child changes your relationship with the child in your mind, in the mental space where you hold the image of the child. This is why Siegel and Bryson (2011), the dyadic developmental psychotherapy (DDP) model (Hughes, 2011), and Fosha (2000) in her work on "minding the child" place so much emphasis on the parent's reflective process. Parental reflection about a child strengthens the ability to develop and sustain a more holistic, multidimensional, integrated image of the child to use as a template for guiding the way to relate to the child. Reflective functioning also helps the parent update her image as the child grows and changes and as the parent–child relationship changes over time.

When a parent adopts a welcoming, empathic, compassionate approach to the child's wild side or worst self, that part that the child typically calls bad or even evil, the parent is communicating to the child that this "dark side" is understandable and even lovable.

When the parent truly gets it that the child's angry self enabled her to survive in a toxic environment, this is key to the process of helping the child heal, integrate her different parts, create a sense of wholeness, of being ok with who she is, safe with all of her feelings and internal states. This internal safety with one's full range of emotions is the core of being a secure, resilient, empathic person.

Helping the Child Feel Safe When Parents Shift from Companionship Mode to Parental Authority Mode

Mistrusting children learned to resist parental authority rather than depend on it. They had to be on guard about relinquishing control, giving power over themselves to an adult who would abuse this power or abdicate parental power through neglect. The hardest part of learning to trust a new caregiver is learning to feel safe with relinquishing control to the parent. To do this, the child has to experience the adult as a benevolent authority figure, not a malevolent or indifferent one. This means that the child has to unlearn his core strategy for staying safe enough around authority figures and stop reflexively resisting parental control.

Parents of mistrusting children often experience an abrupt shift in their relationship with their child when the interaction shifts from a playful one during which there is no real power differential to a parental one in which the parent starts to exert control by giving a directive, such as saying, "Ok, Susie, it's time to get ready for bed." This seemingly innocuous relational shift is a huge change for the child because the parent is implicitly saying to the mistrusting child, "Trust me now with being in charge because my intentions toward you are good and I'm not going to abuse the power that you relinquish to me."

Understanding the difference in a child's experience of us when we shift the relational dynamic from playfulness to authority is an extremely important aspect of the process of gaining a child's trust. The process of making these relational transitions is the source of many of the meltdowns in the parent–child relationship. It is often the parent's innocent exertion of parental authority that triggers what one child called "the Incredible Hulk." This is when the parent needs to really stay empathic with the child's struggle to accept you as a kind boss, a benevolent authority figure whose intentions are good.

Summary

Parenting requires a great deal of brain power and the coordination of multiple brain systems. Parenting well requires that parents feel secure enough in their own selves and in the presence of their children that they can devote themselves to parenting rather than self-defense. Parenting a child in blocked trust requires the often difficult task of inhibiting the development of blocked care. Staying emotionally regulated and sustaining a caring state of mind toward a defensive child are essential for being a trust-building caregiver. In Chapter 9, we revisit parenting to discuss the processes used in DDP to work with parents to help them strengthen their capacity for providing trustworthy care for children with blocked trust.

CHAPTER 4

Attachment-Focused Treatment:
The Core Processes of Change

Changing the trajectory of development is always possible when there is a possibility of accumulating new, more positive experience, particularly when the new experience forces a reorganization of old experiences and thought patterns through the lens of more positive experience.
—Timmer and Urquiza (2014, p. 22)

When you ease the grip of fear, a person emerges who, by his nature, wants to be in relationship.
—Fisher (2014, p. 77)

Attachment-focused therapy uses relational processes to help children shift the trajectory of their development from blocked trust toward trust. This treatment process "works" when adults relate to the child in ways that can awaken the child's brain to the fact that he is now in a safe environment with trustworthy people. This requires disarming the child's overactive defense system that is chronically suppressing social engagement and social emotions. Once this social buffering takes effect, the child's brain can go to school on the relationships with therapists and caregivers to practice and strengthen the underdeveloped potential for social engagement and for feeling those social emotions. Quieting the child's defense system with consistent messages of safety and approachability enables the child's prefrontal cortex in combination with the anterior cingulate cortex (ACC) to come online to support new learning.

This new learning takes the form of processes that neuroscientists call reversal learning, reconsolidation of traumatic memories, reflective functioning, and reappraisal. Think of these processes as the four R's of change.

Reversal Learning

Children with blocked trust have to learn to pay attention to the differences between past and present caregivers and then learn from good experiences with present caregivers to shift from avoiding these adults to approaching them safely. This kind of learning and unlearning requires the activation of the child's higher brain regions, especially the ventromedial prefrontal cortex (VMPFC) combining parts of the orbitofrontal cortex (OFC) and the anterior cingulate cortex (ACC), along with the hippocampus, to help compare past and present experiences, what neuroscientists call "disparity processing" (Morris, 2007). Whenever we learn something very new about relationships, especially if the new learning contradicts old learning, we have to use these higher parts of the social brain, especially the OFC, to incorporate the new learning. Meanwhile the ACC is switched on when we experience conflict between a habitual way of doing something and a new way. When a child starts to have experiences with a caregiver that run counter to those old experiences, his or her ACC needs to come into play to help with the process of inhibiting the old response while trying to do something new: approach a caregiver instead of avoiding or attacking. While the OFC helps with the processes of learning the new "contingencies" of social reward and punishment and storing the new learning to help guide future behavior toward the caregiver, the ACC helps with the process of conflict resolution, monitoring the results of the child's actions for errors caused by reverting to the mistrusting ways (Braver et al., 2001).

These so-called error signals are an essential component of the reversal learning process, alerting the child to pay more attention to what he or she is doing. In this way, the ACC helps the child resolve this internal conflict between the old habit of mistrust and the new, tentative trusting behavior, in favor of the new behavior.

In the early stages of reversal learning, while the old habitual program is actively competing with the child's efforts to learn to approach and engage with adults, it is crucial that the adults understand that the child will be shifting back and forth between the mistrust and the newer, more fragile process of engagement. Allowing the child safe passage between the old and the new ways is vital to help them feel safe with this process of conflict resolution. When the adults embrace this process, knowing it for what it is, they help the child move forward with the new learning and the process of consolidating their capacity to engage and trust. Once the new becomes old, once this learning becomes more of a no-brainer, the PFC withdraws from the process, relinquishing the learning to regions of the brain that can run the well-learned new program automatically, as a habitual way of doing things until new experiences signal the need for another adaptive change in response to a changing environment.

Reconsolidation and Fear Extinction: Safe Exposure to Trustworthy Adults

When children are exposed to very frightening kinds of poor care very early in life, they are likely to be traumatized and develop complex post-traumatic stress disorder (PTSD). This is important to understand because for attachment-focused treatment to work, there has to be a component in which the child's traumatic, often preverbal implicit memories of being exposed to frighteningly poor care have to be reactivated in a safe-enough way that relearning can occur, either in the form of fear extinction or perhaps in the more enduring form of memory change called reconsolidation. The child's memories of poor care have to be revisited, not suppressed, for him or her to begin to feel safe in the presence of a current caregiver. This is what we mean by relational trauma-focused aspects of attachment therapy. This process most certainly is stressful, which is why these frightening memories were suppressed in the first place. Therefore, the process must emerge within the context of relational safety and be a sensitive, gradual process where the fear is co-regulated by a caregiver and/or therapist who is beginning to be trustworthy.

In attachment-focused treatment, reprocessing traumatic memories is relationally facilitated by the way the therapist and caregiver attune to and engage the child to keep the child safe while recalling, implicitly or explicitly, bad things that have happened to them in previous care environments. This involves giving the child the benefit of social buffering of good connections with adults while they are being helped to revisit and reprocess the scary feelings and events that need to be brought up, into the light of day, safely, to be "detoxified." (In DDP other experiences of pride, joy, and curiosity, are also brought up, so that the child is not just a victim, a case, a diagnosis. The child is a real child and all of the child's experiences are privileged.)

Fear extinction is the underlying process involved in exposure-based treatment for PTSD in which the patient recalls the traumatic memory while simultaneously experiencing signs of safety. Applied to attachment-focused therapy and specifically DDP, fear extinction involves helping the child experience the blocked feelings of fear and separation pain while simultaneously receiving safety messages on several levels: (1) internally in the body, (2) contextually from the safe physical setting, and (3) most important, interpersonally, from the soothing, buffering presence of a trusted therapist and a compassionate caregiver.

One of the newer lines of research in the field of trauma studies and PTSD involves what neuroscientists call reconsolidation of fear memories (Quirk et al., 2010; Nader, Schafe, & LeDoux, 2000). *Reconsolidation* refers to the fact that when a memory is recalled, there is an opportunity to change it before it is restored and put to rest again in the brain. There is a window of opportunity while the memory is up and running to alter the firing patterns in the brain that have been keeping the fear in the fear-based memory.

Reconsolidation is different from the more traditional process of fear extinction that has been the dominant model for studying and understanding how desensitization works. In fear extinction, there is not erasure or removal of the fear-conditioned aspect of the memory, but an override in which a new memory—the memory of not being shocked when you touch the kind of thing that originally caused a shock—gets stored in a region of the brain above the amygdala, the subgenual anterior cingulate cortex (SGACC). The SGACC inhibits the amygdala during an exposure process and then apparently stores the memory of the fear extinction process, creating a memory that competes with (rather than erasing) the fear-based memory. In reconsolidation, the memory is actually changed in a more permanent away; when it gets restored in the brain, it is restored without the shock value it formerly had, so it is now a safe memory to recall and be a part of the "safe known" rather than something to be sealed off.

Reflection

Finally, a third region of the PFC swings into action: the middle prefrontal cortex (MPFC), that part of the default mode network (DMN) that enables a person to reflect on new experiences and old beliefs and change her thinking about herself and her relationships with caring adults. The processes of reversal learning and reconsolidation of fear-based memories engage primarily the lower regions of the prefrontal cortex (PFC) and ACC. As these processes unfold, the awakening of the child's prefrontal regions can move further upward to the middle region of the PFC to support reflective functioning, a process that combines affective input with thinking about self and relationships in the light of new experiences and new information. Reflective functioning is the key to the child being able to reappraise old beliefs about herself and the trustworthiness of present caregivers and change her mind and her narrative about herself and the safety of her current environment. The MPFC serves as the working memory zone for what we call "affective/reflective" thinking and dialoguing.

Reappraisal

When the child gains the ability to use the MPFC and the rest of the DMN for safely reflecting on experiences with caregivers, it becomes possible for him or her to use new experiences with caregivers to reappraise old negative beliefs about self and others. This reappraisal process is vital to updating the child's sense of self-worth and building a new self-image rooted in experiences of being safely seen, heard, and touched by a compassionate caregiver. Using this newly acquired capacity for taking a second look at original core beliefs, the child can use top-down, experience-driven thinking to change the way his self-image is stored in his brain, literally changing his brain's stance toward himself and trustworthy adults. The creation of more positive images and thoughts in the MPFC has the effect of quieting the hyperarousal in the child's limbic system that has been driving chronic mistrust (Vogt, 2009). Top-down messages from the MPFC to the amygdala very likely trigger new patterns of gene expression in the amygdala, changing the structure and functioning of that key brain region. This in turn changes the neuroceptive threat detection system, shifting its bias from self-defense toward social engagement.

Enriched Care and the Four R's

Therapy and "enriched caregiving" can help a mistrustful child accomplish the four R's on the journey from mistrust to trust by

1. disarming the hyperactive defense system,
2. awakening the VMPFC,
3. unblocking suppressed social emotions,
4. providing safety to "go inside" to use the DMN,

5. reviving playfulness in the relationship with a caregiver, and
6. providing many opportunities to practice safe engagement and consolidate new learning.

When all is said and done, it actually is harder than it looks!

Disarming the Child's Defense System with Safety Messages

Getting under the Behaviors of Blocked Trust: Emotion-Focused Work
It is crucial that therapists and caregivers understand that blocked trust is essentially an emotional and physiological process, not a behavioral problem. As we explained in Chapter 2, the behaviors that mistrusting children use to deal with poor care originate from the need to avoid the pain of being mistreated and the need to provision themselves, to get what is needed to survive without depending on the good will of an adult to be a provider. Targeting the behaviors of mistrust as a therapist or caregiver rather than addressing the underlying emotional process reinforces the child's emotional experience of being rejected along with the sense of being embedded in shame. It is vital that interventions address the blocked pain, fear, and shame at the epicenter of the child's deep mistrust. When maltreated children block their subjective suffering by suppressing the painful feelings of fear and sadness and rejection, they also block their ability to access these scary emotional states that normally, with good care, would cause the child to reach out to caregivers for comfort. Somehow, treatment for blocked trust has to help these children recover their ability to feel these attachment-related feelings safely enough for them to recover their potential to feel the need for good care, for being comforted and nurtured and experienced as a source of delight and joy rather than as a pain, annoyance, or source of disgust.

Using Eyes, Voice, and Touch to Send Safety Messages
to the Child's Defense System
Parents and children establish trusting, open relationships over time by sharing signals—facial expressions, tones of voice, touch—that

deactivate the brain's defense system and activate the social engagement system. How do these signals accomplish this? In large part, by their power to activate the oxytocin, opioid, and dopamine systems in both partner's brains and bodies. Oxytocin is released from neurons in the hypothalamus, which lies deep in the middle of the brain just below the thalamus, the brain's main relay station. Opioids are involved in relieving emotional pain, as in separation pain, and in pleasurable interactions, such as playful interactions between parents and children. Dopamine is the main neurotransmitter involved in all forms of addictive behaviors, including the process of emotional bonding between people. Together, these chemical systems interact to support attachment and emotional bonding between parents and children as well as between adult partners.

Certain kinds of communication between people trigger the release of oxytocin from the hypothalamus and then oxytocin flows into the limbic system, the social/emotional brain circuitry. When oxytocin reaches certain parts of the limbic system, especially the amygdala, it does something extremely important: it inhibits the flow through to the output region of the amygdala that orchestrates the release of stress hormones and the release of the defensive behaviors of fight, flight, or freeze. The kinds of communicative signals that are strong releasers of oxytocin are mutual gaze, certain tones of voice that are similar to child-directed speech or "motherese," and certain qualities of touch. These signals are at the core of how we relate to infants—reflecting our intuitive knowledge of how central they are in developing trust—and need to be at the core of how we relate with mistrusting older children and teens (modified to be congruent with the age of the child and the child's continuous feedback as to its duration and intensity).

Simply put, caregivers, therapists, and teachers and all who want to earn the trust of children with blocked trust have to become messengers of safety, especially when the child is least expecting kind eyes, kind voice, good touch. When these visual, auditory, and tactile messages are received from an adult in response to a child's defensiveness, the child's brain is confused—discombobulated in the most therapeutic way. This is what we mean by the creation of good surprises as an essential form of habit interruption that can grab the child's attention and help him or her start to process the important news of a difference between these adults and the ones who taught the child to mistrust.

Awakening the Child's Prefrontal Cortex

Error detection is an essential cognitive function for adaptive and flexible behaviors.
—Pourtois et al. (2010, p. 1144)

The power of new experiences to promote new learning depends on the degree to which these new experiences surprise us. If our behavior produces highly predictable, expected reactions from other people, there is no element of surprise, no "violation of expectations"; no new learning is likely to occur. With any habitual way of doing something, the only time we are likely to stop, become aware of, and pay real attention to what we are doing (and maybe see the need to change our ways) is when the habitual behavior creates a very unexpected, surprising result. (Think about driving your car mindlessly until something happens that jolts you out of your reverie and forces you to pay attention.) The unexpected event acts like a kind of wake-up call, what neuroscientists call an error signal, shifting our attention to what we are doing and prompting us to be more careful, more mindful of the situation and the effects of our actions (Tobler, 2010).

In neurobiological terms, this is why it's essential that caregivers and therapists surprise children with how they respond to defensive behavior. In blocked trust, the child's brain habitually expects negative reactions from other people, so receiving negative reactions is a no-brainer: there is no surprise and therefore nothing new to learn. This is why an adult's defensiveness will only reinforce a mistrusting child's expectations of being rejected and block the possibility of positive change based on new learning.

When adults respond nondefensively and empathically to a child's defensive behavior, this triggers what neuroscientists call a positive prediction error (PPE). PPEs are based on the activity of neurons that initially learned to predict negative, unrewarding responses from other people. When these neurons detect the surprising occurrence of a positive response from the adult, it sets off an error message in the child's brain. These error messages help grab the child's attention and make him or her notice this surprising experience. This involves neurons associated with the initial pain-based learning, including opioid cells, and neurons involved in reward-based learning, primarily dopamine cells (Akaro, Huber, and Panksepp, 2007; Steinberg et al., 2013). Research shows that error signals occur deep in the brain (actually within the periaqueductal gray [PAG], which is part is part of the mid-brain defense system) and in high regions of the brain, especially the ACC and the OFC.

These error signals increase in intensity with the maturation of the brain as part of the process of increased executive powers—part of the process of making the prefrontal regions more effective in guiding behavior. This increase in error signaling is part of the stage of brain maturation that occurs from about age 17 into the early twenties, which helps explain why young teenagers and children in general are not as likely to stop and think about what they are doing before they do something risky or careless. Individuals vary significantly in the intensity and thresholds for activating these error signals. Highly anxious people have a low threshold for activating this system, whereas people who are relatively fearless risk takers have a high threshold for triggering these internal "uh ohs."

Brain imaging studies consistently show an electrical pattern of a dip or "negativity" in a region called the dorsal anterior cingulate cortex (DACC) when subjects make errors while performing a wide variety of tasks (Oler, Quirk, and Whalen, 2009). The DACC has strong two-way connections with the basal region of the amygdala, making a brain circuit that promotes increased vigilance following errors or surprises, including "social errors" or the occurrence of unexpected reactions from other people. This brain system helps people make more mindful, careful choices between competing actions rather than just defaulting to some kind of habitual way of behaving. You can see fairly readily how this social error signaling system could play a crucial role in the process of helping mindlessly mistrustful children stop their habitual behavior and pay attention to something unusual taking place in their interactions with a safe person.

Here's how this error signaling process could be helpful in attachment-focused treatment. Imagine that the child is behaving mistrustfully toward an adult who is trying to build trust. When the adult unexpectedly reacts in a positive way toward the child's negative behavior, this "good surprise" registers in the child's brain as a PPE. The adult's unexpected reaction could take the form of some aspect of nonverbal behavior, such as a kind facial expression or an empathic tone of voice just when the child is expecting a negative expression and the sounds of anger or at least disapproval. These nonverbal signals would be rapidly detected by the child's amygdala. The PPE is generated when a message travels upward from the amygdala to the DACC. The DACC triggers the error signal and then activates other higher brain regions in the PFC that can help the child attend to and explore what the heck is going on, what this "weird" response from the caregiver is about. Here we see the awakening of the child's blocked curiosity, which can generate new ways of thinking about self and caregivers, processes of reflection and reappraisal. With this higher brain process up and running, the child can start to use verbal and conceptual processes to make new, better sense of his or her experiences with caregivers, laying the groundwork for editing implicit and explicit narratives about self and the trustworthiness of others.

The element of surprise is often first seen when the child remains defensive—and rejecting and challenging—in response to the therapist's sensitive, warm, and empathic attitude. The child has encountered that many times in the past and expects that his usual defensive response will cause the therapeutic attitude to collapse. But now—the therapist expresses radical acceptance (this expression is primarily nonverbal) of his resistance and the child is surprised! His ability to control the emotions of the therapist and move the interaction into that familiar territory of mutual defensiveness is not working! What does this mean? What is different about this person?

This scenario, then, is a bottom-up process by which the relational emotional experiences create surprising outcomes that trigger error messages which awaken the child's higher brain to news of a difference: something strange is going on between me and this adult, and I need to pay attention to this mismatching experience to learn something new about myself and about caregivers.

> Wow, something weird is going on here when I interact with *this* caregiver that is so different from the way things went with *those* caregivers that maybe, just maybe, it would be all right to trust these guys and stop being habitually, mindlessly mistrusting. Let's see if they keep sending me those safety messages, especially when I least expect them, when I'm showing them my "bad self," my most mistrusting side. This way, I can really put them to the test and learn whether or not they are truly different from *those* guys and worthy of my trust.

Relational Repair to Prime the Prefrontal Regions

> *Reparation of messiness rather than synchrony might be a key change-inducing process in therapy and development. In development, reparation has the effect of the infant and adult coming to experience and implicitly know that the negative experience of a mismatch can be transformed into a positive, affective match, that the partner can be trusted, and that one can be effective in acting on the world. Also, in repairing interactive messiness new implicit ways of being together for the infant and adult are co-created and come to be implicitly known.*
> —Tronick (2007, p. 14)

Children with blocked trust typically have never experienced consistent repairing of misattuned relationships initiated by a caregiver who has hurt them, physically or emotionally. One of the keys to awakening the child's brain to news of a difference in the present relationships is the adult's ability to initiate repair with the child when the adult's reactions to the child's defensiveness are defensive, when the adult inevitably fails, at times, to be empathic and nondefensive with the child. These potentially negative interactions that could simply confirm the child's negative expectations are opportunities for trust-building if the adult is willing and able to initiate repair by taking responsibility for "blowing it," for reacting poorly in the moment. These interactive episodes in which the caregiver's initial defensive reaction is what the mistrusting child expects can be used to create those all-important mismatches, the positive surprises, we see as essential to the process of change in attachment-focused treatment.

When the caregiver comes back to the child with the intent to repair the connection by taking responsibility for becoming defensive, there is an opportunity to give the child a powerful new experience of not being blamed but being valued, being treated in the way that communicates "Your feelings matter and you deserve to be understood, heard, listened to even when you are not feeling or acting nice."

When the adult can initiate these reparative kinds of interactions with clear, unambiguous messages that don't contain negative disqualifying messages ("it's your fault for making me mad"), the child has an opportunity to experience the adult as having good intentions, as caring enough to say "I'm sorry. I was wrong." This applies to the therapist, too! Sometimes the therapist slips and is not able to convey radical acceptance when the child becomes defensive. This is no problem if the therapist quickly owns his defensive reaction and focuses on the repair of their relationship in an open and engaged way. The therapist accepts responsibility for the relationship break and repairs it. The relationship is more important than the break, whatever it was!

One of the authors was supervising a therapist who had initiated individual sessions with a 15-year-old boy, Adrian, who did not want to see a therapist and totally refused to come if he had to meet with her with his parents. He was the third child, and his parents had struggled over the years with their marriage, finances, and challenges from their own histories. Adrian, with good reasons, often felt that his parents did not spend much time thinking or worrying about him. And he gave them reasons for worry, with poor school achievement and attendance, along with a general negative and withdrawn attitude at home. At one point in the third session he challenged his therapist:

Adrian: You don't care! You're just doing this for the money!

Therapist: (*with empathy over his experience, rather than defensiveness over the challenge to her motivation. She expressed empathy in her voice and facial expression*) No wonder you don't want to talk with me! You think that I'm only seeing you for the money! That would be awful if you thought my only reason in getting to know you was being paid for it!

Adrian: Yeah, it is. (*less anger in his voice now; even a bit uncertain about what to say next*)

Therapist: (*still gentle and empathic*) Have you ever spoken with someone who you just knew simply wanted to get to know you, who simply was interested in who you are, what you wanted, what you dreamed about?

Adrian: Yeah.

Therapist: I'm glad. That's what you need, someone who is just interested in you, no strings attached. I am getting paid, so that does make it more difficult to trust me. How would you know if you could trust me?

Adrian: I don't know.

Therapist: Well, if you're willing, let's give it a go. Whenever you think I'm interested in something about you because

I'm getting paid. Or something like I'm asking about something to change you, so you're parents will be pleased. You know, getting to know you with strings attached, would you tell me? Because if you think anything like that about my motives, you won't trust me. And it will have no value to you. Ok?

Adrian: Yeah, ok.

Therapist: Great. Maybe we can just begin with that. Do you think that my main interest in getting to know you is to fix you?

From there, Adrian began to gradually speak openly about his thoughts, feelings, dreams, and doubts. A few sessions later he mentioned that he didn't think his parents knew him like the therapist did. She indicated that if that were true, that would make his life very difficult as he would have to manage important things all by himself. She suggested she would be willing to help his parents get to know him, as she did—with no strings attached—if he wanted her to do so. A few sessions later, he decided to invite his parents in for a session to see how it would go. Adrian saw that his therapist insisted that his parents get to know their son—with no strings attached—and when they began to change, he began to change, too. He now had reason to trust that his parents wanted to know and get closer to him, in spite of the other challenges in their lives, so he could acknowledge that he wanted to get closer to them, too. A key step in Adrian's treatment was when the therapist accepted his belief regarding her motive in getting to know him and he became open to a new possibility. He needed to unlearn his assumptions, and develop new learnings about his therapist, himself, and eventually about his parents as well.

Unblocking the Child's Social Emotions

The most important goal of attachment-focused therapy is to help the child learn to feel safe allowing a caregiver to be a co-regulating emotional partner, a safe, trustworthy source of comfort and joy. This involves an emotional journey consisting of affective movement from states of defensive emotion, often anger, toward the blocked emotions—such as fear, sadness, loneliness—that need to be unblocked to support positive engagement and connection. The therapist has to know how to meet the child in an affective state the child is more comfortable with, often a negative defensive state, and then use this engagement to help the child traverse the fuller emotional terrain, to move the child by co-regulating his affect safely enough into the states of emotion that are conducive to attachment, that activate the suppressed attachment system. This is what we mean by treatment being relational and emotion-based.

In attachment-focused treatment, the therapist's use of self, especially nonverbal ways of expressing emotions, attitude, and intentions, is the main mechanism of change. The ways the therapist uses facial expressions, tones of voice, gestures, and touch—these core processes generate the affective movement in the child and caregiver toward states of emotion and intent that are conducive to attachment, caregiving, and emotional connection.

Of these nonverbal aspects of communication, probably the most powerful is the expression of emotion in the voice. This is called *prosody*. Prosody is regulated largely from the ACC. This is an old part of the mammalian brain that is connected to the limbic system and the brain stem regions that convey messages between the body and the brain. Different parts of the ACC are active during different emotions. Literally, there is a part of the ACC that is on when we are feeling sad, another part that is active when we are feeling happy, another for fear, and another for anger. Through the activity in the ACC, we put emotion into our faces through the facial muscles and into our voice through connections to the vocal cords. From the ACC we make the sounds of sadness, joy, fear, compassion, and anger when we aren't producing the more primitive versions of our emotions (rage and terror) from just our brain stem (Perry, 1997; Vogt, 2009).

This means that the ACC is a critical region involved in attachment, caregiving, and attachment-focused treatment. The therapist has to use his or her ACC in a flexible, attuning way to synchronize with the affective states of the child and caregiver in sessions. This can be called *cingulating* or cingulation, especially appropriate since it is akin to the process of actually using the voice to sing. Prosody is about the musical quality of the voice, and the prosodic nature of our speech provides the moving aspect of vocal communication.

The best way for therapists and caregivers to move children with their voices is to be in a compassionate state of mind toward the child. In brain terms, compassion involves the activation of the MPFC along with the middle or rostral part of the ACC and the front or anterior part of the insula. These regions appear to form a circuit of compassion in the human brain (Craig, 2011; Siegel, 2012). When the adults are able to activate this compassion circuit and keep it on, they are very likely to convey compassion in their voices, facial expressions, and movements to move the child toward a compassionate state toward herself. This is the state we want to induce in the child so that he or she can feel the softer, more vulnerable social emotions that were suppressed when poor care channeled the child's brain into blocked trust.

Making It Safe to Go Inside

The new understanding of the difference between the brain processes of "looking in" and "looking out" has many implications and applications for understanding the developmental impact of having to spend brain power on hyperfocusing on the external environment. Lack of physical and emotional safety in the early stages of development robs the child of the opportunity to develop the DMN because it isn't safe to spend time looking inward, taking attention off other people in the environment whose actions a child has to stay wary of to survive (Sripada et al., 2014). These children are likely to have an underdeveloped and frightening inner life that robs them of the ability to use their minds to reappraise their extremely negative core beliefs about themselves and other people. Therapy has to help them go inside in safety to change their minds about themselves and about relationships with their caregivers based on new experiences that counter the old ones.

The DMN is very likely crucial for the development of inter-subjective relationships, relationships in which both partners tune in to each other's inner life and their own inner life, both able to reflect and share the products of their reflections. When the DMN is underdeveloped for whatever reason, the relationship is likely to be more superficial, more taken up with dual attention to the surface of life, the appearances of people and things, and the readily observable actions or behaviors of others, rather than a focus on the inner life of self and others.

One of the goals of attachment-focused therapy in light of this research on the DMN is to help children experience enough emotional safety to start using this system and developing their inner life, their self-awareness, and their ability to understand their own and other people's minds and safely share this inner life with trusted others. Being able to access and use the DMN is connected with the development of empathy and compassion and the social emotions of remorse and sympathy. Helping a child switch from outer focus to this inner focus system in the presence of safe others is a crucial dimension of treatment.

A powerful way of helping mistrustful children feel safe going inside and activating their DMN is the adult's use of his or her own DMN to engender a compassionate, open, curious state of mind toward the child, a deep state of wonder and interest in the child's inner life that naturally invites the child to shift into this system and out of hypervigilance. When the therapist is in his or her own DMN, thinking about the child, the therapist's voice and facial expressions and body language convey this inner state of compassion and inter-est, the very messages that constitute safety signals to the child's rapid appraisal system and especially the amygdala. Compassionate storytelling and speaking for a child who has no words to express inner experiences are ways to prime the child's DMN and promote safe entry into this inner space. The sounds of compassion are an invitation to another person to enter their DMN and start thinking about themselves and relationships while feeling emotions that are not accessible when we are focused on the external world in a hypervigilant, wary manner. When the DDP therapist starts to use the storytelling mode or speaks for a child to a parent using an emotional tone that conveys vulnerable feelings rather than an aggressive, outward-directed voicing, all three people in the room—therapist, child, and caregiver—are more likely to shift from outer focus to the inner focus. This is when a more intersubjective and affectively positive connection between child and caregiver is likely to emerge.

Reviving Playfulness in the Parent–Child Relationship

Children with blocked trust had to suppress playfulness to survive poor care. Making it safe for them to be playful with an adult is one of the keys to helping them recover from blocked trust. Playfulness is a potent way to disarm the child's defense system for a while and give them opportunities to engage without fear. This gives the child the opportunity to practice engagement and strengthen his or her tolerance for being close to a caregiver without being defensive. This, in turn, can help the child tolerate being close in a state of sadness, in that blocked emotional state he or she needs to feel to recover the ability to seek and receive comfort. Playfulness, then, complements sadness induction, both being processes that help remove the blockage from the social emotions, an essential component of helping the child recover from the blocked trust. During both playful interactions and comfort-seeking interactions, the child gets to experience the healing process of being very close to the caregiver without fear, with the self-defense system suppressed in favor of the social engagement system.

Practicing Social Engagement and Consolidating New Learning

Once the child begins to experience enough safety to engage with therapists and caregivers, it is important to provide many opportunities to practice engagement, both the lighter forms of playful engagement and the deeper forms involving those vulnerable social emotions when the child experiences the need for comfort and empathy. These are the relational experiences that can help revive the child's suppressed potential for caring about self and others, for being "in relationship" where empathy, remorse, and joy of companionship can come into play and help the child shift his or her developmental trajectory from mistrust to trust.

Summary

Children who come into the care of trustworthy adults need to experience the opposite of what they encountered earlier in life when in the care of adults who were not trustworthy. They need to experience a form of enriched care that consistently sends messages of safety into their overly sensitive defense systems to awaken their brains to the news of the critical difference between the present relational environment and the one in which they learned to be mistrustful. The adults who need to be the messengers of safety—parents, therapists, teachers, and others in the child's "circle of security"—need to be aware of the risk of developing blocked care from exposure to these children's habitual defensiveness. By remaining compassionate and avoiding the onset of a mutual defense society, adults can prime the process of change by disarming the children's defense system, awakening their prefrontal regions, and scaffolding the processes of reversal learning, reconsolidation of fear-conditioned memories, reflection based on new information about self and others, and reappraisal of old negative beliefs, all in the service of helping the child make the transition, neurobiologically, from mistrust to trust.

In the next chapter, we describe the relational processes used in DDP and explain how these processes provide the child with the social buffering needed to facilitate the four R's of change. We explain how DDP targets the "epicenter" of mistrust, the child's right brain self-defense system, and provides the social buffering the child requires to feel safe enough to let down the wall of disengagement.

We describe how the relational processes used by the DDP therapist engender the disparate experiences that facilitate reversal learning, make it safe enough for exposure-based reconsolidation of traumatic memories, activate the child's DMN, and promote reflective functioning and reappraisal of old negative beliefs about self and the trustworthiness of adults.

CHAPTER 5

Trust-Building in Parent–Child Dyads

Intervention is where the learning process unfolds. It is about learning your way toward effective intervention for the individual child, adult, and dyad.
—Lillas and Turnbull (2009, p. 33)

W e hope that in the first four chapters we have provided the reader with the basics of a brain-based model for understanding how a young child develops a foundation of trust when receiving good care and how another young child develops a foundation of mistrust in response to poor care. Here and in the following five chapters, we present an attachment-focused treatment, dyadic developmental psychotherapy (DDP), which we believe is very congruent with the brain-based concepts just presented.

The trusting child in the presence of family members is primarily in an open and engaged state of mind; able to access, regulate, and express the full range of his affective states and be actively engaged in his environment; and sharing experiences while learning about his world through his openness to the more highly developed experiences of his older family members. At the same time, he is aware that these family members are interested in him, take delight in him, and are there to assist him whenever he needs some assistance in handling his more intense affective states, whatever their source.

He also notices that just as they influence him, he too is able to influence them.

As we described earlier, the mistrusting child in the presence of family members is primarily in a self-protective, defensive state of mind, being wary and hypervigilant, focusing narrowly on threats to self and opportunities to meet his perceived needs. He is convinced that his safety rests on his self-reliance, which—given his age and lack of resources—is a full-time job. He does not have any leftover time to learn about the bigger world of social-emotional-cognitive realities. Nor does he have the energy to focus inward and thus has limited awareness and ability to use his inner world of reflection. These children have learned to suppress the sadness that comes from feeling alone and unwanted, along with efforts to be comforted when in distress. They also suppress a desire for playfulness and reciprocal joy, no small feat when you imagine the exuberance of active, trusting toddlers. Finally, they suppress the natural curiosity that is seen in most toddlers. They do not have time for such a luxury when they are responsible for their own safety.

So then, to help mistrusting children begin to trust, what might we do? How do we engage them? How do we open their minds and hearts as they were when they were born, or at least when they were conceived? Taking the brain-based knowledge that we've discussed, we might want to approach these wary children with the following goals in mind.

1. Enable them to experience a visceral sense of safety.
2. Enable them to trust enough to recover the ability to experience sadness and seek comfort.
3. Restore their capacity for playfulness.
4. Increase their readiness to be open and engaged with others and with their own reflective abilities.
5. Increase their readiness for curiosity about possible new meaning regarding the frightening or shameful events from their past.

6. Enable them to experience themselves as being a source of delight to others, while also being of sufficient value to be given comfort when in distress.

How might we be present with these mistrusting children to assist them in reaching those goals?

1. Maintain a nondefensive, open, and engaged state of mind, relating consistently with acceptance, curiosity, and empathy.
2. Relate with clear, expressive, nonverbal communications.
3. Establish an attuned, synchronized, matching of affective states.
4. Follow or gently lead the mistrusting child into vulnerable affective states and then provide comfort over whatever emotions are associated with those states.
5. Whenever there is a break in the therapeutic relationship, due to defensive states initiated by the child or therapist, initiate repair so that the child knows the relationship is more important than the circumstances of the break.
6. Establish a varying, rhythmic, voice prosody, while joining the child in co-creating a story about diverse events in the child's recent and past life, and then helping him or her integrate these meanings into a coherent narrative.
7. Evoke a sense of surprise and openness through providing safe, but sometimes unexpected responses to the mistrusting child's initiatives.
8. Provide the child with experiences of delight, while co-regulating any anxiety that might be associated with these confusing, even frightening experiences.

We have presented the general goals needed to address the challenges facing the mistrusting child and her parents as well as the core interventions to attain these goals. Now we describe a therapeutic approach that is congruent with both.

Affective-Reflective Dialogue

DDP is based on ways of communicating that are congruent with how our brains are designed to communicate about events that we organize into meaningful social and emotional experiences. These communications are focused on both our here-and-now experiences of one another in an event (treatment session), as well as the mistrusting child's experiences of shame and fear or joy and pride about a great variety of events. These dialogues consist of interwoven nonverbal and verbal communications between the therapist and client that co-regulate the affective states of the members of the dyad being evoked by the dialogue and co-create the meanings of the events that are the focus of the dialogues. We consider both aspects in sequence, but in reality they are always interwoven, with meaning being co-created as the affect is being co-regulated, and the affect being co-regulated as the meaning is being co-created.

Co-Regulation of Affective States

Following the lead of Daniel Stern, Colwyn Trevarthen, and others, we define *affect* as the bodily expression of our emotional state. Anger, sadness, fear, along with excitement, joy, and love are expressed in different bodily ways so that the other person can infer the emotion by the nature of their expressions. It is very difficult to hide anger from becoming evident in your facial expressions and vocal tone. Not only do those bodily expressions (affects) convey the emotion, they tend to evoke a similar emotion in the person who perceives them. Emotions are contagious largely because their bodily affective expression tends to evoke a similar affective expression in the person who perceives them.

The neuropsychological reality that DDP uses within the affective-reflective (A-R) dialogue is that when the therapist matches the affective expression of the child's anger without being angry herself, the child will most likely experience this as her empathy for his anger.

He is likely to experience this as "She gets it! She understands how angry I am about this!" The child is expressing the emotion of anger with a voice that is likely to be loud and with an intense cadence. He is also likely to show a similar intensity in his face, showing how important this is, how upset he is, and how he really wants you to just get it! When the therapist expresses *her* response with a similar cadence and intensity, equally loud and focused, *but does not experience anger for the child*, the child is likely to feel understood. He is not likely to feel that he is being judged or that his anger is wrong or disrespectful.

If the therapist becomes defensive and annoyed in reaction to the child's anger, the anger is likely to intensify. If the therapist remains calm and detached, the child is likely to feel alone with it, and his anger may intensify as well. If the child's emotional state of anger is dysregulated—the child is having difficulty controlling it, and the anger is beginning to control what the child might say or do—the therapist's defensive or calm response may only increase the dysregulated state. Even if it does not increase that state, such a response is unlikely to help him to become regulated because he will be experiencing himself as alone in his anger. He will not believe that the reasons for his anger are being understood.

By matching the affective state of the child, the therapist is able to co-regulate the affect, along with its underlying emotion. If the child's affect is dysregulated, and the therapist is matching that affective state while remaining regulated, the child's affect is likely to become regulated.

> Colleen was a 13-year-old foster child, in her fourth foster home since age 6. She had been sexually abused by her step-father, and her mother chose him over her daughter. Her current foster placement, with Jenny, seemed different to Colleen, in that she had been there for more than three years, her longest time with anyone. Still, she barely trusted Jenny, thinking it would be likely to end the moment that she

crossed some line that Jenny hadn't decided on yet. She had no use for therapists, but only agreed to come because Jenny agreed to come with her. It was the fifth treatment session:

Colleen: You're just doing your job. You don't give a damn about what I tell you. You pretend you do because you're supposed to, but it means nothing to you! I mean nothing to you!

Therapist: (*responding with the same rhythm and intensity in her voice, without anger*) No wonder you don't want to be here! No wonder, if you think that you mean nothing to me! If that's what you think, of course you wouldn't want to be here!

Colleen: That is what I know! You expect me to believe that you care about me? I don't even think that she [Jenny] really cares about me.

Therapist: If you don't believe that Jenny cares, there's no way that you'd believe that I care! (*still matching her affect*) What would it take to make you believe that Jenny cares for you?

Colleen: How the fuck do I know? You're the expert, you tell me.

Therapist: I would if I could, but I can't. We're talking about your mind and your heart. I don't know what it would take for you to let Jenny in. (*intensity in therapist's voice, implying how important this is to her and how sad she is that she cannot make it happen*)

Colleen: Maybe I never will. (*some sadness too, and resignation*)

Therapist: And I would understand. And Jenny would, too. You trusted your mother, that she'd stand by you and send that guy to jail. Instead . . .

Colleen: She has nothing to do with this! (*with intensity, but not shutting down the conversation*)

Therapist: Ah, I think she does. When you trust someone

as much as a kid trusts her mother, and she violates that trust . . . how can the kid know that she can ever trust anyone else again? (*said strongly, with certainty*)

Colleen: You got that right.

Therapist: Jenny, what would you do if someone tried to hurt Colleen the way her step-father did? (*voice has now changed, quieter and more reflective, inviting Jenny into the dialogue*)

Jenny: (*long silence, as Jenny begins to cry. Finally she seems to find the strength to talk*) I'd kill him . . . but that's no good because you wouldn't let me care for Colleen then. (*another long silence*) I'd put my arm around this girl . . . and I'd walk with her to hell and back . . . until she was ready to stand on her own. But I wouldn't be far away . . . No, I'd be close in case she needed me. I'd be worried about her when she was at school or with friends—like I am now, but more so. And I'd be waiting for her to come home, like I do now. And I'd give her a hug, like I *try* to do now, and do when she lets me.

Colleen: (*staring at Jenny the whole time, with tears, and maybe a bit of shock in her face*) Why?

Jenny: (*moves over on the couch and puts her arm around Colleen who does not pull away*) Because you are you, and I am me. And we're family. And that's what this family . . . that's what I do. And that's no more than what you deserve. No more, no less.

Colleen: You want *me* in your family? (*a bit confused but with a hint of playfulness*)

Jenny: Yes, I do.

Colleen: I want to believe you.

Jenny: And I'm ready to wait.

Colleen: So why do I need to see this therapist? Does she have to fix me before you'll really want me in your family?

Jenny: No, she has to fix me so I can be the mama that you need.

> **Colleen:** You're ok.
>
> **Jenny:** Thank you, sweetie, but I need this therapist. She's my security blanket. She's going nowhere until I know that you trust me.
>
> **Colleen:** Suppose I say that I do.
>
> **Jenny:** Enough of this. Now just let's keep quiet and see what this wise woman has to tell us.
>
> **Colleen:** (*looks at therapist for first time since Jenny began speaking*) She got tears, too!
>
> **Jenny:** Maybe she does care.

Dialogues like this would be a first step in helping a mistrusting teen begin to trust. The first few sentences are the most crucial in getting the momentum going—giving the dialogue a chance to make a difference in building trust. The most crucial element of the first few sentences is the therapist matching the affective expression of the client's words. We're not saying that the therapist's words are not important, but that the words will have less of a chance of being heard if they are not expressed within the same affective state of the client.

Bottom-Up and/or Top-Down

Many trauma therapies are now considered to be "bottom-up" as opposed to being "top-down." These approaches assume that trauma is located within the body, rather than the rational, conceptual areas of our brain. These approaches often focus, especially in the early stages of treatment, on helping the client become more aware of his body's experience of a traumatic memory by asking "Where do you feel that in your body?" or "Describe the feeling in your shoulders now" or "Notice the position of your feet on the floor, or arms on the arms of the chair, describe what if feels like, move your feet (arms) and describe what it feels like." This sensate focus and awareness may lead to new memories or new understandings of traumatic events (bottom-up). This might lead to greater reflective abilities about the trauma, which might influence new bodily experiences of it (top-down).

DDP also emphasizes a bottom-up approach, but the focus in on developing the ways of communicating to build an open and engaged relationship with the mistrusting child. Rather than focusing on the verbal aspects of the communications, the therapist instead focuses on the nonverbal aspects. The eyes, facial expressions, voice prosody, and (when safe and appropriate) touch helps the mistrusting child begin the process of becoming open and engaged with the therapist, regardless of the content of what is being said.

In about 200 milliseconds, nonverbal communication (facial expressions and emotional tones of voice) are processed in the superior temporal cortex, then shunted to the amygdala for appraisal of safety or threat value. When the therapist stays in a nondefensive state of mind toward the child, the nonverbal messages are likely to be processed in the child's brain as relatively safe. These messages provide the child with sufficient safety to stay engaged with the therapist, rather than reacting with anger, distraction, or dissociation. The nonverbal (bottom-up) communication says, "you are safe with me." Only then is the child open to the therapist's experiences of the child and perspectives on the events of his life. Only then is the child open to the possibility of reflecting on the meaning of self and the events (top-down). Such reflections, incorporating the therapist's experience, lead to new meanings of the self, other, and the events. These deeper, integrative meanings are only possible when the child's brain is in a more integrated state, with regions of the prefrontal cortex interacting with subcortical regions, including the amygdala, to enable the child to "feel and deal" (Fosha, 2000), to be in a more regulated emotional state than is typically the case.

Creation of Meaning

As safety is being established, as affect is being shared and co-regulated, as trust is beginning to awaken, increasing space emerges in which to begin exploring the world in new ways and create new meanings of the people and events of our lives, past, present, and future. Since this is a relational process, with new learnings being embedded in relationships, these new meanings are seen as being co-created. Let us step back for a moment and explore the nature of this relational process that generates the core of social and emotional learning. We are talking about intersubjectivity.

Infant intersubjectivity has been discussed in great detail by Trevarthen (2001), Stern (2000), and others and has been introduced into newer developments of psychodynamic psychotherapies. Basically *infant intersubjectivity* refers to how the infant's experiential learning is greatly influenced by the experiences of her parents of the meaning of the people and events the infant is trying to understand. As he experiences his parents' experience of him when they communicate interest, delight, and love, he experiences himself as being interesting, delightful, and lovable. As he experiences his parents' experience of a song bird as being fascinating and enjoyable, he is likely to also experience the bird as being fascinating and enjoyable. As he notices his parents' alert, tense, and cautious response to a loud sound coming from the next room, he experiences the sound as being somewhat frightening and he becomes vigilant. If his parents do not convey interest in a sound, person, or activity, he is also likely to be uninterested in those realities in his life.

Intersubjectivity is thought to have three central components.

1. The first component involves establishing joint affective states. We discussed this when we considered the co-regulation of affect. Stern defined the intersubjective sharing of affective states as attunement, whereas Trevarthen defined those synchronized states as synrhythmia. When focusing on the intersubjective quality of synchronized affect, we notice how sharing such affective states creates social and emotional meanings. The parent's fascination with the activity of the family dog is likely to increase the child's interest in the dog and the meaning of the dog's barks, wagging tail, and rush to the window. More important, the child is likely to resonate with the parent's affective expression of anger, fear, sadness, excitement, and watchfulness. The parent's affective expressions

are seen by her child as being especially important, in part because, through attunement, they become important to the child as well. The child then strives to understand what her parent's anger, fear, or excitement means.

In therapy, the child may sometimes convey an affective state that expresses an underlying emotion of anger, fear, shame, or despair while the therapist is giving expression to being calm, satisfied, confident, and reasonable. The difference in their affective states may make it difficult for the child to experience the therapist as either caring about or understanding him. This feature was discussed with regard to the need to co-regulate affective states to assist the child in being able to regulate difficult emotions and not be overwhelmed by them.

Matching affective states with the child also helps the child feel that the adult understands him more fully. When the child and adult are experiencing resonance, when their brains and hearts are literally in sync, matching rhythms and patterns of activation, the child is likely to have confidence that they are on the same wavelength. Recent brain imaging studies showed that when parents and children are in sync, they show similar patterns of brain activity in their middle prefrontal region, a region associated with relational processes, what Siegel calls the *we* brain (Siegel, 2012). Other research shows that these states are associated with heightened levels of oxytocin in both parent and child (Guastella, Mitchell, and Matthews, 2008; Feldman et al., 2010). Chapter 6 presents the role of attunement in establishing and maintaining a deep sense of safety and connection during the course of the ongoing conversation.

2. The joint focus of attention is the second component of intersubjectivity. When one person focuses on a person or object, she is developing her perspective of the person or object. Her perspective changes as she observes, listens to, or touches the focus of her attention. She may walk around the person or object to obtain different visual perspectives. She may interact with it to see how it changes or responds to different situations or initiatives to develop a more complex perspective over time. She also will bring her history to her per-

spective, either with that particular person or a similar object, or to all other people or objects of that category. It is easy to see how one person's perspective might be quite different from that of another.

When we share perspectives of a person or object, we open ourselves to even more complex understandings about the unique features of that person or object. One person's developing perspective has a reciprocal influence on the developing perspective of the other person. I might visit a friend and be frightened by his dog who did not know me, was wary of me, and began barking at me as I entered the home. If I am alone with the dog, my fear may evoke a defensive response, which causes the dog to be even more wary, bark more, and so on. The dog and I became locked in our initial perspective that the other may be a threat to our safety, and our ongoing responses only reinforced the initial perspective. Then my friend enters the room, talking soothingly to the dog as he strokes him, while welcoming me with a friendly face and voice. My friend is showing—primarily nonverbally—that he is safe with and likes both of us. His experience of each of us influences our experience of each other. Following his lead, I greet his dog differently, and the dog stops barking and wags his tail.

In therapy, the therapist may want to focus on a traumatic event but the child does not. The child would rather focus on something interesting on the therapist's desk or something that happened the day before that he enjoyed, not something that he was in trouble about with his parent. Most children, and many adults for that matter, would often be likely to focus on safe, relaxing themes they are confident will not create any conflicts and will be interesting to the other person, rather than those that might create anxiety or other stressful emotions. This is likely to be especially true if the focus is on the relationship between those in the dialogue. There are a variety of ways that the therapist might facilitate the child's readiness and ability to focus on a given theme.

a. Begin with lighter, relaxing themes before introducing any stressful topics.

b. The child goes first. After exploring what the child is interested in discussing, the therapist introduces a theme.

c. The best conversations involve taking turns. In a playful and/or empathic way, the therapist might mention that to the child and ask for help in making it happen.

d. The therapist is very responsive to any difficulty that the child has in exploring a stressful or shameful theme. Giving the child frequent breaks from hard topics—the child is never "trapped" in any topic—often enables children to explore themes they otherwise would resist.

e. Maintaining the same open and engaged, rhythmic voice tone, or storytelling voice, no matter what the topic enables many children to be fully engaged in conversations about difficult topics they otherwise would avoid or find too stressful if the therapist adopted a stern or serious voice tone. This will be discussed in much greater detail in Chapter 7.

3. The third component of intersubjectivity involves the complimentary intentions of those who are present with and influencing each other. For an interaction to be intersubjective, the individuals are cooperating. They are interacting because they have a common goal. They want the same thing. This may be to enjoy an event together. It may involve one person wanting to learn from the other how to do something on the computer and the other wanting to teach the first person. They may want to complete a chore together or share their resources to accomplish a goal.

In therapy, the therapist may have as his goal to help the child learn to trust, but the child may not have the same goal. He may be certain of his self-reliant, mistrusting view of others and the world and have no interest in beginning to trust his parent or teacher . . . or therapist for that matter, believing that the therapist is really someone working for the parent or teacher.

The therapist may also have the goal of assisting the child in reducing his "problems," whether they involve his social behavior, emotional regulation, self-directed behavior, or ability to focus. Improving impulse control as well as the ability to delay gratification may also be seen as worthy goals by the therapist and parent. Other interesting goals are to help the child learn to do what he doesn't feel like doing, cooperate with others, or learn to share. Many children are not likely to complement the therapist's intention to address those problems by wanting to learn the skills that the therapist is ready to teach.

Better therapeutic goals, more likely to evoke a complementary response from the child would involve simply getting to know him and understand him. Discovering what the child thinks, feels, and wants, and doing so without judging the child's inner life is likely to evoke greater cooperation than are efforts to fix the child. Many of the children with whom we are attempting to engage in a therapeutic relationship—these mistrusting children—are likely to experience intense, chronic loneliness. They are not likely to feel that they are cared for and understood by the adults in their lives, and most likely not by their peers either. When the therapist's goal is to get to know the child—with no strings attached—many children become engaged in that relationship and begin to share their inner lives.

Another, related goal that the child may cooperate with is to explore ways to get along better within the family. This might refer to having fewer conflicts, coming to more frequent agreements about the rules and roles in the family. If the therapist is able to help parent and child recall that they used to be closer, often both will acknowledge that they might want to feel close again. No one is being blamed as to why they are not close.

The following example presents what we mean by intersubjectivity.

> Kevin was a 10-year-old foster boy, He came into care at age four, following experiences of physical abuse, emotional abuse, and neglect. He resided in three foster homes over the next two years and since the age of six has lived with his current foster family, with the understanding that he will remain with them on a long-term basis. His parents have ceased efforts to reunite with their son. The therapist was sitting with Kevin and his foster dad, Randy, and he brought up why he

came into foster care. With Kevin's consent, the therapist described how Kevin's father physically and verbally abused him in front of a neighbor and then locked him in the hall closet. Kevin was asked if it made sense what happened, and he said that it did. Asked how it made sense, he replied that it happened because he was bad. The therapist described the nature of child abuse and the fact that he entered foster care not because he was bad but because his father abused him. Kevin replied with some intensity, "But he wouldn't have done it if I wasn't bad!"

The meaning of the abuse was given to Kevin by the perpetrator of the abuse! Because of the realities of intersubjectivity, Kevin felt deeply that his father's reasons for abusing him were valid. Reason will not change his mind about this. The therapist needed to share his experience of the event, so that Kevin would have an intersubjective experience of it. Kevin had his father's experience ("You're bad and deserve this"). Now he is able to have another.

Therapist: Oh, Kevin, you were four! Four! and you accidently bumped the table, spilling the coffee on your dad. Oh, no! You might have said, "Dad! I'm sorry! I didn't mean to!" and then your dad slapped you, and you fell to the floor. It must have hurt so bad, and must have been so scary! This is your dad! And then he thought that you were being bad! Oh, no! But it was an accident! And you were just running around the kitchen like four-year-olds do! And you believed your dad! He said so and you thought that he was right! You didn't know that dads can make mistakes! And that's been so hard for you! You were hurt and scared! And then locked in the closet! And it must have been so dark in there! Oh, Kevin, (*becoming quieter*) how hard that must have been for you. How hard. So scared, so sad, so lonely. and you thought that you were bad.

The therapist then asked Randy for his experience of that event, and the foster dad expressed empathy and then confusion as to why Kevin's dad did those things. He did not judge him, just was confused that a father would do that to his son. Then he reassured Kevin that he would never do that and he did not think he was bad.

As the therapist and foster father spoke with Kevin, his eyes watered. The therapist had conveyed his experience of that event with voice prosody and facial expressions with a storytelling voice that engaged Kevin and enabled him to be receptive to the experience, making it intersubjective. Randy, taking his cue from the therapist, also shared his experience intersubjectively. Kevin experienced their empathy and may have, for the first time, experienced empathy for himself over what had happened, with much less shame. From the intersubjective experiences expressed by the therapist and Randy, Kevin now had something to raise doubts about the intersubjective experiences that he had with his father. His father had a *subjective* experience of him that was not an *objective* reality. Kevin had an opening to develop his own, new experience about the nature of his past traumas. Those experiences were no longer defined by the perpetrator!

These components—attunement, joint attention, and complementary intentions—when they are present, are quite effective in creating the affective-reflective dialogue that is likely to lead to therapeutic change within the family. However, sometimes it is not as easy as it seems to establish their presence. DDP has found that when the therapist is able to maintain a particular attitude, intersubjective experiences are more likely to be established and maintained during the dialogue. We explore the four features of this attitude, which, when present, are likely to make the dialogue therapeutic. These features are playfulness, acceptance, curiosity, and empathy (PACE).

PACE: Playfulness, Acceptance, Curiosity, Empathy

During the early development of DDP, Dan sought to develop and the describe ways of being present with mistrusting children so they would gradually come to respond to my initiatives and engage with me. I had realized that having rational discussions with children was not likely to capture their motivation or interest, or if they did go along with it, they were likely to be compliant and possibly say what they thought I might want them to say but not be fully engaged. They were not open to my efforts to get to know them and explore the various aspects of their life with them. This led me to thinking about how I had been with my own children when they were infants and toddlers. How did I engage them? Most likely I engaged them the way they wanted me to engage them. How was I when with them that they were likely to respond to? How was I when they initiated activity with me that would make them more likely to initiate more activities with me? Recalling many such moments and interactions, I decided that most of those ways of being with my young children could be described as having been playful, accepting, curious and empathic. Let us consider each of them in turn.

P: Playfulness

When infants and toddlers are open and engaged with their parents, they tend to be playful. They seem to look for opportunities to experience joy. They love the smiling face, the light, high-pitched voice, exaggerated movements and gestures, taking turns, peek-a-boo, and hide and seek. They like things to happen again and again, but they also like surprise. The unexpected—when they are safe in the playful activity—is met with sudden surprise and delight. They like those synchronized interactions—the dance of attunement—that creates and gives expression to shared interests and joy and leads to laughter that seems to be expressing the pleasure experienced by the infant's entire spirit and body. When infants feel safe, they are naturally playful.

Similarly, when the therapist meets a mistrusting child, she is more likely to begin the process of engagement if she introduces a bit of playfulness, inviting the child to respond. If the child does respond, there is likely to be a lightening of the defensiveness that the mistrusting child often demonstrates on arrival. Playfulness conveys the attitude that you are safe and I want to share our experience and get to know each other. Playfulness shows that therapy is not a formal process, goal-directed work that has no room for small talk and exploration of things that evoke pride and pleasure. Playfulness also shows a bit of the therapist as a person, rather than a professional with a narrow goal of fixing problems. It brings in spontaneity, which tends to evoke trust more than does a well-scripted, narrowly focused conversation.

> Johnny was a nine-year-old adopted boy who seldom laughed, never cried, and spent most of his time unhappy over not being able to play video games or saying that he was bored while playing in a little shed in the back yard that he claimed as his own. His adoptive parents would hear him moving things around and talking to himself while he drew what seemed to be designs for his shed. But when they came by, he immediately stopped what he was doing. He did not trust them enough to share anything with them.
>
> During an early treatment session, the therapist was asking Johnny a question about his life.

Johnny: (*yelling*) None of your business!

Therapist: (*matching the intensity of Johnny's voice while raising the pitch, widening his eyes as if he were shocked*) But it is my business! My office is my business and you're in my office! If I'm in your shed, which is your office, then I'm your business! That's how it works!

Johnny: I'm never going to let you in my shed!

Therapist: Not fair! You come to my business!

Johnny: (*speaking quite loudly now*) Pay me like we pay you and you can come!

> **Therapist:** (*taking $5 out of his wallet and giving it to Johnny*)
> Deal! When you're here, you're my business. When I'm
> in your shed, I'm your business! And I'm coming, believe
> me. What are you going to ask me when I come?
>
> Johnny smiled and said, "If you remembered to bring the
> green paint for the walls!" The therapist laughed, and said,
> "You are one clever kiddo!" Johnny laughed and glanced at
> his mother, and they laughed together.
> A few weeks later, the therapist stopped by Johnny's house
> with a can of green paint that he had picked out with help
> from Johnny's parents. He stayed for an hour, looked at
> the plans Johnny had made for the shed and then left, with
> Johnny and his parents laughing as they painted his shed.

Dialogues like this are important because they are not important. They are light, engaging, relaxed, and spontaneous. They show that the child is more than a client, more than a problem. They are equals—therapist and child—in being able to banter, just because they like to. They like to because they are coming to know and like each other. Safe enough to be silly with and interested in each other.

A: Acceptance

Trusting relationships are characterized by acceptance. In such relationships we are safe, knowing that although we have differences, we have confidence that the relationship is stronger than any conflict. We might argue and even state strongly that we cannot accept that behavior, but the relationship is so important we will do whatever it takes to resolve the difference. If we do not always accept each other's behavior, what are we actually accepting?

Affective-reflective dialogues are characterized by the therapist communicating acceptance for *every* experience the child expresses. Each thought, feeling, wish, value, perception, interest, and memory is accepted. These are features of the child's inner life, and he is safe knowing his inner life will be accepted, not evaluated. Qualities of the child's inner life are not seen as right or wrong, they just *are*. There may be significant differences between aspects of the therapist's inner life and that of the child. If the therapist conveys the belief that he is right and the child is wrong, then the child is likely to immediately become defensive and withdraw from the dialogue. If, instead, the therapist conveys the attitude that he accepts the child's experience—his thought, perception, or wish—and he wants to understand it, get to know it, the child is likely to feel safe enough to share it.

If a child says to his father that he is afraid of the dark, the father may want to be helpful by convincing the child that there is no reason to be afraid, thinking that the fear will disappear. The well-meaning father asks specific questions to make it obvious there is nothing to fear. He might even look under the bed and in the closet and conclude there is nothing there to be afraid of. The fear then is "wrong," the father's knowledge that there is nothing frightening in the room is "right." Yet the child is still afraid, and he may become more agitated, with the added fear that his father will not believe him. Suppose instead that the father completely accepted his child's experience of fear. This father is also likely to ask questions, but these questions will convey the intention of understanding the child's fears, not talking him out of them. Knowing that he does not have to defend his fears against his father's evaluations, the child is more likely to speak about them in detail. As they are understood by the father, they are likely to become less or, if not, the child is more likely to accept the father's guidance about how he might manage these fears so that they do not interfere with his sleep.

A mistrusting child may well believe that her mother loves her sister more. She may express her belief through hurting her sister or breaking her toys, as well as screaming at her mother whenever the mother does something that seems to be favorable to the sister. If her mother gets irritated at such a "foolish" belief, the belief is only likely to intensify. If the mother reassures the daughter that she loves her as much as her sister, she is likely to not believe her and now begins to believe that her mother lies to her. Or she will share less with her mother because she is losing confidence in her mother's willingness to listen to her or understand what she is saying. If, however, the mother accepts her daughter's belief as an aspect of her experience, then she is likely to convey an intention to understand her daughter, not change her. As the mother understands her daughter's belief that she is not loved as much as her sister is, the mother is likely to respond with empathy, knowing that her daughter may feel lonely and frightened, and may also believe that her mother is disappointed in her, that she is not good enough. As the mother communicates her empathy for her daughter's belief and related feelings, her daughter is likely to share more. Soon the belief is likely to dissipate, as her mother's empathy and understanding communicates a depth of love that affects the belief much more than anything she could say to talk her out of it. The belief that she is loved less than her sister is likely to get even smaller if her mother expresses a commitment to help her daughter experience her love more clearly so that her doubts might decrease.

C: Curiosity

With acceptance, the therapist is communicating the intent to simply understand the child's inner life, not change it. With curiosity, the therapist begins the journey of understanding. Curiosity is a not-knowing position, with no assumptions, no expectations, no judgments about what is being discovered. The therapist is conveying the attitude of being fascinated with who the child is. The therapist has communicated a deep interest in knowing, "What do you wonder about?" "How do you make sense of that?" "Why did your father say that?" "If you're not important to her, what's that like?" "How do you know?" Such questions, without searching for a particular response, conveys that the child's inner life is important—no matter what it is, it is important—and the therapist wants to know it, to know the child better. Such curiosity is hard for a mistrusting child to resist. Yes, it scares him, and he doubts the motives of the therapist's questions, but he is drawn to those questions. He often does not know the answer, but he begins to wonder, too. How does he know that his mother does not like him? What does his father think about his silence? Why did they adopt him? How will he ever learn whom to trust? And why bother? Gradually, with the therapist's curiosity, the child's own curiosity becomes more active. He never had a reason for wondering before. No one was ever interested in his inner life, so he assumed that there really wasn't any reason for answering those questions. Or if he asked and found the answers, they would lead to realizing that he was bad or unlovable. He would rather not know that.

The child also is drawn to the therapist's curiosity because he is so lonely. Again, he is scared of letting someone know him, but when he can't avoid the loneliness, it is hard to resist sharing his inner life with someone who treats it with acceptance. After years of living with mistrust—out of necessity—he might now have a choice as to whether to trust. He has learned that mistrust has a downside—it really is lonely—and he might begin to consider the other option.

When a mistrusting child is asked why he does something, his first reply is often, "I don't know." Most likely he is telling the truth. He spends so much time not reflecting on his inner life, not wondering about what he feels, thinks, or wants and why he does things that he truly is in the dark about it. Often others are skeptical of this and reply with: "Of course you know, you just don't want to tell me." This often leads to an ultimatum: "You're going to sit there until you tell me." At other times the parent or teacher tells the child why he did it: "You just did that because you always want your own way." Such interactions lead to more shame, more secrecy, and less interest in discovering his motives or telling someone what it is if he does know. Mistrust only becomes stronger.

Contrast that sequence with the following. Sandra is the 15-year-old daughter of Tess and Ray. Sandra had been moody for the past few months and her parents were not sure what to do. They asked her a few times but she did not want to talk about it. One day she had asked to go to the movies with a friend and Tess said that she could but needed to get a few things done first. A few hours later, nothing had been done, and when Sandra asked to go to the movies, Tess said that she couldn't because she had not done what had been asked of her.

Tess: (*with a relaxed, reflective, curious voice that was non-judgmental*) You wanted to see that movie a lot and you didn't clean up the mess you made in the kitchen that had to get done first. What do you think was going on?

Sandra: I don't know.

Tess: OK, that's too bad since I was wondering if something was bothering you. Any idea why it might have been hard to do what I asked?

Sandra: No.

Tess: (*nonjudgmental*) Where you annoyed with me for telling you to do it?

Sandra: You know that I don't like to clean the kitchen, but you made me do it anyway.

Tess: Ah. You're right, I do know you don't like doing it. Why do you think I still told you to do it?

Sandra: Because you don't care about what I want! You just want me to be unhappy.

Tess: Oh, Sandra, no wonder you're annoyed with me. You think that I told you to do that just so you'd be unhappy! (*with empathy, without annoyance*)

Sandra: You and Dad just have everything that you want. I'm not happy and you don't seem to notice! Like you're even glad!

Tess: (*without defensiveness*) I am truly sorry that you haven't seemed to be very happy lately. And I'm also sorry that it doesn't seem to you that your dad or I care! So you've been all alone with it!

> *Sandra:* It's like I can't trust anyone at school anymore. Everyone seems to be just in it for themselves. They turn against you if you do one thing that they don't like.
>
> *Tess:* Oh, sweetie, things have been so hard for you.
>
> *Sandra:* Why, Mom, why do they have to be this way?
>
> *Tess:* (*embracing Sandra, who accepts her comfort*) I don't know. I wish that I did. I wish that I could make things better for you. I wish it weren't so hard now.
>
> *Sandra:* (*quietly, holding her mom tightly*) I know, Mom.

Tess, remaining open and engaged, not defensive, was able to experience empathy for daughter. Her empathy, not reasons, will be likely to cause Sandra to doubt her assumptions about her mom's motive. Sandra felt her mother's understanding for her unhappiness and then was able to rely on her.

Such a sequence is not that uncommon when the parent approaches the mistrusting child with nonjudgmental curiosity. Often, a child like Sandra is able to figure out her motive when the parent simply wants to understand, not criticize. When that child starts to respond to those types of questions, she often ends up providing her assumptions about the motives of the parent in doing something—such as having her do a chore. Other children, who habitually do not trust others, often are convinced that their parent's motive involves rejection, indifference, being mean, not caring, not understanding, or thinking that the child's wishes are not important. Such a child often has very strong negative assumptions about her parent's motives, which might be slower to change.

E: Empathy

The expression of empathy is often the intervention that enables the dialogue to continue, that begins the process of the mistrusting child beginning to sense the possibility of trust. Expressed empathy is more likely to be experienced by the child as empathy when it matches the affective expression of the child's emotion associated with the story he is telling. When the child is angry, the therapist's empathy is expressed vocally with heightened intensity and a more rapid rhythm. We call that "loud empathy." When the child is sad, the therapist's empathy is expressed vocally in a slow and gentle tone—"soft empathy." When the child is agitated, showing anxiety or frantic hyperactivity, the therapist's empathy is expressed vocally with an animated, diverse tone, "containing empathy." When the child is expressing intense distress, the therapist's empathy is conveyed with an equally intense expression that conveys a sense of urgency to understand and be of aid, or "joining empathy." When the child is expressing some pride and excitement, the therapist's empathy is expressed vocally by conveying lightness and energy, or "joyful empathy." These are all aspects of empathy. They all communicate that the therapist is experiencing this aspect of the child's story from the same affective space of the child, and from that space, the therapist is in the best position to help the child trust that the therapist may be able understand the child's story. Since the story may relate to the child's full range of emotional experiences, the therapist's empathic responses need to be varied enough to communicate "I get it" no matter what emotion the child conveys.

Playfulness is a relaxed, light way to feel close to someone that is safer than allowing yourself to give and receive affection with that person. Acceptance also conveys that you are safe with me, I want to understand you, not judge and criticize you. Curiosity is the way that I come to know you, again safely, without evaluating those qualities of your inner life and behavior that are central to who you think you are. So now I am beginning to know this mistrusting child, and I discover how vulnerable she is. She is frightened and lonely, confused and full of shame. She doubts her place within the family, and when she quietly speaks of the endless days that make up her life, she begins to feel the depth of sadness that she has run from, seemingly forever. When I experience these qualities of her experience of self and other, I also experience empathy for the pain she has lived with for years.

It is not enough that I experience empathy for the mistrusting child. I also need to give expression to my experience so that it also may be experienced by the child. By experiencing my empathy, the mistrusting child may become frightened. I am not repulsed by him. I do not hate him. I am not indifferent to him. It is not that I do not know him—he has not manipulated me into thinking that he is better than he thinks he is. No, since he knows that I have experienced his experience, he knows that I know him and feel the pain that he feels, his pain. I do not pull back from it, forcing him to feel it alone once again. Rather, I share his pain in whatever form it is now being experienced—despair, terror, rage, shame, loneliness, confusion—and stay with him in it. From that position, where we are together through his experience of my empathy for him and his life, he begins to awaken to the possibility and the value of trusting me.

Empathy is expressed through nonverbal and verbal communications, and most likely the nonverbal is primary. When the child is safe enough to begin to experience and then express his pain, he is likely to do so nonverbally. His distress will be obvious in his face, his eyes, his voice, and most likely his posture and gestures. We know he is sad when we hear his slow, halting, troubled voice. We know he is sad when his face softens and settles in heaviness above eyes that seem to be working to stay open, maybe wet with the hint of tears. As we are open to experiencing those nonverbal expressions of his sadness, we are likely to convey similar expressions in our bodies. Our expressions are likely to become synchronized with his. As Siegel has said, he begins to "feel felt." Experiencing our experience of his sadness, his experience of it is likely to begin to change slowly. It may feel lighter because it is not felt alone. It may begin to include a sense of hope, since the experience of it is hopeful. As he experiences the therapist's empathy for his sadness, he senses that the therapist has confidence it will change. With hope comes an opening for trust. He may begin to trust that he is accepted, understood, and not alone in his despair, rage, or terror. He may begin to notice that those emotions are softer and less extreme. They may even be experienced—not alone—without causing dysregulation of emotion, cognition, or behavior. It is no wonder that there is probably more evidence for the effectiveness of empathy as a therapeutic intervention and experience than any other intervention that has ever been discovered or developed.

Relationship Repair

Strong attachment relationships provide depths of meaning and intimacy, safety, and discovery. They provide resilience and joy from cradle to grave. They must be tended—nourished and held in our minds and hearts for their central importance in our lives. They must be repaired when they are stressed, when they crack, and when they are in danger of being broken. Repair is needed whenever they are harmed by conflicts and separations, diverging wishes and misunderstandings. Without repair these stressors will put the relationship at high risk of being disrupted. Then these relationships will not provide the safety the child seeks from them. Nor will they provide the opportunity to learn from shared experiences with his parents. Finally, when the relationships are not repaired when needed, it is likely that they will no longer provide the child with the experiences of comfort and joy.

If mistrusting children are going to learn to trust attachment relationships, these relationships will have to be repaired much more frequently than would be needed in relationships with trusting children. Because of the hypersensitivity of the self-defense system, a mistrusting child is likely to experience minor tensions or misattunements as signs of untrustworthiness in the adult, fueling chronic misperceptions of the adult's motives. She is likely to believe that when her parent refuses her request, the refusal is due to her parent wanting her to be unhappy or not caring about what is important to her. If her parent is not available to play with her, she is likely to believe that her parent does not want to be with her or does not enjoy her, and she is likely to consider any other reason as just an excuse made to hide this fact. If her parent is not home for a few days, a mistrusting child is likely to believe she has been abandoned. Even when the parent returns, the separation is likely to make the child anticipate that it will happen over and over again. She will lose confidence in her parent's commitment to remain in her life in spite of short, periodic separations. When the mistrusting child is scolded because of a behavior the parent does not permit, the child is likely to believe that the parent's dislike for the behavior actually represents a more pervasive dislike for the child herself.

A mistrusting child mistrusts attachment relationships. She does not believe that the relationship is "for better or for worse." She does not believe that her parents will strive to do what is in her best interests. While at birth she may have "expected" that an adult would provide safety and nurturance, repeated failures to do so have left her wary about new relationships. She does not trust that a new attachment relationship will be any different from prior ones.

The need for frequent relationship repair is given a high priority in DDP. This is evident in the following:

1. The therapist's relationship with the child is at risk when the therapist introduces stressful themes the child would rather avoid. When the child defends against the theme and believes the therapist introduced it to cause him to be unhappy, create shame, or focus only on what he does wrong or what is hard for him, the therapist pauses in the original exploration of the stressful theme and attends to the child and their relationship at that moment. The therapist relates with PACE to help the child be able to reflect on their current experience together and consider that the therapist might have other, positive motives for bringing up that topic.

2. The theme of the A-R dialogue often brings up experiences that involve a stress or disruption in the child's attachment with his parents. The therapist helps the child explore the meaning he may have given the event (e.g., my adoptive mother said no to me because she does not like me), co-regulates the emotion associated with that event (anger, fear, sadness, shame), and helps the child create new meaning associated with the event

(e.g., my adoptive mother said no because she thought that it was best for me not to do that behavior, and she had empathy for my distress about it because she does want me to be happy).

3. The therapist works with the parent to see the value of relationship repair in response to stress on the relationship at home due to routine discipline and disappointments. The therapist stresses the value of the parent initiating repair so the child knows that no matter how big the conflict is, the parent believes the relationship is more important than the conflict. The parent is committed to the relationship, to the child, and to resolving the conflict and building the child's trust in the parent. By initiating the repair, the parent is not saying she is sorry for causing the conflict (unless she does believe she made a mistake that contributed to the conflict). Rather, she is saying that no matter what happened, she wants to protect and even strengthen their relationship. She is sorry for the doubts and stress caused by the discipline or separation. The rules or discipline might well remain unchanged, but she is available to help the child with managing the distress they cause. By initiating repair, she is conveying to the child that her motives for the child and for the relationship are positive.

4. If the parent believes that his or her own behavior did create the break in the relationship, then the parent needs to go to the child and acknowledge responsibility for the break and apologize if indicated. The parent's behavior may reflect a lack of sensitivity to the child for many reasons: being harsh or punitive, failing to keep a promise, or simply being preoccupied with other responsibilities and forgetting the parental role for a time. When parents are able to acknowledge their mistakes and change their behavior, most of these breaks can lead to an improvement in their relationship.

In each situation, the parent or therapist is encouraged to approach the conflict and need for repair in the following sequence.

1. Describe the event in a relaxed, rhythmic manner without using a stern, monotone voice.
2. Convey empathy for how hard it seemed to have been for the child.
3. Without judgment, begin wondering about the meaning of the event for the child, that is, what made it so hard.
4. Help the child wonder about the motive of the parent in setting the limit or correcting the child. The perceived motive often reflects the child's mistrust of the parent.
5. Express empathy for the child's distress caused by the perceived motive.
6. Ask the child to tell the parent (or offer to say it for him) that he was upset because he perceived the parent's motive to be negative (rejecting, threatening, mean, etc.).
7. Ask the parent to respond, first with empathy, understanding the child's distress if the child's perception of the parent's motive was negative, following with nondefensive information about the actual motive, a commitment to make the motive more clear in the future, and a desire to help the child with his distress and repair their relationship.

The foregoing sequence focused on relationship breaks that might be caused by the child's misperception of the parent's motive. There are other reasons for breaks that also need to be discovered. These include the child believing the parent does not understand how hard things are for the child, the child having difficulty regulating and expressing strong emotions, and the child not knowing what she wants and blaming the parent for her unhappiness. When children mistrust relationships, the relationships are vulnerable to frequent breaks and the child needs the parent's initiatives to frequently repair them.

By tending to the need for relationship repair, the DDP therapist emphasizes the ongoing need to build and restore trust whenever the normal stresses of any close family relationship are perceived by the child as reasons for mistrust. The DDP therapist does not say to the child that the reasons are wrong. Rather, the therapist and caregiver express empathy for the child's distress caused by his perception of the motives of the parent with regard to the conflict or discipline. The child's experience of empathy for his distress—similar to the infant's experience of comfort when in distress—goes much further in helping him to begin to trust again than does any explanation given by the parent for the discipline. To understand why, let's explore comfort more fully.

> Anthony was a 16-year-old boy, living with his mom and 7-year-old sister. His parents had been divorced for six years and during that time, Anthony spent less and less time with his father. He had poor grades and was increasingly withdrawn from his mother. He did not experience therapy as being helpful, and he thought that if he needed to talk with someone about something bothering him, he would tell someone he knew, not a stranger. At the fifth session Anthony attended with his mother, he seemed to become more open and engaged, and he spoke in some detail how bothered he was by not seeing his father very often. He expressed hope that this might change because his father had invited him to go camping with him over the upcoming weekend and he was excited about it. When he was much younger, he and his father often went camping, something his mother did not enjoy doing. The therapist got many details about the camping plans and conveyed understanding about how important it was for Anthony.
>
> In the sixth session, Anthony initially was very engaged and expressive about something he had done with a friend the day before, as well as a movie he and his mother had watched. As the session progressed, he spoke less and less and seemed to be increasingly detached and irritable. The therapist asked him if something was bothering him, and Anthony denied it.

The question only seemed to make him more upset. The therapist reflected about what Anthony's withdrawal might mean and then he had a guess:

Therapist: I'm sorry, Anthony, I forgot to ask about your camping trip with your father. How did it go?

Anthony: Don't worry about it.

Therapist: Anthony, I really am sorry. That trip seemed to be very important to you last time and I should have asked about it as soon as I saw you.

Anthony: Why didn't you, then?

Therapist: I've had a lot on my mind the last couple of days, but none of it justifies not asking you about you and your dad. That was important to you, and I should have asked you as soon as I saw you. You are important to me, Anthony, and during our sessions, I need to be aware of what's on your mind. I wasn't, I let you down and you deserve better than that. (*silence for a few moments*) Would you be willing to tell me now? I really want to know about the trip with your dad.

Anthony began telling the therapist, and within five minutes his voice and enthusiasm expressed how important the trip had been. Not sure of his importance to his dad, he also was not sure about his importance to the therapist, who did not appear to remember or be interested in what Anthony had told him the week before. The open apology from the therapist went a long way to helping Anthony to begin to trust the therapist again. He did develop confidence that he was held in the therapist's mind, something very important to him and to all of those we treat in therapy.

Creating Space for Comfort and Joy

Over the years, the authors have had many early morning discussions about children who had been born into families who were not able to provide them with the early experiences to facilitate their development—emotional, cognitive, psychological—along with the key neurological developments of infancy. Jon casually commented that these children were especially vulnerable to the lack of development of their uncinate fasciculus. This brought a gasp from Dan that here was another esoteric brain part that Jon had neglected to mention that most likely was worth discussing.

"What is that, and what makes it important?" asked Dan. The uncinate fasciculus (UF) is a bundle of fibers that connects the amygdala and the hippocampal region to the lower regions of the prefrontal cortex, especially the orbital PFC and the lower ACC, and the VMPFC we always talk about. The UF is like a brain highway between the lower PFC, the amygdala, and the hippocampus and is important for processing emotionally relevant information and putting this information into the context of time and place. On the right side of the brain, the UF is primarily involved in the process of regulating negative emotions that would typically lead to avoiding a harmful or threatening thing, including another person. On the left side, the UF is more involved in regulating "approach" functions, such as social approach emotions involved in attachment. It's very interesting that there are now studies showing that socially anxious people have a less developed UF on the left side, and this also has been shown to be true of children who spent up to a year or more in an institutional setting (like an Eastern European orphanage) prior to adoption (Chugani et al., 2001; Eluvathingal et al., 2006). In other words, the UF appears to require social stimulation and interaction with an attachment figure to develop in a more typical fashion (Braun et al., 2000). Underdevelopment of this fronto-limbic circuit may be a factor in the problems that maltreated children have with attachment and social engagement (Chen and Miller, 2012; Chen et al., 2012).

Of course the question that follows involves the type of experiences that infants need from their parents that facilitate the development of the VMPFC–amygdala circuit, the core link between the bottom of the prefrontal cortex and the deeper emotional regions of the brain, the link that enables a child to regulate strong emotions rather than flipping out. The answer involves a range of experiences easily summarized by two words: comfort and joy, those relational experiences mediated by opioids and oxytocin and dopamine. The presence or absence of comfort and joy in the infant's life has crucial meaning for his entire lifetime, including his readiness to live a life of trust or mistrust. Experiences of comfort and joy are central in the child's ability to trust his parents, most likely in part because they are central in the development of the VMPFC–amgydala circuit.

An infant's cries of distress have multiple causes: cold, hunger, needing a diaper change, or uncomfortable emotions they are not able to regulate—they just seem to get bigger and bigger—emotions such as fear and helplessness in response to some sensation, either sudden and unexpected or long and discomforting. What the child needs from the parent at that moment is action that will manage and remove the source of discomfort and fear—a bottle, a dry diaper, a blanket. Just as important, the infant needs an affective response from the parent that acknowledges the distress and communicates that the parent will assist the child so the distress is removed. This response is known as *comforting*.

By comforting the infant, the parent is communicating that the infant's distress is important and the parent is committed to ensuring that whenever the infant is in such a state, the parent will make it better. This happens again and again, consolidating a call-and-response cycle that engenders in the infant the knowledge that a parent will be close, available, and responsive to the infant's expressions of distress. Through repetitions of this cycle, the parent learns the meaning of different distress signals and how to respond to them in the most effective way. The parent goes further than making it better; she also communicates that she understands the baby's distress. She communicates comfort for her infant through her soothing, rhythmic, voice; her soft, loving, facial expression; and her gentle caress. Her comfort is experienced through the infant's eyes, ears, and skin, with all three sensations integrated. Comfort also results from the fact that her sensitive expressions are in synchrony with the infant's motor expressions. The infant's and parent's joint, complex sensory-motor experience provides the infant's brain with an equally complex experience that begins the integration of the lower regions of the cortex with the amygdala and joining regions. The parent's attuned response to the infant's state is contingent on the infant's decreasing distress and creates a sense of trust in the parent which, when it occurs again and again, is strong and lasting. Not only is the parent's voice, face, and touch synchronized with the infant's expressions, these expressions of the parent are unique, enabling the infant to form an attachment that is differentiated from that with other adults. The infant trusts that this particular person will be available, sensitive, and responsive to him in his expressions of need (Mayes et al., 2009).

In DDP the therapist and caregiver are also available, sensitive, and responsive when a mistrusting child gives expression to the distress associated with the experiences of abuse, neglect, and abandonment. In DDP comfort is demonstrated through expressions of acceptance, curiosity, and empathy which are attuned to the expressions of the child's distress. The therapist's voice, attuned with the mistrusting child's expressions of terror, despair, rage, or shame, matches the affective expressions of these emotions, which enables the child to feel deeply understood and feel the therapist's compassion. The child is not alone, possibly for the first time, in the memories of the horrific experiences of his young life.

In DDP the therapist does not simply observe and express reflections on these experiences of the child; rather, he joins the child in these experiences. The therapist remains regulated while leading the child into similarly regulated affective experiences of previously dysregulated states. The therapist reflects on these experiences which the child previously was unable to reflect on while being alone and overwhelmed by them. The therapist's voice is both affective and reflective, has nonverbal and verbal components, is expressed in a modulated, rhythmic way that tends to become attuned with the child's expressions. In this manner, the attuned, affective-reflective dialogue is similar to the expressions of the parent as she joins her infant's distressed state and provides comfort. Very likely, the A-R dialogue truly does facilitate the development of the UF and the integration of the amygdala with prefrontal regions, helping the child develop the capacity for self-regulation from his experiences with having an effective co-regulator (Hofer, 1994, 1995; Insel and Young, 2001; Hostinar, Sullivan, and Gunnar, 2014).

Joy is not often thought to be an important therapeutic experience, but it definitely is in DDP, just as it is in the infant's neuropsychological development. A mistrusting child has had too few experiences involving pleasure, laughter, and delight that are shared—and created—within the interactions with his caregiver. The therapist looks for opportunities to include such experiences in the therapeutic session. She notices and then invites such joint experiences, but she does not force their presence when the child, caregiver, and therapist are focused on the sources of the child's mistrust. The opportunity for experiences of joy may be present:

- At the onset of the session, during light small talk or explorations of experiences of success, fun, and humor.
- During transitions in the A-R dialogue when the exploration of a stressful theme has come to a natural ending and there is need for a light pause before exploring another difficult theme.
- Toward the end of the session, when the therapist is reflecting on "a job well done" and all present take some time to enjoy their joint accomplishment and sense of emotional closeness. All may playfully turn their focus to enjoyable experiences that lie ahead after the session.

Joy does not require intense laughter or happiness. Such intensity may be present at times, while at other times joy is expressed with a reciprocal smile and affirming eye contact. These joint experiences of joy enable a mistrusting child to begin to regulate positive emotional states through the co-regulation of these states with the therapist and/or caregiver. A mistrusting child habitually does not trust the emotions of happiness, joy, and affection, which often evoke anxiety and withdrawal. By co-regulating these states of joy, the child increases his capacity to regulate them just as he learns to regulate states of fear and sadness when these states are co-regulated with comfort. Thus, attuned, A-R dialogue increases a mistrusting child's ability to regulate the full range of emotional states and also to reflect on a full range of relational events that led to mistrust in the past.

The Integration of Affective and Reflective Experience and Communication

Through DDP and A-R dialogue, made more engaging and meaningful through intersubjectivity and PACE, the child begins the neuropsychological process of integrating the more cognitive with the more emotional regions of his brain. This enables him to attain an experience of his therapist and caregiver that generates greater safety and its closely associated state of being open and engaged. The child is now open to new learning about the differences between his current caregiver and his prior caregiver, who created his sense of mistrust. The child is also more able to regulate any associated emotional states and be more receptive to experiences of comfort and joy that occur with the caregiver and therapist. The attuned communications between the child and the caregiver or therapist create the confidence that the adult understands him and experiences empathy for his prior experiences. This process involves the simultaneous development of these parallel processes:

1. Integration of regions of the cortex and amygdala,
2. Integration of affective and reflective states,
3. Integration of the experiences of child and adult through intersubjective communications, and

4. Confident awareness that the adult understands and feels empathy for the child's experience. The adult is becoming trustworthy.

Mistrusting children have great difficulty trusting anyone enough to rely on them for assistance in developing the skills to address the source of the mistrust. It takes trust to be able to benefit from psychotherapy, and these children do not have that core ability. DDP first establishes that basic sense of trust in the therapist and caregiver by providing and developing those immediate self and other experiences that enable the child's mind and brain to unlearn habitual mistrust and develop selective trust.

The DDP therapist approaches this core trust-building task with the same open and engaged attitude; expressive, nonverbal communications; and the intention to create the conditions of safety and new learning that are present when a capable and committed parent is engaged with his or her infant. The expressions may differ based on the age, history, and manner of engagement expressed by the mistrusting child, but the core stance is highly similar. Throughout this entire process, the therapist is sensitively responsive to the child's expressions of mistrust, co-regulating the emerging affect and co-constructing new possible meanings about the nature of adult–child relationships.

As the child's trust in the therapist and caregiver gradually increases, the child becomes open to new learning about self, other, and the world. The perspectives of these two adults adds to the child's limited perspective (limited by his age and narrow experiences, made more narrow by his need to attend primarily to sources of threat) and enables the child to begin to discover the world only visible to those who feel safe. Gradually, the child, with the support of the therapist's and caregiver's regulated stance and new perspectives, begins to attend to the past events that taught him to mistrust. The new, interwoven perspectives of the child, therapist, and caregiver regarding those events, enables the child to begin to revisit and re-experience those shaming and frightening experiences from a safe place, in connection with these accepting, empathic adults.

With a mistrusting child, this process does not occur easily. The therapist knows that the child will have difficulty experiencing her as benign and well intentioned. Understanding the adaptive nature of the child's mistrust can help the therapist appreciate the child's need to resist engagement. DDP recognizes that the child's defensiveness is well earned, serving the child in a family experienced as untrustworthy. The therapist begins with no other agenda than to help the child feel safe enough to engage, even if the level of engagement initially is light and tentative.

Moment to moment in the treatment session, the therapist needs to continuously send the nonverbal message: "You are safe here and now with me." The open and engaged stance of the therapist —while not responding to the child's defensive stance—evokes a similar stance within the child. The therapist's rhythmic voice and interested, accepting facial expressions say again and again: "I enjoy being with you and getting to know you. You are safe here and now with me." The synchronized responses to whatever affect is expressed by the child say: "I notice how you are with me, I understand your experience here and now, and you are safe in our here and now together." Whatever the child's affect—sad, mad, frightened, confused, excited, vulnerable, full of shame—the therapist conveys the message "whatever you are experiencing now with me, you are safe with me in your experience and its expression, and I want to understand and stay with you in this moment together."

Safety is conveyed in DDP with an intersubjective stance that says: "I like you and being with you no matter what you think, feel, wish for, remember, tell me, or plan for the future. I will like you while I stop you from hitting me if you intend to do that, and I will help us both understand why you tried to hit me." With DDP the therapeutic stance is not ambiguous or neutral. Such a stance would only leave the mistrusting child more anxious and create more defensiveness with anger or withdrawal.

With the mistrusting child, new learning also occurs with difficulty. Teaching the child problem-solving skills with cognitive coping strategies tends to rely on parts of the brain that are poorly developed in these children. Teaching such skills does not address the child's needs for motivation, confidence, and a core grasp of what something means for him at an experiential level. He needs such experiential learning if he is to be willing and able to do the hard work required to change perceptual, cognitive, emotional, and behavioral habits he developed to keep himself safe. New learning must be embedded in nonverbal communications of their value, meaning, and likelihood of success. New learning about past events that led to mistrust must be embedded in empathy and a compassionate understanding about how hard those events were for the child, how he did not deserve them, and how he can discover the value and possibility of trusting this therapist and caregiver. Such communications, again, must be embedded in nonverbal communications. These say: "You are safe with me, here and now, and we will learn together ways that you might discover another world where you come to know who I see when I see you, and what we discover together when we recall your past, observe the present, or imagine the future."

CHAPTER 6

Practicing Openness:
Awakening Trust and Engagement with
Relational Processing and Fear Extinction

Seeing lives which one had thought irremediably blighted suddenly bloom into a wonderful renewal.
—Sacks (1990, p. xxv)

In our brain-based model, the goal of attachment-focused treatment is to reawaken and nurture the child's dormant potential for open engagement and trust. Mistrustful children need for adults to know that beneath their defensive exterior is the blocked need for comfort and companionship, the child's inherent potential for engagement that needs reawakening. Think of the shy boy at his first school dance. He's standing in the corner, watching his peers twist and shout, frozen and showing no outward signs of wanting to dance. But don't be fooled; on the inside, he is, indeed, an exuberant dancer, just needing something, someone, to help him unfreeze so he can hit that dance floor with a ferocious passion to move freely with the music. Children with blocked trust are much like this frozen dancer—they need someone to help them feel safe enough to join the dance of connection.

We borrow the concept of awakenings from Oliver Sacks (1990), the gifted neurologist who early in his career helped victims of the early twentieth-century encephalitis epidemic recover, at least transiently, from their seemingly lost capacity for social engagement by giving them medicine that triggered their dopamine system. Other awakenings can be seen in recent work with Alzheimer's patients using music to activate the social engagement system when all hope of reviving this capacity seems lost. In DDP, the therapist uses relational processes to awaken the child's capacity for engagement.

Fear Extinction and Relational Trauma Processing

Ellen was providing dyadic developmental psychotherapy (DDP) to a nine-year-old foster child, Anita, who had developed a life of mistrust during her first six years when she was experiencing chronic neglect and periodic abuse. Now she was very distractible and kept busy going from one activity to another. She was diagnosed with attention deficit/hyperactivity disorder, for which she was receiving medication. Periodically, Ellen would refer to those early years, and each time Anita would change the topic or become involved in another activity. Her foster mother indicated that Anita never spoke about her life prior to entering her current foster home 18 months before.

During one session, Ellen commented, with complete acceptance and nonjudgmental curiosity about Anita's avoidance of any exploration of those early years.

Ellen: (*with some animation, matching the high energy level that Anita routine demonstrated*) Gee, Anita, I've noticed something, I've noticed something! (*Anita paused as she usually did for a moment when Ellen seemed to be interested in something*) I've noticed that whenever I talk about when you were a little girl . . . *little* . . . like when you were three, or four, or five. Whenever I do, you talk about something else. Every time! And I wondered about that.

It seems to me that you really, really, really do *not* want to talk about those early years when you were little. Am I right?

Anita: (*pausing, seeming to be gazing into a far away place, then replying in a quiet, matter-of-fact tone*) That's when I was dead.

Ellen: (*now much quieter, matching Anita's voice*) Oh, my, Anita. That's when you were dead. Dead. How sad that must have been for you back then. When you were little . . . to be dead. I wonder if you felt all alone then.

Anita: I was.

Ellen: So alone. To feel dead.

Anita: I was.

Ellen: Do you still feel dead?

Anita: No.

Ellen: I'm glad, Anita. I'm so glad that you don't feel dead now. Why do you think you don't feel dead now?

Anita (*looks at foster mom, Ruby, and smiles. Ruby smiles back, with tears*)

Such a stark word, *dead*, to so clearly describe a life without comfort, joy, emotions, and relationships. That moment in that session helped Anita to begin the journey of coming alive again. Her relationship with Ruby began to gradually become the source of comfort and joy. Her distractibility and hyperactivity greatly decreased and she successfully stopped taking medication. As she gazed back, with the help of Ruby and Ellen, at those early years, she began to make sense of them and form a narrative that involved resilience and relationships.

Reawakening the suppressed need for connection in maltreated children is one of the most moving experiences therapists and parents can have. Scenes in which children, closed off for years, disengaged and chronically defensive, start to feel the pain of this prolonged isolation rising up through their defensiveness and urging them to finally seek comfort from a caring adult, can be stunning to witness. These are dramatic moments of reawakening that are vital to the process of healing from blocked trust. It's important for therapists and caregivers to realize that any experiences of open engagement for the deeply mistrustful child are probably going to trigger preverbal, implicit fear memories that led to the need to block the social engagement system in the first place. In a very important sense, the reawakening of the child's need for connection in a safe context with caring adults is a relational trauma-focused exposure process in which the child's old fear-based memories are made available for reprocessing and fear extinction. The authors have had many experiences with moments in treatment when children were beginning to feel those "forbidden" feelings of separation distress and in the next moment wanting to hide or flee. These are crucial moments in attachment-focused treatment when the adults in the room need to pay exquisite attention to the child's level of distress and titrate the process of helping the child safely tolerate staying open long enough to receive comfort and experience unexpected care and compassion. This is the process of safely revisiting and revising implicit fear-based memories often stemming from infancy, memories that cannot be reprocessed in a strictly cognitive-focused trauma treatment model because these preverbal memories are not accessible for this kind of remembering. These memories have to be recovered relationally and reprocessed relationally, primarily through nonverbal communication with safe adults who know how to send safety messages into the child's limbic system even as the child is reexperiencing the fear.

While these moments are just openings to the possibility of trust, not a cure for blocked trust, the process of "sadness recovery," of restoration of the child's capacity to feel the need for help from a caregiver and then receive real comfort, is a vital step in the journey from mistrust to trust. Recovery from blocked trust is a multiphased process involving the drama of such awakenings and the less dramatic practicing of engagement light, when children are helped to sustain safe-enough interactions with adults in recurring "doses" to strengthen their fragile, underdeveloped capacity for openness. These lighter, "moving along" moments of the therapy create within the child an open and engaged stance with his caregiver that enables him to initiate and be responsive to the deeper experiences of comfort and joy that are available to him.

Synchrony and Attunement

Just how does this movement toward synchrony work within our brains? As we noted in the last chapter, attunement represents the sharing of affective states when two people are interacting. The nonverbal expressions, the body's expressions of intentional movements, tend to be responded to in kind by the other person, and a dance quickly develops where the two people become matched in rhythm and intensity of expression. At a preconscious level, each senses what the other is experiencing. The experience of one becomes contagious within the other. The states become matched. In part, this state-matching process is facilitated by the mirror neuron system that neuroscientists discovered in the 1990s in monkeys. Humans have a rich mirror cell system, and we use it to tune in to each other's internal states and intentions without awareness of doing so, at an implicit, preconscious level (Rizzolatti and Craighero, 2004).

When one person expresses an emotion of anger, sadness, or fear, the other person also tends toward feeling angry, sad, or frightened. In this situation, their emotions are synchronized. However, it is possible for the affective expression of the emotion to become matched while the two individuals do not experience the same emotion. If the adult matches how the child expresses the emotion of fear, sadness, or anger (by resonating with the rhythm and intensity of the expression), without experiencing the emotion himself, the child is likely to feel the adult's empathy. Thus, if a child yells at an adult, "I don't like it that you won't let me leave!" and the adult responds with a very similar degree of intensity and rhythm in his expression, "I get it! You are angry with me for saying that you cannot leave until you finish your chore!," the child is likely to feel the adult's empathy for his anger, much more than if the adult said the same words in a calm and reasonable manner.

Giving "Safe Passage": Staying Open

Mistrust, the child's dominant reaction, does not go away quickly. Recall the earlier discussion of the job of the child's amygdala to help her stay safe? This fast appraisal system detects the lowering of defensiveness in the presence of a caregiver as an immediate threat to safety, and this unconscious threat detection can quickly turn that brain switch from openness to defensiveness in milliseconds. This is an inevitable reaction that a deeply mistrusting child cannot control in the moment. Indeed, this is the beginning stage of a therapeutic process in which the child experiences intense conflict between the fragile urge to engage and be open and the robust urge to defend himself by avoiding open engagement. Literally in the child's brain at the point, the social engagement system and the social defense system are competing to "decide" whether the child should be open or defensive. Because the defense system is overdeveloped, this is not a fair competition: the defense system will often prevail until somehow, the child's limbic system gives enough of a "green light" that he can stay open for longer periods of time.

In our desire to see a child be open to the present, we may naturally resist his or her "relapse" into defensiveness. This can be especially challenging for caregivers who may be experiencing open engagement with the child for the first time after years of trying to have such moments. Naturally we want the child to notice the opportunity that is provided for her to learn something new, to play, cooperate, and share in something of value. We want her to be engaged with us and with what is provided—to take advantage of it. When she resists staying engaged with us, we may push her to do so. We might push through encouragement, advice, and showing the advantages in doing so. Later we might push through becoming stern, adding rewards and consequences, and becoming a bit annoyed ourselves. After all, if we are going to do so much to give the child the opportunity to improve her life, doesn't she owe us a positive, grateful, effortful response? We tend to forget at those times that a mistrustful child is likely to become more defensive because she does not feel safe, that she is likely to push back or shut down and resist our efforts to be of help, which are not experienced as helpful.

If we do not want that mutually defensive struggle, where do we turn? We focus on remaining open and engaged during the interaction until slowly the child's defensive stance is likely to begin to weaken until the child seems to awaken in our presence and also becomes open and engaged. What gives us confidence that if the adult is able to remain open and engaged throughout the dialogue, the child will follow? Research shows that our brains are designed to synchronize with the brain of the person with whom we are interacting (Mills and Conboy, 2009).

Because we all give priority to our safety, if one person is defensive, the other person is instantly likely to become defensive. It is important for the adult to recognize this, be aware of the movement toward defensiveness, and quickly become open and engaged again. Then, if the adult is able to resist the tendency to become defensive, his or her open state of mind can help the child shift into a more open state of mind through the emerging process of synchronization. In this way, the adult can use his or her state of mind to lead the child out of defensiveness and into openness. Remember, the *adult's* ability to send messages of safety to the child's defensive brain is the driver of change.

Mistrustful children are so habitually defensive that when we are able to assist them in becoming open and engaged, they are often eager, at least in those moments of openness, to learn what might improve their lives. They are sometimes excited by this opportunity: there seems to be a new world out there they had not known before, a world they are safe to explore and learn to live in. Most likely this will not happen in one try. The excitement is likely to be combined with anxiety, with the stressful feeling of having let down the guard wall. In the child's brain, the awakening trust is likely to meet resistance from the habitual state of mistrust, generating a state of internal conflict. The child is likely to "hear" in his mind, "Do you really think that you can trust him? He's most likely going to change his mind. Or he's deceiving you about this being a better way to live. He'll only hurt you in the long run and if you trust him, it will hurt more." The therapist needs to remember that the child is doing the best that he can in the conflict between open engagement and defensiveness. Rather than trying to push the child to remain open and engaged, the therapist needs to trust the process. Namely, if the therapist is able to truly accept the child's emerging defensiveness, with his own open and engaged state expressing a bit of curiosity or empathy, this acceptance is likely to cause it to soften and awaken the open and engaged state again.

> Roger was 11 and struggling to stay in his fourth foster home. He was tired of moving, he seemed to have a few friends at school and his foster parents weren't bad. In his eighth treatment session with his foster mom, Janet, and his therapist, Ben, he sat quietly, listening to Ben's gentle, rhythmic voice describe some of the hard times he had with his mother. Roger's face softened, his eyes watered, and he stole a quick glance at Janet, who gazed at him with compassion and care evident in her face.
>
> **Roger:** *(looking away, seeming to become defensive and regaining control)* I'm good.
> **Therapist (Ben):** *(seeing Janet look disappointed that Roger was covering his vulnerability and rejecting her desire to comfort him, he wanted to protect the soft moment that had just occurred)* Yes you are, Roger, yes you are. *(maintaining the same open and gentle tone)* You've learned to be strong to be able to be "good" even in tough times. And I don't think that you'll ever lose that. And now you might be learning to let Janet give you a bit of a hand with it too, once in a while. And that also takes being strong,

Roger, and you are, and I'm glad. (*Roger glanced back at Janet for a moment and she was now communicating compassion again, her disappointment having passed quickly from her face. Tom added, with a small smile*) I think we're all good.

In that brief sequence, some healing had occurred with a bit of the trauma having been integrated. In that brief sequence a bit of comfort was shown and received. A small movement from defensiveness toward joining Ben and Janet in an open and engaged relationship had occurred. A bit of trust started to form.

This is why it's so important that the adults anticipate the child's "relapses" into defensiveness and stay open to the child's struggle with this internal battle between openness and self-defensiveness. What will help the child gradually move toward greater openness is the adult's ability to accept, with compassion, the child's need to go back and forth until openness becomes safer as the child gets the benefit of the adult's contagious openness. The child needs "safe passage" to move between openness and defensiveness, movement made safe by the adult's ability to move with the child through these changing states without getting stuck in defensiveness. If adults shift from open engagement into defensiveness, they need to repair the break as soon as possible and become open and engaged again. Only in this way will the child be able to respond to the many relational experiences that will lead him—step by step—toward a state of trust.

Cindy was a 16-year-old girl who had experienced many difficult years in an orphanage in Europe before being adopted by Gwen and Thomas when she was seven. She was distant, withdrawn, and irritable with efforts to help her become engaged with her parents when she was first adopted, and this only got worse as she moved through adolescence. At times she would seem to be happier and communicate more openly with them, but this usually was short-lived. Various efforts with individual therapy were not very helpful, and her parents recently approached a therapist certified in DDP.

After a general discussion of routine events, the therapist turned her attention to Cindy and was able to make some connections between her current states of unhappiness and her very difficult first seven years in the orphanage. She started to cry quietly, and the therapist spoke soothingly with empathy. Suddenly she started laughing.

Therapist: (*waiting until her laughter stopped; speaking gently*) Any idea why you started to laugh? (*Cindy started to laugh again. The therapist again asked, still very gently*) It's ok to laugh, I just wondered why you might be laughing.

Gwen: (*whispering, with a bit of frustration in her voice*) She does that whenever things get too hard.

Therapist: (*seeing Cindy abruptly freeze when she heard her mother's tone of disappointment*) I'm sorry, Cindy, I did not realize that it was getting too hard. Your mom knows you better than I do and she can tell it was too hard. I'm sorry. (*Cindy began to cry again. Then the therapist turned to Gwen*) I don't think that you and I will ever be able to know how hard Cindy's life has been. (*Cindy cries even harder. Gwen moves over and puts her arm around her daughter and they cry together*)

This scenario is an example of how important it is to accept the child's experience whether it reflects engagement or disengagement. It also suggests that if we are frustrated by the child's defenses, but then repair the relationship by accepting where the child is functioning at the present time, that the child is likely to be open to reengaging.

Surprise: The Value of Positive Prediction Errors

In our biobehavioral model, the process of creating unexpected moments of compassionate care to trigger positive prediction errors is a key component of treatment. When we expect something in our interactions with another person and it occurs, our mind goes on automatic pilot. There is no news of a difference that commands our attention. Since what we expected happened, the next series of interactions are also likely to happen. When we were correct in guessing what was likely to happen, we are more confident that we can predict what will happen after that, and after that. . . . We really don't have to think about it much then because we're not likely to learn anything new. Importantly, the child in this scenario is not going to become curious about what is happening between him and the caregiver and we want to engender, to revive, the child's blocked curiosity, a higher brain function than habitual blocked trust.

Mistrustful children assume that adults will interact with them in certain ways, and when adults respond in those ways, the child anticipates—usually quite accurately—what will happen next. And what happens next most likely confirms his reasons to be mistrustful. There are two major sequences the mistrustful child is likely to put into place in his interactions with adults, and each is likely to end with the child again experiencing another adult to not trust.

The first sequence involves either the child or adult initiating a bit of friendly, smiling, interested, and cooperative stance. The adult might be genuinely open and engaged, wanting to get to know the child, build trust, and begin a trusting relationship. The child might begin with the same friendly, cooperative stance, but rather than it reflecting an open and engaged stance, more than likely it represents an effort to discover what the adult wants so if the child gives that to him, the child will be safe. There is a manipulative, deceptive quality to the child's surface friendliness. This is a survival skill— if the adult likes me, he will not hurt me. I have to be nice to be liked, and I can do that. The adult really does not know me, only the play-acting I can be good at. If the adult knew me, he would no longer like me. After a bit of this surface friendliness—when I begin to show the qualities that define who I believe myself to be—the adult will show that they really were not interested in me, only in my pretending that I am good. When I begin to lie, fight, express my habitual negative moods, refuse to do what I am told, make excuses, or ignore the adult and stop talking, the adult will respond in a way that has defined my relationship with adults for years. At first he will be increasingly defensive. He will focus on what he does not like about my behavior—about me—and sternly tell me not to do that. When I continue, he will become more obviously annoyed with me and begin to give me consequences that will teach me what I need to do, how I need to be. When these do not work—did he really think they would?—his mood begins to change, and I seldom see that early friendliness. He will consistently be angry with me, afraid of me, give up on me, or feel inadequate with me because he just does not know what to do with me. He will call me—or think this way even if he does not say it—ungrateful, selfish, mean, manipulative, and unmotivated.

The second sequence skips the initial friendly stage of the inter-action. The adult may have gotten to know the child because of his misbehavior and may believe the child just needs a fair, but strict hand that will set him straight. Here the child is likely to either fight back immediately or be compliant for a time while working out the best way to control this situation. The child is not likely to work to earn the positive relationship he is told will result from his good behavior. He has no trust in such relationships, so why should he work to earn one? He might follow the rules for a while, if only to avoid tough consequences or attain rewards, but when he gets bored with these or when his anger, fears, and loneliness gets stron-ger again, he will lose interest in this conditional arrangement and elicit the anger, anxiety, despair, and sense of inadequacy from the adult that he knows so well.

There is a third way that avoids these sequences. The adult does not respond to the child's initiatives in a manner that will inevitably lead the mistrustful child to increase his mistrust. In this way the child is not able to control the responses of the adult, not able to lead him into defensiveness and increasingly negative sequences. In fact the child has a difficult time anticipating how the adult will respond and thus finds his own controlling survival skills to not be effective. The third way begins with creating the element of surprise in the interactions. With surprise, the adult is able to activate regions and systems in the child's brain that might lead him from mistrust to trust.

Playfulness, acceptance, curiosity, and empathy (PACE) is an extremely effective stance for generating surprise within the mistrustful child. The child is expecting a stern and serious response, and our response involves playfulness in a light and engaging manner. We respond in a way that emphasizes the connection with the child, rather than any annoyance over challenging behavior. Acceptance communicates that we are attending to the child himself, rather than his particular behavior. The behavior might be addressed or responded to, but only in the context of the overall relationship with him. He had anticipated that his behavior would be evaluated immediately and if it was found to be inappropriate, he would be evaluated negatively. With acceptance, it is clear that he and our relationship with him are more important than his behavior.

With curiosity, we turn our attention to our child's words or behavior, without judgment. He had anticipated that if his actions or words conveyed a negative, challenging attitude, we would immediately respond defensively in kind, without bothering to try to understand what his behavior meant. With curiosity, we show that we are first interested in understanding its meaning. The behavior is seen as communicating something about the child's inner life that may be important. We may choose to respond more to the meaning of the behavior, rather than the behavior itself. The behavior would be addressed immediately if it suggests a lack of safety, but otherwise it is responded to in the context of the overall situation. Finally, empathy conveys to the child that if his behavior reflects something that is difficult for him, we understand and support him in his distress. He is not feeling the distress alone. With curiosity, we show that we understand the meaning of the behavior, and when the meaning suggests that he is in distress, empathy is the core of our engagement with him at that time. The behavior might still be addressed or limited, but with empathy, we are communicating an understanding about the reasons for the behavior that is likely to create a gentle and caring response along with the limit.

When we respond to a child's challenging behavior with PACE, rather than defensiveness, he is left experiencing his relationship with us as being safe and important, regardless of his behavior. The relationship, or relationship withdrawal, does not become part of the discipline. A conflict or significant misbehavior—something that a mistrusting child anticipated would hurt the relationship—does not do so. That experience, embedded in surprise at the adult's unexpected response, is likely to increase trust in the adult and the strength of the relationship.

Conflict Resolution and Social Buffering: Follow-Lead-Follow

Many therapists adopt a stance that is primarily either nondirective or directive. There are sound theoretical reasons for each stance. A nondirective approach tends to place the emphasis on the value of safety and the client being in control of the content of the session. The client chooses what is important for her to talk about as well as when to bring it up and how long to stay with it. This stance assumes the client ultimately knows best when she is willing and able to explore something that she decides is important, though difficult, for her. There are reasons for thinking that this stance would help the child feel trust in the therapist and the process of therapy. She will not be pushed to do something she does not want to do. The directive approach places more responsibility on the therapist to assess what topics are best to address and then initiate such discussions in a manner that is sensitive to any anxiety associated with them. The directive stance believes that many difficult themes may well be avoided indefinitely if the child finds it difficult to think about those issues, which might be embedded in shame or fear. Such avoidance might be even more pervasive in the mistrustful child who does not have the habit of relying on any adult to explore difficult issues.

With follow-lead-follow, the therapist conveys the attitude that the emerging therapeutic dialogue is a reciprocal process with ongoing interactions of initiating and responding between therapist and child. They create a dialogue together, and as it continues, they co-create a story about the events of the child's life. This process is similar to that of the parent with a young child. When the child is safe, the parent tends to follow the interests and expressions of the child, supporting his or her spontaneous desires and sources of delight and fascination. The adult experiences these with the child—in an intersubjective manner—so that his experiences contribute to how the child develops his own experience of the other person, object, or event. When the child begins to lose interest in or disengage from the current focus of attention, the parent is likely to lightly lead the child toward something new to experience. The therapist presents it to the child and then responds to the child's response to the invitation. Or, if the parent realizes the child might be in need of something that will keep her safe and comfortable—food, warmth, sleep—the parent may more actively lead the child toward this new situation, having determined that it is in her best interest to do something she might not really want to do. Such leads are best done with patience, understanding, and empathy over any distress that comes with the parent's lead to do something the child is showing she does not want to do right then.

With the therapist taking an active stance in co-creating the story, the dialogue often has greater momentum and energy than if the child is responsible to take the lead mostly on her own. With the child's initiatives being given such interest and intersubjective response, she is likely to contribute a great deal more to the momentum than if she were passively following—or actively resisting—the therapist's initiatives. This joint, reciprocal process, with the therapist being open and engaged throughout, facilitated by PACE, tends to create the most suitable setting for generating the affective-reflective dialogue that emerges from the interactions of two synchronized neuropsychological beings. This leads often to a true awakening from mistrust to trust—an awakening where the mistrusting child is safe to discover and explore who she and her parents are, along with the wonderful possibilities of a relationship where they are open and engaged in the joint process of being together.

Windows of Opportunity to Build Trust

Therapists and caregivers need to be prepared to use emergent small windows of opportunity for helping a mistrusting child experience the novelty of safety and the unexpected trustworthiness of these particular adults. One of the ways these windows open is when children with blocked trust get what we call "false alarms" from an adult's nonverbal communication, especially shifts in tone of voice and facial expressions. Here's an example:

> **Don't Fight:** Dylan, age eight, had been badly abused and neglected by his birth parents. After three foster placements, he was adopted by a warm, loving couple who are now in family therapy with a DDP therapist. In this session, Dylan flits about the room, constantly scanning the little space for signs of danger so he can preemptively intervene to keep things safe. Always keeping one eye and one ear on the adult conversation, he suddenly leaves the back of the room where he is playing and comes toward the adults, saying, "Don't fight." The adults are surprised by his reaction because they weren't fighting, but then they realize that as their voices took on a serious tone, this shift in their prosody instantly registered in Dylan's hypersensitized amygdala as a threatening sound signaling impending anger and violence. His brain was doing its utmost to keep him safe by alerting him within milliseconds to potential harm so he could nip it in the bud and keep the adults from hurting each other and him.

Dylan's brain was trained by experts in mayhem—his biological parents, who frequently fought in his presence, teaching him well how to know, before he knew he knew it, that bad things were about to happen. Fortunately, his brain's rapid threat detection system, the neuroceptive process we described earlier, was working pretty much from birth, enabling him to start learning to connect the sounds of angry voices, the movements of eyebrows, and the body movements that preceded painful encounters with adults so he could take preemptive action, becoming the one in the family who devoted all of his developing brain powers to keeping things safe when everyone else was making things dangerous.

But now Dylan was in a home with no violence where the adults take care of children rather than the other way around and he is needing to learn to turn off his threat detection system and relax into this safe new world. But it's hard, so hard, because when he starts to let down the protective wall that served him with his biological parents, his defensive brain instantly takes this as a threat and prompts him to stay vigilant and ignore those "false signs" of safety that tricked him for a moment. How will he ever learn to live in safety?

When Dylan's therapist coaches his caregivers to use PACE and especially be curious about his false alarm reaction to the change in their prosody when they are discussing something serious, Dylan gets a chance to experience their care without being judged for mistrusting them or lectured about why he should know by now that they don't fight in this family like people did in his first family. Their curiosity can help Dylan become aware in the moment that something is very different in this family, something that is worth paying attention to and learning about while feeling safe in this context of nonjudgmental acceptance.

From surprisingly new experiences like this, Dylan can

start to make new meaning about himself and the trustworthiness of caregivers. He can begin to create a new, positive story to replace the old negative, fear-driven narrative. The next chapter looks at the power of storytelling and story voice to promote change in attachment-focused treatment.

CHAPTER 7

Healing Stories: Prosody, Integrative Narratives, and Co-Creation of Meaning

A healthy mind builds proud memories in loving company with specially trusted family and friends, making a good story.
—Trevarthen (2013, p. 206)

Jimmy is a 12-year-old boy who spent the first six years of his life in seven different foster homes. Now he lives with his aunt and uncle and attends a day treatment program at a local mental health facility. At the moment, he has his head on his desk while his teacher is trying to explain the process of long division. Earlier in the day, he had to be restrained when he blew up after he couldn't understand how to read the instructions for his reading assignment.

Now something quite amazing is about to happen because it's story time. One of the sterner members of the staff, a grandmother in her sixties who is known for her creative scoldings when she catches the kids "being bad," moves to front of the room and opens the story book as the kids gather on the floor at her feet. "Once upon a time," she begins in an engaging musical voice that she doesn't use otherwise during the work day (typically speaking in a gruff, flat tone). Suddenly, Jimmy is all ears and eyes: head up, leaning forward, hanging on her words. The magic of storytelling is at work; for the next 15 minutes, Jimmy shows no signs of being a traumatized, angry, disengaged, mistrusting boy. Rather, he looks much like a healthy child who loves to hear his parents read and tell stories. One day the staff noticed the effect that telling stories had with children, and they began to think about ways they might extend that influence into their daily routines. One of the staff members had attended training in DDP, and she suggested that the voice prosody used in telling the story might be as important as the actual content. They decided to see if they could bring a similar way of talking with more rhythms, inflections, pauses, and variations into their regular speech and then see if the children responded differently. They found that they did. Cooperation increased with more open engagement. There were also fewer angry outbursts and restraints.

As the authors came to know each other, we realized that we both like stories—the telling and the hearing. Our stories contained many elements of humor and distress, pride and failure. When we discovered that we were born within two days of each other, we devised many stories of origin including the likelihood that we were blood brothers—stories that involved treachery and loss, bravery and reunion. When we discovered that we both loved baseball and played with varying degrees of skill but a consistently high level of passion, our stories took on a more epic dimension.

Humans love stories. We live our stories and we create them to make sense of how we live. Our minds and hearts are joined in our love for stories. Our brains—with neurological connections to every part of our bodies—find that we understand the events of our lives better by establishing their meanings in stories. When we communicate to our friend what is important to us, we often do so with a story. When we are influenced by a friend in our efforts to decide on a path forward, we often find that friend's greatest gift is in helping us create a story that will enable us to be open to the possibilities ahead while sensing the best path to take. When we want our friends to "just listen," we are asking them to help us in our efforts to create our story. When a friend knows us well, his or her listening mind actually has a part in co-creating our story. When we can see our own life through our eyes and our friend's eyes at the same time, these interwoven (intersubjective) perspectives often create a space where a more coherent and meaningful story may evolve.

Now we intend to look at stories for a while, noting their important components and their impact on us. We will see why they are central in dyadic developmental psychotherapy (DDP) as well as the biobehavioral journey from mistrust to trust.

Co-Creation of Meaning

Neuroimaging studies of what goes on between storyteller and listener shows a process of synchronization between the two people's brain activity (Zak, 2012). That is, the storytelling and listening process brings the two people into matching states of mind where in essence the boundary between teller and listener is blurred and they are deeply engaged, in sync. This is why the use of storytelling for engaging mistrustful children can be so helpful, such a powerful process for helping deactivate the child's self-defense system long enough for a compelling narrative to be completed. In DDP, the stories are always co-constructions, often beginning with the therapist conjecturing about dramatic things that happened long ago, then blending in whatever a child may offer up to tailor the story to the individual child. When the therapist is using "story voice," the child is typically paying rapt attention, as if the drama unfolding is so engaging that the child "forgets" to disengage, temporarily shutting off the self-defense system and connecting with story and the teller.

Describing the narrative process, Siegel wrote,

By the third year of life, a "narrative" function emerges in children and allows them to create stories about the events they encounter during their lives. These narratives are sequential descriptions of people and events that condense numerous experiences into generalizing and contrasting stories. New experiences are compared to old ones. Similarities are noted in creating generalized rules, and differences are highlighted as memorable exceptions to these rules. These stories are about making sense of events and the mental experiences of the characters. Filled with the elements of the characters' internal experience in the context of interactions with others in the world, these stories appear to be functioning to create a sense of coherent comprehension of the individual in the world across time. (Siegel, 2012, p. 364)

Research by Zak (2012) showed that stories trigger release of cortisol and oxytocin. Oxytocin is released when the listener experiences empathy for the characters in the story. This probably helps explain why stories are so compelling and also why, perhaps, people higher in oxytocin are more drawn to stories, understand them better, and are more moved by them. Think about the difficulty that people on the autism spectrum have understanding stories that have to do with people's emotions and interpersonal relationships. They much prefer physicality, physical action. Autism is known to involve atypical oxytocin activity (Bartz and Hollander, 2006).

The power of dramatic stories to engender a compelling combination of stress hormones and oxytocin helps us understand why in DDP the use of stories and story voice is so effective in creating and sustaining mutual engagement with defensive children. The drama of the narrative arc—the brave young child faced with having to play defense to survive poor care, learning to take care of himself, and then finding himself in a safe place, but not knowing how to feel safe—plus the narrator's dramatic tone, is an extremely engaging form of communication. What will happen to the hero? Will he

Figure 7.1 Stories on the brain

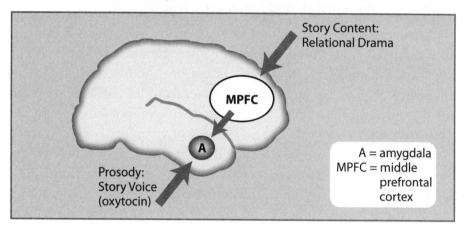

learn to feel safe and live happily, or will he stay forever mistrustful, afraid to connect? Stay tuned. Hooked by the tale and having to hear the ending, the child is engaged and temporarily freed from blocked trust. As in music, the story creates tension that needs to be resolved to feel relieved, satisfied. Stories create a "safe emergency," a safe form of exciting uncertainty rather than the terrible uncertainty of real and imminent danger. Dramatic stories are a form of playing with danger, uncertainty, and possible calamity, while feeling safe enough to know that the scary stuff isn't really happening. (For older readers or younger movie historians, think of watching *Psycho*, especially the shower scene at the Bates Motel, while chomping on your popcorn. This creation of "safe fright" is what makes mystery writers and creators of scary movies rich.)

When the therapist combines story voice with story content, the combination provides co-regulation of the child's affect (safety messaging to the amygdala) with co-creation of new meaning (engagement of the brain region that supports reappraisal and relational thinking). The activation, in turn, provides top-down inhibition of the child's hypersensitive amygdala. See Figure 7.1 for an illustration of these twin processes.

Nonverbal and Verbal Communication

With the exception of pantomime, stories involve words. But what an exception! Pantomime is able to convey complex stories conveying intricate emotions, thoughts, intentions, and actions, without any words. Nonverbal communication tends to be overshadowed by words, but its importance in creating stories cannot be overstated. The storyteller knows this. The content of the story may be interesting and relevant to the listener. But the story comes alive when the teller uses the full range of her voice, facial expressions, gestures, posture, and timing to build suspense, surprise, anticipation, and deeply felt meanings. We express the meaning of a story with our friend more often nonverbally than verbally. Our friend knows the impact that an event has on us when our voice slows, pauses, and then takes on a force of expression that leaves no doubt about how touched we were by what happened. We convey our deep sadness through our quiet, slower movement through the words as we struggle to complete the sentence and the thought. We convey a sense of urgency to understand through rapid movements of gestures and bursts of words that seem to be seeking a meaningful whole. We convey a sense of urgency to be helpful to our friend with focused animation on his tale, showing that there is nothing more important to us than understanding his story right now.

The voice can be a musical instrument that sets a tone and creates an atmosphere with our child or friend that enables the communication to touch us both deeply. In fact, our voice easily creates contagion where we find ourselves in the same affective state, with the same focus of mind and a complimentary intention. Our voice, when it is rhythmic, soothing, and deeply engaging, may foster a sense of trust with the mistrusting child in a manner that words would never be able to attain alone. Knowing how our brains are integrated and function, the importance of these nonverbal communications should not be surprising.

Voice *prosody*, referring to the nonverbal component of the spoken word—the cadence, rhythm, variations of beat, and intensity of the vocal expression—contains much of the personal meaning of the communication. These variations of tone and rhythm have the ability to generate a sense of safety while holding our interest in the momentum of the dialogue. With infants our voice tends to have a musical, sing-song quality that draws their attention and maintains their engagement. We tend to elongate soft vowel sounds, as in "awwwwww," and exaggerate changes in pitch, from high to low and back to high. This unique quality is known as infant-directed speech by some and musicality by others (deHaan and Matheson, 2009). When we speak to infants in this manner, they seem to experience safety with us and quickly understand implicitly that we are intending to communicate something positive. We might say we are exaggerating our nonverbal expressions so they are better able to understand the meaning and intentions of our communication. When we talk with our friends in a relaxed and engaged way, communicating that we accept them and the current interaction, they also experience safety and a deeper level of engagement. In contrast, research shows that infants of depressed mothers whose prosody is flat show depressed-looking electrical patterns in their brains via scalp recordings of these patterns (Mills and Conboy, 2009).

When we understate nonverbal expressions, we tend to be more ambiguous about our intention and the person we are speaking with, especially if that person tends to be mistrustful or might become anxious in response to this uncertainty. Many therapies have stressed adopting this ambiguous stance to minimize the communication of our experience of the client, with the goal of encouraging the independent development of his experience. The assumption was that the client would assume our experience was similar to that of key people in their lives and they would respond as they did with these important people. In psychodynamic therapies this process is known as transference. The therapist would then have a better sense of how the client related in those other relationships and might share the perceived meaning of these interactions with the client.

With DDP the therapist is quite expressive in his therapeutic communications and responses to the child's communications by relying fully on voice prosody to convey the therapist's experience of what is being communicated. The words themselves may carry much of the content of the dialogue, and the nonverbal expressions—central to which are the variations, rhythms, and inflections of the voice, or the voice's musicality—carry how the therapist communicates his experience of the content being explored. Now experienced by the child intersubjectively, this enables the child to experience herself through the therapist's eyes. The child is not likely to simply repeat what the therapist says or believe something to be true if that was the therapist's experience, because central in the therapist's communications is the priority that he gives to the *child's* view of what is true for him. The therapist is clear that he accepts and even encourages the child to express a different view when that is the case. When the therapist is conveying—nonverbally—his sense that the child is brave, persistent, caring, honest, lovable, clever, creative, and hopeful, along with other qualities, the mistrusting child is likely to begin to reexperience his sense of self that had been organized around fear and shame and expressed in anger and despair. He is open to this new way of experiencing himself and creating his story.

Storytelling often enables children to revisit scary experiences from a safe-enough distance, embedded within social buffering, while helping them make new meaning of their past. In brain terms, the therapist's compassionate voice during the storytelling process helps disarm the child's defense system, enabling him or her to identify with and empathize with the "hero" of the story, him- or herself. This can promote a reawakening of the blocked potential for experiencing the pain of separation and the need for comfort, a reviving of the attachment system as part of the child's journey from mistrust to trust.

Flowing and Deepening

Now that we've explored how much of the intersubjective meaning and energy of the dialogue emerges from voice prosody and other nonverbal expressions, it is time to notice the process of the therapeutic communication itself. The spoken communication can be measured as sine waves—the smooth, repetitive oscillations in the spoken word—that resonate between the therapist and child. The sine wave has a horizontal dimension to it, measured as the frequency (number of oscillations per second), and a vertical dimension, measured in amplitude (peak deviation from zero). We look at the horizontal dimension, or the flow of the dialogue, and the vertical dimension, or the deepening and lightening qualities of the dialogue.

The dialogue's horizontal flow can be seen as having a certain momentum to it that enables it to go forward with a sense of ease and forward movement irrespective of the content. This momentum often enables the child to continue to be engaged in the dialogue regardless of how stressful the content may be. The therapist, as she moves from the lighter to the more challenging content, continues to convey an open and engaged attitude. This attitude conveys confidence that the content is not too difficult for the child to attend to. It also conveys a certitude that the dialogue itself will be therapeutic—it will enable the child to participate in the process of integrating the events being explored into his narrative in a way that will reduce any shame and fear associated with the events and enable the narrative to become more coherent.

Sometimes therapists tend to become anxious about the anticipated distress for the child over the experience of exploring a stressful or traumatic theme. This might create an intersubjective experience in which the therapist's anticipated anxiety is experienced by the child, which creates the very distress the therapist wanted to avoid. If the therapist is able to remain confident that the emotion associated with the event will be regulated and the meaning will be sufficiently reflected on as a part of a coherent narrative, then—again, intersubjectively—the child is more likely to have confidence that engaging in the dialogue will be positive. If the child shows anxiety greater than the therapist might expect from the discussion, the therapist simply co-regulates the anxiety, follows the child's lead to lighter content, or initiates the lead himself.

The vertical dimension of the dialogue refers to moving the focus to the deeper emotional meanings within a given event. The horizontal movement (the frequency of the sine wave) is now slower, while the energy goes more into the depth (the amplitude) of the dialogue. This is often done by the therapist emphasizing greater curiosity about the event being explored or greater empathy for its impact on the child.

While being curious about the event, the focus is more on the various aspects of the experience of the event rather than more details about the event itself. The therapist may wonder, for example, about any or some of the following:

- How do you make sense of your mother saying that?
- Does that bring up any other memories?
- When you think of that now, what emotions are you feeling?
- When you felt that sad in the past, how did you usually handle that feeling?
- Were there ever times that you wondered if somehow this was all your fault?

Through such questions, the therapist temporarily pauses the forward movement of the dialogue and goes more deeply into the meanings—making them more complex—of this specific event. It is not simply the words in the questions that deepen the dialogue, but how the questions are asked. The therapist actively evokes the child's sense of suspense and wonder about where the story might be leading through animation, pauses, wide eyes, or patting her hands on her legs while exclaiming, "Wait! Wait! Wait! . . . do you think, maybe, when your mom didn't come to your game because she was shopping with your brother that you thought that she did that because she *loved* your brother more than you! . . . and that might be why you broke his video game?" Or with a softer voice and gentler expression, "I wonder if . . . sometimes after your dad swore at you . . . and then didn't come home for a few days . . . that maybe you thought that it was because your dad just thought you were a bad kid . . . that he just didn't want to be your dad anymore?" The emotional tone of voice and facial expressions direct the child's attention to his possible experiences of the events, rather than the events themselves. The questions are put forward tentatively, with much opportunity for the child to express a differing experience. In fact, the therapist's active wondering about these possible experiences often causes children to become aware of what they did experience at the time. Frequently, with a level of absorption in the story equal to that of the therapist, the child responds, "No, I thought . . ." making it clear that he was not simply agreeing with the therapist's guess about his experience but had discovered within his own mind what his experience had been.

The questions are also expressed with gradually increasing intensity of meaning. For example, the question, "Did you think that maybe your mom didn't love you?" is likely to be the last in a chain of questions, not the first. It might be preceded with, "Do you think maybe your mom didn't know how much you wanted that?" Followed by: "Do you think maybe that your mom didn't care how much you wanted that?" Followed by: "If she didn't care how much you wanted that, what do you think that meant?" Followed by: "Do you think it might have meant that she just didn't care about you right then?" At any stage of this sequence, the child's response might move the line of questions into an entirely different direction.

Similarly, when the therapist expresses greater empathy for an event, the exploration tends to move toward more meaningful and integrated experiences of it. The therapist may highlight his expression of empathy by slowing the cadence of his voice and placing greater emphasis on empathic words or phrases that enable the child to deeply know that the therapist gets it. The therapist's empathy also helps the child stay with any stronger emotional states that are emerging along with the deepening experiences. The therapist in this way is co-regulating emerging emotional states, which frequently involve shame and fear (with empathy), and co-creating new meanings of traumatic events (with curiosity).

Moving It Along: Talking For and Talking About

Individuals who are securely attached have the skill of simultaneously reflecting on attachment-related experiences, organizing them into a coherent narrative, and communicating this narrative to another person. This complex mental task is likely to be much too difficult for a child who mistrusts his parents and has not experienced the safety needed to make sense of frightening and shameful events. This child has neither the emotional vocabulary nor the emotional regulation skills to identify and reflect on the traumatic events of her life. Lacking this access to her inner life, she is not able to make sense of and communicate how she has come to experience these events. Thus, it is not only very hard for her to recall being abused by her father without experiencing dysregulating emotion that prevents any dialogue about it; she is also unable to make sense of how that abuse has affected her by making it hard for her to trust her adoptive father. For these reasons, the mistrustful child needs the active assistance of the therapist in learning to make sense of and communicate her inner life. Therapists tend to focus on the child's extreme difficulty with the joint process of reflection and communication about her inner life regarding stressful or traumatic themes. However, we should not forget that the mistrustful child is likely to have difficulty engaging in this process around routine events, too. These children have difficulty simply having a conversation with an adult about ordinary topics. Often, when they begin to enjoy and actively engage in routine conversations, they start to show increased ability to manage difficult situations. Helping the child develop this skill around these lighter events will make it easier for her to regulate, reflect, and communicate about the more difficult events of his life.

By helping a mistrustful child understand his explosive behavior, the therapist actively guides him through a nonjudgmental exploratory attitude of what he was experiencing at the time of his aggression, regulating associated shame and making sense of the reasons behind the behavior. For example, after evoking the child's curiosity about the strength of his anger at his adoptive father for scolding him, the therapist was able to help the child recall how he thought that his adoptive father was disappointed in him. The therapist's engaged, animated curiosity even helped the child reexperience his fear that his father did not want him anymore. When the therapist asked him to tell his father that, the child's fear about what his father would say made it hard for him to express himself. The therapist asked for permission to talk for him, and when the child agreed, he told the child to correct him if he got it wrong. The therapist turned to the father, and using the child's voice, with an emotional tone in his voice consistent with the words, said, "Dad, I did get mad at you! Really mad! I thought that when you were angry with me because I left your tools outside . . . I thought that you were disappointed in me! I even thought . . . I thought that maybe you even didn't want to be my dad anymore! That's why I said I hated you! I thought that you were going to throw me away!"

When the therapist talks for the child, she does so after developing with the child his experience of the sequence of events that led to the behavior being explored. She tentatively guesses how these experiences are organized in a way that led to the behavior. If the child agrees, she suggests that the child tell the parent what he thinks/feels; if the child is too anxious to do so, the therapist speaks for the child. Such sequences often lead to the child being vulnerable with the parent, sharing an aspect of his inner life that he had not been aware of before the dialogue began, which now calls for a response from the parent, even though the child might be terrified about the anticipated response.

The child's emotional state tends to mirror the vulnerable emotions expressed by the therapist when he speaks for the child. Thus, when the therapist expresses the child's anger toward the parent, he does so only when he is also able to express some of the fear, sadness, and/or shame that lie under the anger, which the child had previously acknowledged. Of course the therapist will not evoke the child's willingness to be open and engaged in such a vulnerable state unless he is certain the parent will also be open and engaged with the child and respond with empathy. Such empathy would then be followed with curiosity, and possibly information, support, and ideas to deepen the parent–child relationship in a way to handle such events together more successfully in the future.

Talking for a child in this manner tends to deepen the affective experience of the memory of the event and the immediate relationship between the child and parent. There is also value in helping the child reflect on the developing memory of the event being explored as well as the current parent–child experience. Talking about the child with the parent often facilitates this reflective experience.

When the therapist talks about the child to the parent—in front of the child—the child is likely to listen in an open and engaged manner. He does not have to prepare a response, he does not even have to listen. But he does. The therapist's relaxed, rhythmic voice about the child's emerging memory as well as his experience at that moment may deepen the child's intersubjective experience of the therapist's perspective, and so he absorbs the therapist's attitude of PACE and his experience. When the child is so open and engaged to the therapist's communication, he often remembers what is being said word for word and allows it to enter his narrative and influence its movement toward integration.

> Eight-year-old Michael was adopted by Abe and Ken when he was six. He was a quiet boy, seemingly tense and wanting to please his dads. This was understandable. He had lived with domestic violence and physical abuse the first five years of his life and then moved to three foster homes. "Being good" was an important survival strategy for Michael if he was not going to be hurt again. Yet at times he would scream at his parents and sometimes hit Ken. When this happened, he often remained angry for nearly an hour and then withdrew in silence for even longer, before engaging them again as if nothing had happened. The therapist was able to gently

recall a recent event in which Michael was enraged at Ken. He was able to evoke his curiosity about the strength of his anger, which had occurred after his dad had mildly scolded him for not putting away some toys before dinner.

Therapist: Oh, Michael how angry you were then! I wonder why? I wonder why you were that angry when your dad said that you should have put away your toys. I wonder why? (*building suspense of the story*)

Michael: (*with tears and much intensity*) He didn't like me!

Therapist: Oh, Michael, I'm beginning to understand now why you were that angry. You thought that your dad didn't like you! How hard that must have been for you. You might have even worried that your dad might not like you for a long time!

Michael: He might give me away!

Therapist: Oh, Michael, you even worried that your dad might give you away! That would be *so hard* to worry about that! *So* hard. (*waiting a bit while Michael sat quietly*) Did you tell your dad that, Michael? Did you tell him that you thought that he didn't like you and might give you away? (*Michael shakes his head no*) Could I tell him for you, Michael? (*He nods*) Dad! (*adopting a child's voice and the affect appropriate for the emotion expressed*) I got so mad at you, Dad! *So mad!* Just because I didn't put the stupid toys away. You got mad at me. And I thought . . . I thought that you didn't like me. I thought that you really didn't like me . . . and then Dad . . . then I thought you might not want me anymore and you might give me away. That's why I said that I hated you, Dad. That's why.

Ken: Oh, Michael! I didn't know that you thought that I didn't like you and might give you away! Thanks for telling me that, son. That would be so hard if you thought that I would give you away! Now I understand why your anger was so

187

big. Thanks for having the courage to tell me that. I will never give you away, even if I'm angry at something you do. And I will always love you, even if I don't like something that you do.

After talking for the child to the father and evoking the empathic response from him, the therapist waited while Michael and Ken hugged and talked quietly and eventually giggled a bit. The therapist decided to talk about what just happened to Ken to assist Michael in reflecting about the experience that happened at home as well as what just occurred in the session. Talking about the child to the parent often facilitates the child's reflective functioning about a particular theme and enables the child to integrate it better. As in every aspect of the A-R dialogue, the therapist's voice has a rhythmic quality that enables the child to remain openly engaged as he safely listens to the therapist's communication of his experience.

Therapist: (*to Ken*) I think your son is very brave. He was able to let me tell you how his anger at you was so big because he was afraid you were disappointed in him and that you might not want him to be your son anymore! He might have worried that you would say he was right and you did regret that he was your son, and he still let me talk for him! Then you told him that you understood so much better why he became angry with you and you were sad that he was not sure how glad that you are that he is your son. Then when you showed him how special he is to you, he got quiet and calm, and seemed so happy inside to know that you want to be his dad. And then I saw you both! How you both seemed so happy. I felt lucky knowing you two—father and son. And Ken, while you are helping your son learn to trust you, you have to be patient. This might take some time because his birth dad used to really hurt Michael. It might be a while before your son knows that you are different. You will not hurt him like that and you will never throw him away. Will you be patient, Ken, and give your son time to trust you?"

DDP attempts to make the therapeutic dialogue (A-R dialogue) as natural as possible, similar to how we might be communicating with a good friend over lunch. The ebb and flow of the dialogue creates an open and engaged experience that enables any emerging emotion to be co-regulated and the meaning of events being explored to be co-created. The focus is on the events of the child's life, past and present, easy and difficult, with associated emotions and possible meanings. At the end of the day, it is simply human communication, occurring in an atmosphere created for trust, that invites the mistrustful child to learn to live safely in his family. DDP simply uses the structures and functions of the remarkable human brain to regain the capacity for trust that it had at birth.

Dirt Girl: Amy is in her third session of attachment-focused therapy with her adoptive mother, Lucy. After her usual still-face beginning, Amy grins when the therapist teases her about her oversize handbag. As Amy starts to engage, Lucy says, "Tell him about what you were telling me about your birth mother."

"All of it?" Amy asks.

"Sure, all of it," Lucy says.

"Well, I was two," Amy begins, "and I was reaching for my mother, crying, and she was being mean. She wouldn't hold me, so the meaner she got, the more I tried to get her to be nice, but she never was. And then she gave me away."

"Wow," the therapist says, "that sounds so hard, Amy. You were reaching and reaching and you couldn't get your mother to show any love. Why do you think she was so mean to you?"

"Because I'm dirt," Amy said, very quietly, so quietly that the therapist had to ask Lucy what Amy said, so she repeated, louder, "I'm dirt."

"Dirt!?" the therapist almost gasped.

"Yes, she gave me away because I'm dirt and she couldn't love dirt."

"Amy, we have to think hard about this, really hard. This is a huge mystery and you are so smart and you used your kid brain to find an answer to why your mother was so mean to you. Let's see if we have any clues to try to see if maybe, just maybe, you aren't dirt."

Then, Lucy says that Amy was born with hepatitis. "Wow, Amy," the therapist says, "This could be a big clue. Let me think, how could a little baby before she's born get hepatitis? Oh, that could happen if your mother was using drugs, the kind you take with a needle, like heroin. Amy, do you know what happens when a mother uses heroin?"

"No," Amy says, big-eyed now and paying close attention.

"The heroin blocks the mommy's love. It makes her love the heroin more than she can love her beautiful baby."

Amy gets up, walks toward the therapist, and looks into his eyes.

The therapist asks Amy, "Is it all right if I touch your face?"

"Yes," Amy says, still looking into the therapist's eyes.

The therapist rubs two fingers down Amy's cheek, then looks wide-eyed at these fingers. "Nope, Amy, no dirt. No dirt came off. Maybe I need to rub harder." The therapist rubs both cheeks and then Amy's arms and then checks again. "None. This is weird. You've been so sure that you were dirt, but no dirt is coming from you."

Amy looks confused, but maybe a little relieved. She goes to her mother and hugs her tightly. The therapist sits quietly as Amy seems to be experiencing herself absorbing her mom's love, without any dirt getting in the way. Then the therapist gets out a piece of paper and says to Amy, "You know how you asked for my autograph the first time 'cause I 'wrote the book'? Well now I want your autograph because you're writing your story and it's a great one."

So Amy smiles, and Lucy smiles, and Amy signs her name. As they are leaving, Amy, who is very short, looks up into the therapist's face and says, "You are a very friendly man."

CHAPTER 8

Playing in Safety: Strengthening Attachment Bonds with Delight and Co-Regulation of Affect

Rough and tumble physical play and/or chase-and-dodge teasing play are intrinsic, experientially refined faculties of every mammalian species, which help promote social affiliations and epigenetic development of fully social brains.
　　　　　　　—Panksepp and Trevarthen (2009, p. 112)

A t a pub in Edinburgh, Scotland, Colwyn Trevarthen—who has done pioneering studies of infant development for decades— asked one of us (Dan) if it was accurate that therapists tend to focus on unhappiness when they are assisting their clients. When told that generally it might be fair to say that therapists do attend the most to various themes of unhappiness, Trevarthen wondered: if a client tended to be experiencing unhappiness in much of his daily life, why would a therapist not try to make him aware of some experiences of pleasure and joy? In the presence of Trevarthen's sharp mind and a pint of stout, Dan had to agree.

This book is about helping mistrusting children begin to trust again through experiencing comfort and joy, among other relationship experiences. There is no evidence that comfort must precede joy or joy precede comfort. For the infant, these experiences tend to be present in a given day, even in a given hour. They are likely to be cyclical, with the experience of one often enabling the child to be more open to the experience of the other. They represent different ways of being close to another person, types of closeness that in their own way develop a sense of trust in the relationship with the other. When we are in distress and experience comfort from another, the distress tends to decrease and the trust in the other's helpful presence increases. When experiencing joy that is shared with another, joy increases, which also makes trust in the other increase. An individual who is able to increase the experience of happiness and decrease the experience of unhappiness is truly likely to be trusted.

> Breanne was a high-energy, seven-year-old girl who had not much reason to be happy. Years of maltreatment were followed by three foster placements in 14 months. She complained a great deal about everything. Her foster mother, Ruth, had little confidence she could do anything that would evoke a smile and contentment from Breanne. Therapy was even worse. Her therapist wondered about things that she might want to talk about, even things like why she liked yellow shoes and what she had for breakfast two hours earlier. Once, when her therapist made an innocent comment about a toy that Breanne had brought with her, she said with annoyance:
>
> **Breanne:** Don't talk about it, it's mine! Stupid!
> **Therapist:** (*With a bit of laughter, a higher pitch to his voice, a shocked facial expression, along with a playful smile*) Girl! You can't treat me that way! There are rules of therapy and one of the rules is that you can't give your therapist such a hard time!
> **Breanne:** (*not missing a beat*) You are not my therapist! You're my thera*pest*!

Her therapist roared with laughter as he leaned back in his chair. Ruth laughed as well! Breanne looked puzzled for a moment and then she laughed, too. Ruth gave Breanne a hug, and her therapist reached over and squeezed her hand.

Therapist: Thanks, Breanne, that was one of the funniest things anyone has ever said to me!
Breanne: (*replying immediately with laughter*) Pest! Pest! Pest!

This was the first of many such moments when Breanne learned that it was safe enough to laugh. It took a while longer before she felt safe enough to cry. As time went on, she even learned why she had been too full of shame and fear to laugh or cry.

Play on the Brain

Brain research shows that play triggers the release of opioids and dopamine, chemicals that combine to make play pleasurable and memorable. The opioid response makes the play feel good, and the dopamine response helps the players learn what makes the play fun, what causes the play to break down, and how to use this learning in future playful encounters. Meanwhile, mutually enjoyable play keeps the players' defense systems off, providing relational practice with being open and engaged. Not surprisingly, research shows that when a parent and a child are engaged in the most exciting, playful kinds of interactions, they show peaks in their oxytocin levels. When play triggers laughter, the opioid system is strongly activated. In short, play appears to engage a cocktail of brain chemistry that helps make it a powerful social process.

Furthermore, play in animals is known to promote brain development, especially development of the prefrontal cortex. Panksepp (1998) in his studies of play in rats, showed clearly that young rats deprived of play show underdevelopment of their prefrontal regions and deficits in executive functioning, including social skills and impulse control. Importantly, as he and others emphasized, the kind of play that seems to be such a brain builder is "free range" play, not highly structured kinds of play. Apparently, the spontaneity, creativity, and attention to the unfolding of playful sequences of interaction make free play uniquely effective at promoting brain development. You only have to spend a little time near a playground to hear the continuous sound of joyful shrieking emanating from young children exuberantly engaged in free-ranging play.

Panksepp (2013) recently took this research to the level of exploring epigenetic effects of play. This line of research reveals that free play promotes certain patterns of gene expression that are probably the underlying molecular process leading to structural differences in the brains of young people with access to lots of free-range play versus those deprived of play. It is probably not unrealistic to think that playfulness in attachment-focused therapy promotes epigenetic changes in a child's brain that help undo at least some of the effects of early life adversity.

Play and Trust

Most important for attachment-focused therapy, reciprocal play promotes a great deal of social learning that is essential for learning how and when to trust others. In primates, including humans, play is based heavily on reading nonverbal cues—facial expressions, prosody, touch, and gestures. Through reciprocal free play, participants learn to read each other's intentions and know the signs that indicate "This is play, so let's keep it going. This is not real fighting. No harm intended. Trust me."

Fear suppresses playfulness. Lack of a reciprocating safe play partner leads to underdevelopment of social skills, problems with mentalization and mindsight, which are "intention reading" skills. Trust is built on the ability to read the intentions of other people accurately. Children with blocked trust are poor at this, because their chronic defensiveness biases them toward overdetecting bad intent in others and underdetecting positive intentions.

Play and playfulness, then, are essential components of treatment for children with blocked trust. In this sense, the playful aspects of treatment are serious business, serious in the sense that these playful encounters are an essential element of the change process in therapy, having a key role in lifting the block from blocked trust and helping the child learn how to trust and how to stay in connection.

Through play sessions with therapists and parents, the child gains practice at participating in reciprocal social engagement while learning the subtleties of nonverbal communication that need to be mastered to stay engaged and not shift into defensiveness when there is no real threat. Children with blocked trust have to have playful encounters with adults to desensitize them to facial expressions, tones of voice, touch, and body language that are actually safe, not the signs of danger they had to become so vigilant about. In neurobiological terms, free play probably helps the child with blocked trust improve vagal tone, strengthening that smart vagal circuit that is the foundation for social engagement, that neural system supporting the ability to stay open enough during intense interactions to avoid the brain shift into self-defense. When combined with practice at seeking and receiving comfort when distressed, playfulness can help the mistrustful child develop a stronger neural capacity for social engagement.

Teasing is a form of verbal play in which the play partners take the "game" to the edge of hurtfulness without actually being hurtful. This is a process that can strengthen one's ability to trust a teasing partner without experiencing true social pain, that feeling of rejection that is such a powerful component in the development of blocked trust. Teasing is a natural process in children and in parent–child dyads in which the partners practice keeping the teasing within the bounds of playfulness. During teasing episodes, the mistrusting child has to suppress the habitual tendency to overread bad intent, pay much more attention to what is actually being communicated, and practice distinguishing between real signs of bad intent in a partner and signs of positive, playful intent that actually signals "I like you and like engaging with you and having fun."

Play and Safety Messages:
Helping the Child Recover from Safety Blindness

In a very important sense, you can see how teasing and other forms of free play with a parent helps the mistrustful child recover from the safety blindness we described earlier by enabling the child to see, hear, and feel the strong, unambiguous safety messages that a parent sends so strongly during bouts of mutually enjoyable play. These safety messages in the form of laughter, smiling, shining eyes, warm touch, and funny kinds of movements are big and bold during playful encounters, making these messages easier to detect, very similar to the way parents of infants make their facial expressions, gestures, and tones of voice bigger and more exaggerated so that the baby experiences interaction as safe and delightful. A playful tone of voice is one of the most powerful ways to send safety messages into the limbic system of a defensive child, as long as the child is not in a state of deep anger, fear, or sadness.

The adult has to titrate the playfulness, gauging from moment to moment how the child is reading intentions and making instantaneous adjustments when the child starts to shift into real defensiveness due to misreading the intent behind the playfulness. Adults who cannot read the child's feedback accurately in real time will inevitably trigger the child's sensitized defense system and inadvertently reinforce blocked trust.

Play has had a long history in therapy with children through its ability to help a child express his or her inner life though metaphor. Symbolic play introduces an "as if" quality to the interaction, where the child can begin to make sense of traumatic experiences in a safer manner. The symbolic play is one step removed from the child's direct experience of the trauma, and the play is amenable to the child gradually attaining mastery of the event by using imagination to modify the story.

Symbolic play definitely has value in helping children safely begin the process of reexperiencing trauma, though regretfully some children have limited readiness to use symbols in that manner. Their inner lives tend to be too rigid and lacking in meaning-making skills, so they are at risk of simply reenacting the trauma in a repetitive, compulsive manner.

No matter whether symbolic play is of value for a child in therapy, the play and playfulness we describe here are different. It is the interactive, intersubjective stance of the therapist that conveys reciprocal joy and delight. It is of value in building sufficient trust for a child to become more fully engaged in treatment. This play is similar to how we play with toddlers and is characteristic of a model of therapy for children known as Theraplay. This is the presymbolic play of toddlers, or the immediate, reciprocal sharing of laughter and delightful experiences that all of us enjoy engaging in with a trusted friend.

Engendering the Experience of Being Delightful to a Parent

This form of expressive play with a child enables him to discover special qualities of self that he is likely to only experience when he is with an adult who experiences and communicates delight in him while the therapist discovers and responds to his spontaneous expressions of openness, joy, and fascination with here-and-now activities. How can he not feel safe when this adult communicates a degree of acceptance and interest that causes him to feel cherished?

In addition to this sense that he is unique and special to the therapist, there is value in having play and joy be integrated into the therapeutic experience.

- Laughter and play generate positive emotional experiences, which children need to learn to regulate as much as negative emotional experiences.
- Sharing laughter and joy is often a safer way to begin to feel close to someone than is the experience of affection.
- Easier themes, often associated with positive emotions, may be

safer to begin exploring at the early stage of the development of the relationship than are more stressful themes.

- A joint, playful attitude tends to carry hope and confidence that we can get through these hard times together.
- Playfulness is likely to be expressed in a spontaneous manner that increases the sense of safety in the here-and-now experience. That sense of safety in the present makes it easier for the child to maintain attention when focusing on stressful themes.
- Playfulness tends to evoke a sense of acceptance and gentle pride in the self, qualities that are crucial when shame-related memories and experiences are addressed.
- Playfulness in therapy helps the child experience the therapist as a person who enjoys him and is genuinely interested in him, rather than someone who is simply trying to fix him.
- Playfulness gives the child a break from the stress of addressing difficult memories and experiences. It enables the therapist to maintain the natural ebb and flow that characterizes most good conversations.
- Playfulness affirms the strengths and successes of the child's life, qualities the child may seldom experience when he has a traumatic history and his present relationships hold many problems.
- Shared joy contributes to a sense that life is worthwhile. It generates a sense of resilience needed for trusting that life will take a turn for the better.
- Playfulness generates a sense of openness to experience, anticipating with pleasure what might happen next. The child feels safe enough in the moment to be surprised with what is to come. This makes it less likely that the child will become defensive in response to themes of shame, anger, sadness, or fear that are being explored.

The purpose of bringing play and playfulness into the therapy office is not to distract from, minimize, or avoid the traumatic aspects of the child's life that led to mistrusting adults, but to expand the therapeutic gaze toward all aspects of the child. This gaze fosters the child's self-gaze so that he may discover qualities of himself that are delightful, enjoyable, and worthy of trust. Often the mistrusting child's sense of shame prevents him from trusting adults because his prior trauma has caused him to believe he does not deserve good care. Why should he trust adults if he is not worthy of trust? If the gaze of the therapist is only on his challenging behaviors or traumas, he is likely to think the therapist is only doing his job. The therapist is being paid to convince him that he is worthwhile and that he can trust others. He is not likely to trust motives or honesty if the therapist does not show that he enjoys being with him, if they do not share moments of joy, laughter, and mutual delight.

When the therapist has had moments of joint playfulness with the child she is treating, she may rely on these moments to generate the momentum needed in the dialogue for the child to move into and through exploration of distress or trauma. With experiences of shared laughter, the child is more likely to trust the motives of the therapist in moving his attention into moments of fear, shame, or sadness. Yes, playfulness can lead to the child increasing his trust of all of the therapist's motives. A similar process occurs when the infant is securely attached to his parent. When she disciplines the infant—now a toddler—her child trusts that while he does not like the parent's intention to limit his behavior, he trusts her motives. She is not doing it to make him unhappy or hurt him. He senses that she says "no" because it is something that would not be good for him or others if he does it or because she wants him to develop a habit that will be best for him in the long run.

> **The Mistrustful Point Guard:** Marcy is a 16-year-old girl adopted at age 2 from an orphanage. She spent the first week with her new parents crying at a high pitch and resisting all attempts to comfort her; she hasn't cried in the presence of her adoptive parents since then. She is a "tough cookie," the point guard on her high school basketball team. When she

first meets the therapist, she gives him a cold stare and a minimal "hi."

Pretty soon, when the therapist expresses a keen interest in her basketball skills, she starts to soften a bit, as her stressed-out mom looks on, wanting her to be appropriately friendly and responsive, to be "nice" and "respectful." "Can you shoot?," the therapist asks. Marcy rolls her eyes and the therapist starts to fear an angry shutdown, but instead, she says, "Can I shoot? Does 50 percent from three-point land mean anything to you?"

"No way!" the therapist says. "You mean you make half your shots from long range? That's amazing! Mom," the therapist says, "is she putting me on?"

"Nope," says Mom, "she's really good."

"Do you like watching her play?" the therapist asks.

Mom says, smiling. "I love it".

"You sound proud of her," the therapist ventures.

"Yep, very proud," says Mom, her face softening a bit as she speaks.

"You know anything about basketball, being old and all?" Marcy says to the therapist.

"Hey, you're talkin' to a former high school point guard at this very moment".

"No way," says Marcy with a little smirk. "I didn't know basketball was invented then." She leans in close, making the therapist wonder for a second if she's going to sock him, and pulls out her cell phone and starts showing pictures of her team. "We could be pretty good this year."

In this scenario, the therapist had one goal only: find a way to start liking Marcy as soon as possible. The use of playful banter, a little teasing, gets this "likability discovery" process under way and fortunately bears fruit. For a little while, Marcy's social switch gets shifted from self-defense to open engagement, and as this happens with her, it also happens with her mother. Maybe therapy could be helpful to this relationship that went south several years ago, sinking into a mutual defense society of blocked trust and blocked care.

Summary

Play is not a therapeutic technique to build a relationship with a child so that she will be more receptive to the real purpose of therapy, which is to focus on problems. Play is an integral part of dyadic developmental psychotherapy. It facilitates the child's ability to become engaged in a reciprocal conversation, begin to explore all aspects of self, move easily into a synchronized rhythm with the therapist (which is often maintained around stressful themes), and experience herself as being liked for who she is, not for "being good" or "cooperating." The spontaneity and joy of play are often key aspects of the child's journey toward trust.

CHAPTER 9

Treating Blocked Care:
Guidelines for Working with Parents

If children in the midst of adversity find positive role models who teach them that the world has others that they can depend on and trust, they are more likely to use reappraisals to change how they think about stressful situations.

—Chen and Miller (2012, p. 136)

Dialogues with Parents Alone

In the best of times—with the picket fence, plenty of money, a great relationship between parents—parenting is hard. In the worst of times, parenting is very hard. Parenting is a very important part of how we define who we are and what is central in our lives. When we struggle and begin to worry that we might fail at being a parent, it is very hard to face this and try to make it better. When we try to raise a child who does not trust us, the challenges to parenting well may be extreme (see Alper and Howe, 2015).

Readers might notice that we are careful not to understate the difficulties of parenting well. We are doing so because it is crucial that we professionals understand what parents who enter our offices are facing and how difficult it is for them to make an appointment to speak with us about their challenges. Seeking treatment for oneself is hard, but seeking treatment for a child—for a family that is struggling—is especially difficult. Parents often feel shame in acknowledging that they are failing and are seeking help. Knowing they might be judged to have contributed to their child's problems makes it harder still. It takes great courage and commitment to a child to face the challenges of seeking professional help.

Since many professionals who offer to assist parents are parents ourselves, it is probably wise to acknowledge to ourselves our own challenges, past and present, in being a parent in a way that makes us proud. This humble self-awareness will help us experience and communicate empathy for the parents who seek our help. They are in our office to speak with us about their family struggles. They might be defensive. They might have a punitive attitude toward their child and place responsibility for the problems on their child or the other parent. They might challenge our qualifications, knowledge, ideas, or recommendations. We must remember that under their defensiveness, they are vulnerable. If they feel safe with us, they may begin to express their vulnerability—their desperation to be successful as parents. They will only begin to feel safe with us if they experience our empathy for them and their family.

The Parenting History

Who actually were these parents before they began to care for a child who does not trust them, and possibly never did? It is important for the therapist to explore the original hopes and dreams of the parents to have a better sense of how parenting began for them. Often adults become parents with a dream of a strong and nurturing family that will bring deep meaning to parents and children. They hope for happiness and success for their children and for years of shared joy and satisfaction with meaningful, interwoven lives. When these dreams become uncertain and the hopes do not appear to be realistic, parents may enter a stage of intense doubts, eventually leading to despair and grief that the dreams will never come true. This puts them at risk for ongoing states of shame—shame over their inability to experience the satisfactions of bringing joy or comfort to their child, over not helping their child manage their challenges, over not being loved in return, when they provide their child with seemingly endless love. Finally, they experience blocked care. Then the shame becomes embedded in daily life.

When the failings that emerge while parenting a mistrustful child meet a parent's sense of failing when they were children in relationship with their own parents, there is a risk for a perfect storm of blocked trust and blocked care. When a child yells at us for perceived harshness or unfairness, it is easy to experience this criticism as being similar to what we may have felt if we were harshly criticized by our own parents. If anger was not managed well in our family when we were children, then anger is likely to be difficult to manage when it is repeatedly expressed at us by our child. If our parents gave us the silent treatment when they were annoyed with us, then our child ignoring us is likely to be very stressful. If conflicts and other breaks to our relationships were not routinely repaired by our parents, it is likely to be challenging when our child needs us to initiate repair in response to relationship difficulties. Thus, parents may face significant challenges in parenting a mistrustful child because of both a failure to attain their parenting hopes and dreams and the activation of their unresolved attachment distress.

A Matter of Trust

If the parents who seek our help are to be successful in helping their children learn to trust them, they need to be able to trust us. If they are to continue to care for their children when their children do not want their care, these parents need to experience our care for them. If they are safe with us during a session, their children will be more likely to experience safety with their parents and with us. Thus, our first goal in the initial session is to help parents trust us, accept our care, and be safe with us. To do so, they need to know that we see their strengths, including their willingness to become vulnerable in acknowledging their difficulties to a professional—a professional who is also a stranger and might be judging them as being responsible for their child's problems. They need to know that we know they are good people who do the best they can and are deeply committed to their children. Only after they have confidence that we perceive them in that way will they be able to become open and engaged with us and reduce any shame they felt in seeking help. If they engage us without shame, they are likely to truly want our help and be open to our influence in exploring new ways of being engaged with their children.

PACE (playfulness, acceptance, curiosity, empathy) is the core therapeutic attitude that dyadic developmental psychotherapy (DDP) therapists hold for parents, just as we hold that attitude for their children. At times playfulness generates laughter, an experience that can keep us going when times otherwise seem bleak. Playfulness carries a lightness and sense of hope that we can move through this challenging time and eventually attain our goals. We need to continuously express acceptance for the parents' intentions, wishes, and goals for their child and their family, even when we are not able to accept some of their behaviors. Many times we have said to a parent that we seem to have the same intentions and goals for their child though we might disagree over the best way to achieve those goals. Parents are then more likely to be open and engaged as we discuss our differences.

Our curiosity for parents is conveyed in many ways, and it facilitates the parents' ability to hold the same curiosity toward themselves and their children. Example questions are many:

- How do you find the strength to keep going?
- Where do you find the support and comfort that matters?
- What other possibilities might explain why he does that?
- How else might you respond to that?
- When you get in a situation like that, does that remind you of anything similar when you were growing up?
- Does it seem like I'm blaming you when I ask you that?
- How can we disagree about how you handle that behavior, while you still know how much I respect your parenting?

Empathy for parents, deeply experienced and communicated clearly and fully, helps parents experience our care and begin to trust us more than any other therapeutic intervention—certainly more often than just information and advice. Our empathy enables parents to feel that they are not alone in their terrors, despair, or rage. Experiencing us being present with them provides the coregulation and social buffering they need to help modulate their negative emotions. With this support from us, they can shift from defensiveness into more openness, and experience feelings of sadness, or fear, or anger while safely connected with us. This is the same trustbuilding process we want to help these parents engage in with their mistrusting children. Just as the children need to have novel, unexpectedly positive experiences with their parents, the parents need to have novel, unexpectedly positive experiences with us, especially if they come to treatment with blocked care.

> After a number of very difficult, challenging weeks trying to raise her 12-year-old adopted son, Erica looked at her therapist and exclaimed, with a mixture of despair and rage:
>
> **Erica:** Sometimes I just wish that I never adopted him! Sometimes I even wish he had never been born! (*Erica seemed shocked by what she had just said and expressed a painful sigh as she began to cry*)
> **Therapist:** (*after a minute of silence, with a voice that matched the emotional distress conveyed in her expression*) Oh . . . oh my . . . how painful that must be for you . . . how painful to know that you sometimes wish that your son had not been born . . . You never imagined . . . when you adopted him . . . when you felt so much happiness and love . . . that you would ever have those thoughts and wishes . . . yes, how painful that must be for you.
> **Erica:** (*a few minutes later, with a look of sadness and gratitude*) I've had those thoughts for a while now and I never thought that I would tell a soul. Now I've told you. And

> I'm not afraid of them. I feel a lot lighter . . . I want to keep
> working at this. I have to be able to help him to get a life.
>
> **Therapist:** (*after more silence, spoken quietly and slowly*) I
> am grateful that you had the courage to tell me that you
> have those thoughts and feelings. It must have been so
> hard to tell me that. Somehow you face your rage and
> your despair and you find the strength . . . the strength to
> keep going. Where do you find it?
>
> **Erica:** I try to remember that no matter how much pain I am
> carrying, he is carrying more and has been for a much
> longer time. I know love, I know family. And he doesn't
> know those things . . . yet. I want to teach him. And I
> want you to help me . . . and help him . . . help us.
>
> **Therapist:** I will work as hard as I can, for as long as you do.

The therapeutic alliance is crucial in all forms of therapy and especially necessary if we are to work with parents to help them with intense family challenges that emerge from attempting to raise a mistrustful child. This alliance begins to take root with a foundation of acceptance, and it deepens and expands with the interwoven experiences of curiosity and empathy. Playfulness—in the background and sometimes up front—adds some sunlight to give a break from the hard work of living in the gray times and really make things blossom.

Once PACE has enabled the parents to experience trust with the therapist, the therapist is able to provide suggestions and another perspective. These suggestions might be regarding other approaches to discipline and ways to communicate so that the child is able to trust the parent even when the parent is saying "no." They might involve ways of expressing anger without shaming the child and ways to repair the relationship after a conflict. They might involve ways of communicating affection for a child who does not want expressions of affection, or communicating affection when the parent is not comfortable with physical affection because he or she was not raised with it. These suggestions might simply be verbally given, but are also given through modeling, coaching, and having the direct experience of the therapist relating to the parent in that manner. The alliance is truly strong when the parent and therapist are able to disagree, neither becomes defensive, both engage in making sense of a way forward, and they repair the relationship so it is stronger than before.

Often, by the time that parents seek assistance for their child's challenging behavior, they have become discouraged, angry, and worried and are experiencing blocked care. This may have led to them solely focusing on their child's behavior, without any curiosity or empathy about the possible reasons for it. They only know that they want the behavior to stop! As their perceptual focus becomes only on the behaviors, their behavior toward the child may have become harsh and punitive or anxious and avoidant. They may have lost sight of their child's strengths and forgotten many special moments they have had with their child in the past.

When parents are in this state of blocked care, one danger is that the professional will quickly give them cognitive-behavioral remedies without openly exploring what the behaviors mean and without developing confidence that the parents will be able to follow the suggestions when still in blocked care. Another danger is that the professional will only see the parents at their worst with regard to patience, empathy, and understanding and not be able to perceive of the past strengths of the parent–child relationship. As a result, the professional may judge the parents' present attitude toward their child as the source of the child's mistrustful behavior and not understand that the parents' present attitude followed the child's mistrust, rather than preceding it. It is crucial that the professional not make assumptions about the past or the parents' core states based on how they seem in the present. Without such assumptions, we are less likely to judge the parents, and they will be more likely to trust us. With this safety, they will be more likely to begin to show self-at-best, rather than the self covered with shame, fear, and anger.

It is also important when the parent is in the midst of great discouragement and despair and conveys a sense of wanting to give up, that the therapist not push the parent for motivation and change when it is not there. Parents do not need a cheerleader; they need someone who is with them in their pain, truly with them, until the joint presence in the pain reduces its intensity and the parent takes the initiative in moving forward.

> An adoptive mother, June, was in despair over how hard she had tried to reach her child for the past four years, without any sign that her efforts were making a difference regarding her son's ability to trust her. Many times she felt like giving up. That's what some friends told her to do. Others said that she needed to try something new: be stricter, be easier on him, spend more time with him, expect more of him. The therapist sensed that June needed to go more deeply into her mind to discover what she needed to do. She needed to know that only she had the best guess as to what was best for her son, herself, and the family. The therapist hoped that she would know she was not being pushed to make any particular choice.

> **Therapist:** (*with gentle, quiet empathy*) Your heart is so big and it has so much to give. I think that it may be possible that you are asking too much of your heart.
> **June:** (*after silence, truly without sound for what seemed like a long time*) Are you sure? Are you sure that I am asking too much?
> **Therapist:** No, I'm not sure.
> **June:** Then . . . (*with a newfound strength in her voice*) then I'm going to keep on asking. I think that it might be bigger than you and I think.

When parents decide to keep trying to parent their child by finding a way to keep caring or beginning to care again after they have stopped, it is not because someone talked them into it, saying it is best for the child or they will never forgive themselves if they give up. If they try for that reason—a reason outside of their own mind, heart, and character—their efforts will only stop again, and sooner rather than later. When parents make a commitment to keep trying or try again, it is often because they were safe—truly safe—to make the opposite decision.

Prior to beginning the joint sessions, the therapist will also be telling the parents what to expect in the sessions with their children, including how PACE and the affective-reflective (A-R) dialogue are central to the session. The therapist is likely to give examples of these dialogues, possibly role-playing one using a typical interaction that occurs at home. The therapist will also ask the parents for permission to interrupt them if the therapist thinks the parents might be doing or saying something that might hurt the relationship with their child. The therapist will suggest saying something different that might strengthen the relationship. The therapist will ask for permission to guide, coach, or even speak for a parent during the session with their child. The parents will be encouraged to be equally open with the therapist if they think the therapist might be saying something that might hurt the parents' relationship with their child.

Dialogues with Parents and Their Children

The treatment of the parent and child together—the core of family therapy—begins when the therapist believes the parents are experiencing safety with the therapist and are ready to join the therapist in providing safety for their child. If the parents are not safe in the room, the child will not be safe. The therapist is confident that the parents will be able to accept the therapist's guidance when necessary to ensure safety for their child and the effectiveness of the dialogues.

The therapist's primary task is to facilitate affective-reflective dialogue within the session, so that parent and child feel safe, understood, and confident that each is committed to improving their relationship. The message developed between parent and child is that the relationship is bigger than, more important than, the conflict.

The therapist is not focused on problem solving, mediating, and developing communication skills, though these may have a small, though important, place later in some sessions.

> Billy, age nine, became agitated and annoyed when his mother, Sue, said he could not play with his friend after school that day because Billy had broken his friend's toy in anger and the friend's mother said that she did not want them to play together for a few days. Noting Billy's annoyance, the therapist wondered about it:
>
> *Therapist:* You seemed upset that your mom told me that, Billy. What bothered you about her telling me?
>
> *Billy:* She only talks about the stuff that I do wrong. She never talks about the stuff that I do right!
>
> *Therapist:* Oh, Billy, if your mom only talks about your mistakes and not about what you do well, I can see why you'd be upset. If she does . . . if she only talks about the things you do wrong . . . why, Billy, why would she only talk about what you do wrong?
>
> *Billy:* Because she wants me to be perfect, that's why! She only looks for my mistakes because it makes her crazy when I make one! Like no other kid does!
>
> *Therapist:* Oh, Billy, if that's right, if your mom wants you to be perfect . . . how hard that would be. You'd never be able to please! That would be so hard! So awful!
>
> *Billy:* It is! I'm not good enough for her!
>
> *Therapist:* When you tell her that, Billy, when you tell her that you think that she wants you to be perfect . . . what does she say? (*pause*) You haven't told her! Billy, we have to know what she would say. Would you tell her now or let me tell her that's what you think if you don't want to tell her yourself. (*Billy nods his head*) Thanks, Billy, I'll speak for you. (*speaking with a child's voice*) Mom . . . Mom! This is really hard to say! But I want to say it! I

need to know! Mom . . . sometimes when I do something wrong and you talk about it . . . sometimes I think that you're disappointed in me! That you think that I'll never be good enough for you. I'll never get things right. I think that you're disappointed in me and that it will never change!

Sue: Oh, Billy, thanks for telling me that! I didn't know that you think that I want you to be perfect. I didn't know, and I'm so glad that you have the courage to tell me. It would be so hard for you if you thought that I'm disappointed in you because you're not perfect. So hard.

Therapist: (for Billy) Well, it seems to me that you are disappointed in me! Are you?

Sue: I know that I get annoyed sometimes, Billy, when you do something wrong. But I'm not disappointed in who you are, and I don't expect you to be perfect. Sure you make mistakes, we all do, and that's ok, even if I fuss about them. I love your courage, and how you don't give up, and how much you care for your family and your friends. I do know that, Billy. I guess I have to show you that more often and more clearly. Thank you, Billy, for telling me this!

Many therapists might think that such a response from Sue would be unlikely to happen. However, such a dialogue is likely to have been role-played in the sessions with the parents alone. Also, if the parent does provide information or reassurance (i.e., "I don't think you're bad, Billy") without first expressing empathy and understanding for the child's experience, the therapist will interrupt and ask the parent to begin with empathy. Children tend to accept such guidance from the therapist to the parent, without questioning the parent's honesty or intention. If they question the parents' motives in saying what the therapist asks them to say, the therapist then addresses the child's doubts with further PACE and A-R dialogue.

Also it is important to note the therapist did not agree with the child's perspective about the parent's thoughts, feelings, or behavior. Note that the therapist used the word "if" often to stress that it is the child's experience that the therapist has empathy for, not that the therapist is agreeing with any objective truth of that experience. Note that the therapist, when speaking for the child, tells the parents about the child's experience, rather than asking the parent if the child's experience is accurate. This tends to evoke greater empathy from the parent than a question would.

In focusing on A-R dialogue, the therapist constantly monitors whether both parents are open and engaged, rather than defensive. If defensive, the therapist turns her attention to the defensive comment, often with curiosity and empathy, and that sometimes becomes a focus of the dialogue. If the parent becomes very angry with the child or therapist, the therapist addresses the parent's anger with PACE. Sometimes this might be hard to address in front of the child, in which case, the child is directed to the waiting area (if it is safe) while the parent and therapist address the parent's distress.

The joint sessions tend to begin with a light and positive event and move toward a more stressful, often shame-related event that has created a break in the parent–child relationship. The momentum of the dialogue is crucial in keeping the discussion moving from the easier to the more difficult themes. The therapist does not change tone, rhythm, or intensity of voice as she moves from the lighter to the more stressful events.

The therapist tends to begin the dialogue around a specific event and deepens it to include associated thoughts, feelings, perceptions, and attributions about the motives of the other. As the meaning of the event (i.e., how it is experienced) to the child and/or parent is explored, links to previous events are often made. These links might connect to similar experiences in the current relationships or to the experiences that were present in the distant past in this or other important relationships. If an adopted child had been told in words and deeds by his birth parents that he was bad or unlovable, then there is great value in helping him see why he believes his current parent thinks he is bad when he does something wrong. Children—

and their parents for that matter—often do not see the connection between current behaviors (symptoms or behavioral problems) and past life experiences. When they begin to see those connections, they have less shame about current behaviors and past abusive experiences, and they have more motivation to explore and resolve those past experiences of abuse.

In the first part of each session, the therapist tends to focus on developing a momentum to the conversation with storytelling voice, moving the dialogue to the experience between the parents and child involving a stressful event, deepening it with the emergence of vulnerable emotions, understanding them with PACE, and finally experiencing comfort and closeness. Joint experiences of joy might be explored and deepened, especially in later sessions. Toward the end of each session the therapist reflects on what happened, enabling both parents and child to experience the therapist's experience of the session and so reflect on it themselves in an additional way. The therapist might give some suggestions that fit the theme being explored, to encourage carrying out these experiences at home. Suggestions might involve informing an absent parent of what occurred in the session. Cognitive-behavioral strategies to help change some perceptions or behaviors might be suggested. These strategies tend to be more effective if they are given after the meaning of the behavior has been understood and the joint desire to resolve the conflict has been made clear. When the therapist has been able to truthfully express her perception that the A-R dialogue showed how much parent and child wanted to feel close again, like they felt in the past, the motivation of parent and child to remember and do the strategy is greatly enhanced.

Parents Who Abuse and Neglect:
The Issue of Reconciliation

Most adults who harm their children are not sociopaths or severely mentally ill people. Most of the time, they come from abuse, neglect, and lives of chronic stress, and their brain development is essentially the same as that underlying blocked trust in children. In short, many of these adults were children with blocked trust who did not get the care and help they needed to recover from their own developmental trauma.

In many cases, the authorities who get involved with abusive and neglectful parents have a goal of returning the children to the care of these parents. Typically, the parents are given a number of things to do to facilitate the return of the children. This usually involves a list that includes parent counseling and maybe individual counseling for the parents plus supervised visitation with their children. What this list typically does not include is intensive, trauma-focused therapy for these parents, a form of treatment designed to help these adults reprocess their traumatic histories and recover from blocked trust and blocked care sufficiently to enable them to be truly safe parents for their children. If and when these parents undergo treatment successfully, they are ready to begin a process of repairing the damage they have caused in their relationships with their children, a process of beginning to establish some basic trust. Clearly, an essential step in this process is for the parent to take complete responsibility for the harm done and for creating the mistrust their children have toward them. Short of these processes of in-depth treatment for the parents and their willingness to take responsibility for repairing the damage they have caused, there is no reason to believe that parent counseling and visitations in a "safe place" are sufficient to create real safety in these parent–child relationships. Indeed, making children have visits with a parent who has not even begun the process of owning responsibility for the damaged relationship is often just a recipe for further traumatization of the child. This well-intentioned process is rooted in a failure to understand that safety is not just freedom from physical attack but more fundamentally involves creating emotional safety while the child is in the presence of a parent who has harmed the child and is a constant source of perceived threat.

Until the whole field of child protection, including family court systems, embraces the science of attachment and developmental traumatization, the approach to reconciliation remains insufficient to ensure the safe return of abused and neglected children to the care of the adults who mistreated them.

Teamwork in Family Treatment: Addressing Parental and Couple Issues in Attachment-Focused Treatment

Parents often need to work with the therapist without the child present until they reach the point where they are ready to engage in the trust-building process with the child. Depending on the parent's history and state of mind toward the child, this process of preparing for joint work with the child may be short or long. Full implementation of the DDP model requires that therapists be available for "deep work" with caregivers who need it, especially when they come to treatment with unresolved trauma from their own childhoods. A team approach can make the difference, where two therapists work together with the family, one working primarily with the parents in the early stages, the other with the child, until all are ready to be together for conjoint attachment-based work.

The principles and interventions of DDP apply equally well to children and their parents. Another model of treatment has been developed for adults that relies heavily on emotional and relational interventions. This treatment, developed by a psychologist, Diana Fosha (2000), is known as accelerated experiential dynamic psychotherapy (AEDP) and has many similarities with DDP. It could easily be considered a brain-based model of treatment congruent with neuropsychological research and theory. The same may be said for a treatment model for couples, emotion-focused therapy (EFT), developed by another psychologist, Susan Johnson (2004).

Error Signals: Jump-Starting the Learning Process in the Child

Parents have to be able to provide unexpected acceptance and empathy to create disparity between the child's deep mistrust and strong expectations of negativity or neglect from would-be attachment figures. It is important to remember that blocked trust is an anticipatory process in which the child's prior learning during experiences of poor care comes to predict poor care in the present and future. The brain is an anticipation machine with the job of helping us see what's coming before it arrives. As we explained earlier, the quicker the child's brain detects signs of negativity in the parent, the quicker the child can deploy those well-honed defensive skills. Children with blocked trust see rejection, criticism, invalidation, or outright physical and verbal abuse coming before these reactions or behaviors actually occur and frequently when these behaviors are not about to occur, as in false alarms.

This is why it is vital that the parents understand this dynamic and are prepared to respond in ways that trigger what neuroscientists call "error signals" in the child's brain. Error signals are generated in regions of the brain above the quick appraisal defense system. Specifically, these signals apparently come from regions in the anterior cingulate cortex (ACC) and perhaps from the orbitofrontal cortex (Bush, Luu, and Posner, 2000). The stronger these ACC-generated error signals, the more likely the child is to stop, pay attention, and start being curious about this surprising event. This is why error signals are so vital to learning how to change behavior and beliefs based on new and very different experiences from what we expected.

Error signals occur when what we expect to happen doesn't happen. The greater the expectation of negativity the child brings to the interaction, the more powerfully the parent's accepting, empathic responses trigger these vital error signals. Error signals triggered by empathic, mindful, PACEful parenting are essential to the process of helping a mistrusting child learn from new, positive experiences to trust. "No error signals, no learning" is a fair statement.

How do parents create these error signals in the child's brain? By consistently violating the child's negative expectations with positive responses. This is why it is effective when the child is the most mistrusting: this is when the parent's acceptance, understanding, and empathy is so surprising, so shocking, so unexpected.

PACEful parenting, then, is a style of parenting a mistrusting child that is likely to produce robust error signals and prompt the shift in the child's attention from just seeing signs of threat and negativity to seeing, hearing, and feeling signs of safety, acceptance, and understanding in the parent's eyes, voice, and touch. These are the signs that can get to that epicenter of defensiveness in the child's brain, the amygdala, and turn the dial away from "defense" and toward engagement, toward "safe to approach."

Remember how sensitive the amygdala is to eyes and emotional sounds in the voice? PACE is like "brain whispering" or "amygdala whispering," a form of enriched nonverbal communication that goes deep into the child's brain, straight to the center of mistrust and helps the medial amygdala switch from social defensiveness to social engagement, that open engaged state in which the child can see signs of safety and tolerate sharing personal space with a caring caregiver.

Parental Stroop Test:
Why PACEful Parenting Requires Higher Brain Powers

The Stroop test requires the ability to override a habitual way of responding to something in favor of a new, nonhabitual way of responding. The basic Stroop task consists of words printed in different colors with the instruction to say the color of the ink instead of reading the word (the habitual, mindless overlearned response to seeing a word).

When you take a Stroop test, you have to engage higher regions of the brain to inhibit the habitual reaction while holding in mind the rule for the task: say the color, not the word. In an emotional Stroop test, the words are emotionally tinged, like *murder*, and the task requires you to inhibit your emotional reaction and just respond to the color of the word.

In real life, a Stroop test occurs whenever we have to hold back a habitual reaction to something and respond in a new way. In parenting, the challenge of not responding defensively to a child's defensiveness, but responding with openness and compassion, is a robust emotional Stroop test, at least until responding compassionately becomes your new habit, your new "no brainer" way to respond to your child's negative behavior. This is akin to what Marsha Linehan (1993) tries to teach highly emotionally reactive people to do: opposite action. When someone is being mean to you, respond kindly. When you feel afraid and your habitual response would be to avoid the feared thing, go toward it.

Parenting defensive children is often a very challenging emotional Stroop test requiring opposite action. When the child is being habitually defensive, try to be nondefensive: inhibit the reflexive urge to be defensive and instead, be understanding, kind, compassionate, understanding, PACEFul, while still (if necessary) taking action to protect yourself and the child from physical harm. This is a tall order, requiring a mature and healthy brain. With a very stressed-out brain, you can't do this because you won't be able to access the higher regions and functions required to hold back the habitual reaction and do opposite action.

Learning to be PACEful in the face of a child's very unPACEful behavior takes a lot of effort, especially when you are first learning to resist your own self-protective, defensive reactions. Therapists need to appreciate how hard this is and be ready to do a lot of coaching while being empathic and PACEful with parents during this difficult learning curve. Making the shift to PACEful parenting begins with embracing the concept of connection before correction. Putting PACE into practice requires a lot of effortful, intentional work, including the parent working with the hot triggers that typically cause them to go defensive.

Practicing being PACEful in the face of a child's triggering behaviors should promote changes in the parents' brains. Like practicing any other skill, with enough reps and intentional practice, the brain circuits activated with PACE should be strengthened. This would happen through epigenetic processes and increased myelination of the pathways connecting the different regions of the brain that make up the PACE circuit in the brain. These are probably the pathways and regions that are seen to be strengthened in brain imaging studies of people who practice compassion meditation.

> Mary is having a parent session with the therapist who is working with her and her adopted daughter, Janine, who is 16. Mary is venting about how frustrated she feels as she thinks about Janine rolling her eyes and avoiding real engagement when Mary tries to address problems with her. As the therapist works hard to listen empathically, without judgment, Mary starts to soften her tone, and soon tears well up in her eyes. She says, "I never thought it would be like this. Janine was so delightful when she was little and she seemed happy. Now, I can't do anything right in her eyes."
>
> Gently, the therapist starts to talk with Mary about the theme of connection before correction, which they have reviewed before. Feeling heard and accepted, Mary stays open to this discussion, and she and the therapist start to think together about how she might find opportunities to surprise Janine with playfulness or by being unexpectedly nondefensive when Janine rolls her eyes. "Maybe," the therapist suggests, "you could ask her to teach you to roll your eyes and you two could have an eye roll contest." Mary laughs quietly, picturing this silly scene.

We ask a lot of parents, and parents ask a lot of themselves, in providing good care for mistrusting children. We and they must remember that they will make mistakes. They will have bad days. It is best for parents to acknowledge that to themselves and their child. Repair the relationship when necessary. It is crucial that the parent not go into shame about this or he or she will end up only experiencing anger at self and child. It's better to simply acknowledge making a mistake, repair the relationship, and move on. While remembering that parents will make mistakes, therapists might also remember that they will too! When the therapist is inattentive or misunderstands a situation and provides poor recommendations, it is crucial that the therapist repair the break with the parent that he caused himself. This will help the parent to continue to trust the therapist in spite of the error while also modeling for the parent the value of their repairing their relationship with their child.

CHAPTER 10

Therapeutic Presence:
Brain-Based Approaches to Staying Open and
Engaged with Caregivers and Children

As we have stressed throughout this book, a mistrustful child will begin to trust his parents when he is able to move into an open and engaged state of mind, accessing his social engagement system, rather than his social defense system. What will help him greatly is for his parents to be able to remain open and engaged with him when he interacts with them in his defensive, mistrustful way. If the therapist wants the child and caregiver to relate in an open and engaged manner, then the therapist also needs to be open and engaged.

Why might it be difficult for a dyadic developmental psychotherapy (DDP) therapist to remain open and engaged when doing therapy with children who are experiencing blocked trust and with their parents, who might be experiencing blocked care? If a therapist simply focuses on doing our job, shouldn't it be easy to be open and engaged when a parent and/or child is defensive? If we do our job by focusing on the problem, determining the intervention required to manage the problem, and then implementing the therapeutic strategy—all in a scripted, rational manner—this might be possible. Or if we adopt a primarily receptive position, being nondirective regarding the emerging dialogue, then it also might not be too difficult to stay open and engaged. In either case, a detached attitude will protect us from becoming defensive in response to the defensiveness of the parent or child. But if we do that, most likely the parent will not begin to care again and the child will not begin to trust.

The processes we therapists need to activate with mistrusting children and their possibly anxious and defended parents are emotional and relational. We are trying to activate a reciprocal process where the trust-enhancing engagement of the parent meets the awakening attachment experiences of the child—where the spontaneous experiences of delight and joy in the one resonate with similar delicate emerging experiences in the other.

As Allan Schore (2003) emphasizes in his description of what is needed in emotional and relationally focused treatment, this is predominantly a right-brain form of treatment in which the right brain of the therapist engages with the right brains of children and caregivers to promote engagement, emotional shifts and visceral changes in internal states. To attain the goal of helping a child with blocked trust in attachment-based work, the therapist has to be a real presence and engage with children and caregivers in ways that are immediate, unambiguous, emotional, sensory, affective. This is not nondirective or interpretive work, not behavioral or skill-directed work; it is, at its heart, relational through and through, requiring the therapist to attune from moment to moment to the quality of engagement with child and caregiver. To achieve this level of attunement, therapists must put aside all other agendas. When therapists relate in this highly resonating, relational manner, they are at risk for becoming pulled into the parent and/or child's defensiveness unless they are able to establish and maintain a state of mind that is similar to the adult who is autonomously (securely) attached. They must have the capacity to sustain a compassionate and reflective state of mind toward the caregivers, children, and themselves to evoke a similar state of mind within the caregivers and children they are treating.

To maintain this open and engaged, compassionate and reflective state of mind, the therapist must feel safe. The moment the child or parent perceives the therapist becoming defensive, their own defensiveness will become more intense. To maintain such a consistent sense of safety throughout the session, the therapist needs to understand the nature of the parent's and child's defensive actions toward him and be aware of therapeutic responses to the client actions that will be effective in maintaining his safety and initiating his clients' safety. These will be discussed next.

Success at maintaining this state of mind also depends on a therapist's own attachment history and current adult attachment status. This is especially true with regard to the therapist's exposure to trauma. Trying to work with children with blocked trust and caregivers with blocked care inevitably triggers a therapist's hot buttons and, like a heat-seeking missile, targets the therapist's own vulnerabilities. This will be discussed shortly. Therapists are not immune to the risks of experiencing social pain and feelings of impotence from helping mistrustful people recover the ability to feel safe and to trust. It is imperative that therapists be helped to create a safe environment within a supervisory relationship and a treatment team capable of exploring and sharing attachment histories and supporting each other in strengthening the capacity to do this difficult work mindfully and openly.

The key here is to apply the knowledge and processes described earlier in the book toward creating emotional safety for everyone involved in the work, from therapists and child workers to caregivers, to the children who are ultimately the target of treatment. There needs to be a constant commitment to engendering and sustaining this circle of security if the treatment process is going to be effective (Cicchetti, Rogosch, and Toth, 2006). Importantly, this means creating safety for therapists with each other and their supervisors to address conflicts constructively and repair connections when inevitable misattunements occur.

Team building, then, is an essential component of developing an effective attachment-focused treatment program. Nowhere is this more evident than in a residential or intensive outpatient program where team members have to work together under intensely stressful conditions and be able to withstand pressures to split their loyalties, take sides between caregivers and children, and so on.

Being Safe:
Knowing What's Happening and What to Do About It

The experience of safety is jeopardized by uncertainty about what is happening and what is about to happen. It is further jeopardized when we don't know what to do about what is happening. If our clients interact with us in a defensive way that we did not expect, do not understand, and do not know how to respond to, we are at risk of becoming anxious, angry, or detached and limiting ourselves to doing our job. We will be defensive ourselves. Of course we might also give up and refer the person to someone else if we lose our sense of safety too frequently.

What Is Happening?

To maintain our sense of safety, we need to have a fairly inclusive understanding of who our clients are and the meaning of their interactions with us. Once we give meaning to what is happening, we are likely to immediately experience safety. Ideally, the instant the client is defensive with us, we know what it means and we are able to remain open and engaged. Realistically, once in a while the client will be defensive and we will react defensively; hopefully we understand the meaning of the interaction fairly quickly and can reestablish an open and engaged stance.

To strengthen the ability to maintain a sense of safety and be open and engaged, we therapists need to understand:

- The nature of blocked trust (see Chapter 2), including its adaptive origins and how it manifests in behavior.
- The nature of blocked care (see Chapter 3) and how it manifests in behavior.

- The influence of the caregiver's attachment histories on their behavior.
- The effects of our open and engaged presence on our clients' behaviors.

With this knowledge, combined with a general knowledge of therapeutic interactions and the therapeutic process, we are likely more capable of establishing and maintaining our sense of safety.

What Do We Do about It?

Often therapists have a sense of the meaning of the client's behaviors but still become defensive when they are uncertain as to how to respond to a client's defensive actions. What do we say when our client says that we really don't care, we don't understand them at all, we're not competent, or we're blaming them and only taking the side of the child (or parent)? What do we say or do when a child refuses to talk, looks out the window, or stares at us with contempt? What do we say or do when the parent screams at the child or maintains a critical, shaming, attitude throughout the session? What do we say or do when the parent or child communicates nonverbally with changes in posture, breathing, facial expressions, voice tone, eye movements—in response to our communications or the communications of each other?

Here are some ideas as to what to do, mostly given elsewhere in this book. If we are skilled with such responses, they need to rest lightly on our tongue or fingertips to be expressed when needed. Better yet is when they represent our usual therapeutic stance and activity, so we are more likely to remain safe in responding to the various challenges that we might expect.

PACE

PACE (playfulness, acceptance, curiosity, empathy) frequently prevents or quickly lowers defensiveness in our clients. PACE is most effective when it is a habitual manner of engagement with our clients, not a technique that we turn on and off as needed. Our playfulness is genuine and sensitive, conveying hope and openness, and diminishing a sense of threat in our clients. Our acceptance for the inner life of thoughts, feelings, and wishes is complete and becomes our way of being in therapy. We only evaluate behavior. Curiosity represents a deep desire to understand our clients, a fascination with who the clients are. It is a *not-knowing* stance that allows us to be flexible in discovering the uniqueness about this person. Empathy is not a technique to use or give to a person. It is a way to experience another's challenges and vulnerabilities, join them in the emotion, and clearly communicate the experience to the child and/or parent. Sensitivity and communication involving nonverbal expressions are primary in all aspects of PACE.

Co-Regulation of Affect

Therapists are at risk of becoming defensive when clients act toward us with anger, distress, shame, or disgust. These emotional states, expressed affectively through voice, facial expressions, posture, or gestures, activate the therapist's limbic system before the therapist is aware of being affected. When we are able to match these affective expressions in rhythm and/or intensity of our expression (without feeling the emotion itself), often the emotion of the client remains or becomes regulated; then the person may gradually become engaged with us in communicating their stressful experience more openly. Such matching of the affective expressions of clients' emotional states is often experienced as empathy. The behavior of the client or child can be very intense and can easily create a defensive reaction in us. If we are able to match the intensity and convey a sense of urgency to understand, urgency to be helpful, or urgency to repair the relationship with the client, we may avoid a defensive reaction, and the client's intensity is likely to dissipate.

Affective-Reflective Dialogue Along with Follow-Lead-Follow and Story Voice

DDP strives to develop an integrative (involving emotional and cognitive) dialogue about the stressful events of the person's life, co-regulating their emotional components and co-creating new meanings that are not shameful or terrifying. When challenged defensively by our client, if our focus is on integrating what was said to us into a story that makes sense—is more coherent—our mind is likely to remain open and engaged. If our curiosity is strong about the meaning of the challenge being expressed, it is much easier to sustain the internal state of open engagement rather than moving toward defensiveness. Our curiosity inhibits our defensiveness, helping us keep our social engagement system on. If the person says we really are only seeing them for the money, it is easy not to become defensive if we are focused on understanding the roots of that perception and how it is experienced by the person.

Leaning Toward
Often we are at risk of becoming defensive when the client verbally attacks our knowledge, action, or motivation. One defensive reaction is to pull away from the attack by literally and psychologically becoming more distant, passive, or compliant. Another reaction is to be intrusive in return by psychologically pushing against the person's attack. A middle way is to psychologically and physically lean toward the person, with acceptance, curiosity, and empathy, being clear that our attitude is to assist them in their distress. We are assisting them even when they say that we are the source of their distress. If we are closely attuned, the degree to which we lean toward the client will match his sense of personal space, experienced as an open engagement, with containment, rather than being intrusive.

When We Slip

It's great when we are able to remain safe in the instant our client is defensive. It's important that this happens the great majority of the time. Sometimes we will not remain safe, but become defensive ourselves. What do we do then?

- Be aware of it, without shame. If we make a mistake and are ashamed of it we are likely to deny the mistake to ourselves, become defensive and try to hide it from our clients. Yet, it probably was detected by our client. When we do not admit it, our client will experience us as being deceitful and trust us less. If we are able to accept our mistake and any efforts at a "cover up," we will be able to openly acknowledge it to our client and repair the relationship. Do so with empathy, and then openly invite their response. If we are not defensive while openly admitting that we had been, being a bit vulnerable ourselves because of our slip, the client is likely to trust us more. If anything, a brief bit of defensiveness—acknowledged openly without defensiveness—will improve our relationship.

- Notice any pattern of defensiveness. We may have particular difficulty remaining open and engaged around certain situations. A particular emotion, criticism or theme might place us at risk for responding with defensiveness. It is crucial to become aware of this pattern, understand what makes it difficult and know how to address it. Such patterns might well result from our own attachment histories, which we will now discuss.

Therapists Have Attachment Histories, Too

The attachment themes that we have focused on here—trust and caregiving—involve helping families in treatment move from blocked trust and blocked care to restored trust and restored care. Attachment themes are so crucial in the passage of abuse, neglect, and marginal care from generation to generation because the attachment patterns tend to be passed down by generation. Attachment patterns are highly contagious. If we provide treatment to a parent who has a dismissive attachment pattern, that parent's style of relating tends to evoke a similar or opposing style within the therapist. We are aware that if parents have been raised in a very strict way, they are at risk to raise their children in either a strict manner or in a manner that is overly permissive. When therapists have been raised in a very strict manner, they are at risk to intervene with very strict parents in a way that either strongly criticizes them or barely notices that their child-rearing approach is not creating safety, is not open and engaged. Being triggered by our own history does not mean we had a traumatic history. Indeed, we are always affected by our own history, in positive, adaptive ways and sometimes in ways that hinder our ability to stay open and engaged. Being triggered may simply reflect some stressful times from our past that are awakened by similar events that emerge in the family we are treating. After all, our brains, like our clients' brains, are always comparing the present moment to past experiences to see if there is match. This is the normal process our brains employ to help us know what is going on and what to do about it.

> Stephen was a certified DDP therapist providing treatment to a single mother with a very oppositional 12-year-old son. In DDP, the therapist approaches whatever relational problems are present in an open and engaged manner, with PACE. The therapist tends to try to make sense of the child's behavior in the context of the relationship, and often this involves helping the child become aware of his assumptions about his parents' motives for setting a limit or expressing an expectation. When the child becomes angry with the parent in the session, the therapist is likely to match the affective expression (intensity and/or rhythm) of the child, establish a co-regulated affective state, and then become engaged with the child in co-creating the meaning of the event that led to the conflict. The supervisor was watching the video of the treatment session, and at one point the child became angry with his mother over a limit that he thought was unfair. At that point, Stephen immediately became angry with the child and said that he should not speak with his mother in that manner.

> **Supervisor:** Any idea what was happening there?
> **Stephen:** He was pretty intense with his mother and I thought that he expressed his anger in a way that was disrespectful to her authority.
> **Supervisor:** Ah, so that's why you got angry with him?

Stephen: I guess.

Supervisor: Any other options?

Stephen: Probably could have wondered about it. Maybe why it was so intense. What made it so hard. Maybe asked how his anger at his mom has a downside for him, her, and their relationship.

Supervisor: Why do you think you became angry with him instead?

Stephen: I don't know.

Supervisor: His anger at his mother seemed to be hard for you. What's that about?

Stephen: (*quite reflective, pausing, starting and stopping, and then, with some excitement*) That's it! He reminded me of my little brother, yelling at my mom when I was a teenager! My father was seldom home and my mom would be worn out with having to take care of everything at home and there were four kids. I was the oldest and felt responsible to help her with the younger ones and sometimes I really yelled at them for giving her a hard time!

It only took one reflective look into his attachment history for Stephen to avoid reacting in a similar way in subsequent sessions. For him to be able to do that, he needed to feel safe with his supervisor. His inner life needed to be met with PACE.

As therapists, most of us had professional training that makes us quite sensitive to how the adults we treat are influenced by childhood experiences within their families. We are aware of various childhood experiences—discipline, losses, affection, comfort, relationship repair, emotional recognition and expression—that may be particularly relevant for understanding how a parent may be interacting with their children. We are aware of how defensive parents get when they are asked to explore connections between their child's behavior, their response/reaction to it, and their own family of origin. We work to help them look at their childhood without feeling blamed and without shame. Now we need to direct the same degree of nondefensive reflection to our own childhoods. We need to be open to the possibility that our own childhood is creating a bias in our perceptions, interactions, or goals in treatment. If we are committed to therapy that uses the principles of DDP (intersubjectivity, holding an open and engaged attitude, PACE, the characteristics of A-R dialogue) and we find ourselves struggling to be fully responsive to our clients, we might consider our attachment history to be involved. Examples of questions we might ask ourselves are:

1. Do we value the parents' authority over the child challenging this authority (or vice versa)?
2. Do we rescue the child from parents who may have different child-rearing practices than our own but are not abusive or extreme in one direction or the other?
3. Do we rescue the parents from children who are very defiant or disrespectful of them?
4. When the parent or child expresses vulnerability through sadness or fear, do we respond with reason, reassurance, or distraction, rather than empathy?
5. When the parent or child expresses shame, do we respond by talking him out of the feeling and thus preventing its exploration and resolution in a more meaningful way?
6. Do we focus on fixing the problem with consequences, tighter rules, or lectures which are similar to how we were raised?
7. Are we routinely anxious whenever any member of the family expresses anger toward another member of the family or toward us?
8. Do we experience ongoing shame when we make a therapeutic mistake, and does this shame prevent us from learning from the mistake or from repairing the relationship?

When the parent or child is frustrated or annoyed with our interventions their annoyance may certainly be because we are not taking their side or we are addressing something that is challenging for them. Another possibility is that we are not open and engaged with their experience but are responding within the limits created by an aspect of our own attachment history.

> Susan was an experienced therapist who had been practicing DDP for a few years. In supervision her supervisor observed a video of a treatment session, in which the mother comforted her daughter over her troubles with her friends. The supervisor asked Susan if the girl's father was equally supportive, and Susan indicated that she did not know because she had not met the father. The supervisor wondered why and Susan said that she asked the mother a few times and the mother replied that her husband tended to be quite busy and she thought it was not necessary for him to come. Susan accepted what the mother said without further questioning. When the supervisor suggested that Susan might approach the mother again and indicate that he needed to come to at least one session and maybe more, regardless of how difficult it is, Susan appeared resistant.

Supervisor: You don't seem comfortable with my suggestions.

Susan: Well, the family does have a lot going on, and dad is not involved in the day-to-day much anyway.

Supervisor: Would he like to be more involved?

Susan: From what mom says, probably not.

Supervisor: How does that affect her?

Susan: She seems resigned to it.

Supervisor: So that might be causing a problem in their relationship.

Susan: Probably.

Supervisor: Which might be affecting how the child is doing, apart from whether it might bother her that her father does not seem to be that engaged with her.

Susan: Ok, I get it. I'll ask harder for dad to come in. At least for me to meet him and decide how important it is for him to be there more regularly.

Supervisor: Why do you think that you didn't?

Susan: I just accepted mom's view that it was not that important.

Supervisor: Would you mind telling me, Susan—how involved was your father in your life growing up?

Susan: (*looks surprised, then smiles, then seems a bit embarrassed*) Not very much. He worked a lot, then seemed to have various projects that he was involved in that did not involve the kids.

Supervisor: How did that affect you?

Susan: I just was used to it. I never talked to him about stuff, I always went to my mom. And she said that dad worked hard and was very independent himself growing up so he wasn't likely to change. But he was a good man and we should just accept it. He loved us.

Supervisor: How did that affect you?

Susan: (*again a bit surprised by the question, followed by a smile, and then some sadness*) I never felt that special to him. I knew that he loved us, but I didn't feel it. Even mom. She seemed to put what was best for him above what might be best for the kids. But that's how she was raised.

Supervisor: And this mom in the therapy might be a bit like your mom, and you might be supporting her with her child, that dad has too many other responsibilities to spend time with the kids. By not asking dad to attend the sessions, you might be suggesting to the girl that she shouldn't be bothered that her father is not more involved in her life.

Susan: (*with much thought*) I think that I need to get dad into the session. And maybe help the girl to be aware of any possible sadness and doubts over his not being present very often. And then to express whatever is there and see how the parents respond.

Supervisor: (*smiling*) Sounds like a good plan.

When Susan realized that her assumption might not be in the best interests of the child, she consciously focused on having the father present in the sessions. She was also able to attain a much higher participation of many of the fathers in her treatment families than she had before. This aspect of her history, now reflected on, no longer led to assumptions that were not based on the experiences of the families that she was treating. Whatever makes up the history of the therapist, if it leads to understanding and integration, need not impair the ability to provide good treatment. Rather, our histories, brought into self-awareness, can be an asset to becoming more successful as a therapist.

In DDP the therapist's central tasks are to create an open and engaged reciprocal relationship with all members of the family while focusing on collaborating with them to create a coherent narrative with respect to their ongoing attachment-caregiving relationships. One of the therapist's tasks is to set a tone where strong emotional states of terror and shame, rage and despair are co-regulated so that they do not impede the open exploration and discovery of aspects of the story that prevent it from becoming coherent. While maintaining the safety that comes from co-regulation of these emotional states, the therapist openly explores the meaning of events as they emerge without these emotional distortions or restrictions. Within such joint explorations, the therapist maintains a state of not-knowing curiosity, helping the child or family become aware of their assumptions or judgments and their impact on the story. For example, a child—after engaging in A-R dialogue with the therapist—might tearfully express to her parent: "When you said that I couldn't see my friend over the weekend, I really felt that you just wanted me to be unhappy." Her mother, hearing her daughter's expression of her assumption about her motive, while remaining open and engaged rather than becoming defensive, might reply with empathy: "Oh, honey, that must have been horrible for you if you thought that I said 'no' because I wanted you to be unhappy. No wonder you got so angry! Thanks for telling me what you thought about why I said 'no'!"

Such dialogues are central in DDP, and the therapist takes an active role in helping the story unfold. The therapist wonders with the child about the nature of her emotional response, her perceptions of her mother's expressions, and her assumptions about her motives. When the child is confused about the event and says she does not know what she felt, what she thought her mother felt, and other aspects, the therapist makes tentative, educated guesses about the child's inner life at the time of the incident, watching carefully for the child's responses and helping the child develop her story. It is crucial for this active therapeutic stance to be an effective act of discovery of the meaning of the event and not a therapeutic distortion of it. The therapist must be truly open and engaged with the child's and parent's experiences and not be influenced by bias emerging from her own attachment history. Her guesses should be tentative and the parent and child must know and trust that the therapist will not be disappointed or annoyed if they disagree with her guesses. The therapist needs to focus on activating the child's and parent's reflective abilities about the event, not lead them in a particular direction that is similar to an aspect of the therapist's own attachment history!

> Rebecca was engaged in supervision regarding a 17-year-old girl who was developing her narrative regarding the very difficult years of her childhood and the meaning of the abuse and neglect she experienced from her biological parents. Rebecca recalled that in the previous session the girl said that she was convinced that her mother never loved her from the moment of her conception. She had responded to the girl that her mother must have loved her, at least a bit at her conception if not during or immediately after her birth.
>
> **Supervisor:** What makes you so sure of that?
> **Rebecca:** (after pausing and with some confusion) Doesn't

every mother love their child at least for a moment when they realize they are pregnant?

Supervisor: I wouldn't think so. But what makes you think that?

Rebecca: (*after a great deal of reflecting*) Many times when I was growing up . . . after a conflict with my mother . . . she would not let the conflict end until I said that I knew that she loved me.

Supervisor: So your mother did not allow you to have any doubts about her love.

Rebecca: No. I never thought that was right. But it was very important to her and I had to agree. When I got older she told me that she spent much of her life thinking that her mother did not love her and that she wanted to be sure that I didn't have doubts, too.

Supervisor: So you might have assumed that your client was better off believing that her mother loved her, at least at some point in the pregnancy, rather than believe that she was never loved.

Rebecca: Yes, I guess I did not want her to have doubts.

In the next supervision session, Rebecca referred back to her treatment of that teenager. "Remember last time I mentioned the teenager who said that she thought that her mother never loved her, even when pregnant and at birth. . . . Well I told her that I was sorry for having said that her mother must have loved her then. I told her that I didn't know and that she had to trust her gut as to why her mother treated her as she did over the years . . . Do you know what she did? She cried. And then said that was the only way that things made sense to her."

Therapists are rightfully cautioned not to tell their clients what they feel, think, or want. Our inner lives need to be held respectfully and delicately in the minds of others, especially in the minds of therapists! As a result, therapists have been urged to take a very receptive stance, with open-ended questions that will be sure not to lead the client down a certain path. In DDP, with children experiencing blocked trust who have spent little time developing their reflective functioning and have little motive or ability to communicate their inner life, the therapist often needs to be more active—not receptive—in initiating such explorations. She makes light, tentative guesses about the inner life of the mistrusting child, communicates complete acceptance of the child saying "no" about the guess, and works only to facilitate the child's ability to reflect and discover what makes sense to him.

This active process exposes the therapist to an increased possibility that her own attachment history will be in play and will influence the mistrusting child's developing narrative in ways that distort and restrict it to developing similarly to the therapist's own narrative. It is crucial that the therapist's own narrative be coherent, resolved, and open to self-reflective abilities. The therapist's own history will influence her person—who she is—and because of the nature of intersubjectivity, she certainly influences the child through her experience of the child, which she is communicating nonverbally and at times verbally. Central to what she is communicating is her confidence in and respect for the child's own autonomy, along with honoring their different perspectives and her value in the child being the author and editor of his own narrative. She is not going to write his story for him, nor substitute her story for his.

What the Therapist's Brain Needs
Trusting Relationships

It is not likely that therapists will be able to help mistrustful children begin to trust if they we are not themselves in trusting relationships. Just as parents and kids need to feel safe and have a trust-based relationship with the therapist, therapists need to feel safe with their colleagues and supervisors—deeply safe, safe enough to go through the learning curve of what may be a radically different way of understanding and working with people, safe enough to tell their own attachment stories, safe enough to help each other work toward increasing levels of security and resilience as a team and as an individuals. Therapists tend to be empathic people, but they are still human and subject to the same defensive reactions as everyone else. Since DDP requires the ability to regulate affect and to sustain a PACEful state of mind toward people who are often defensive or disengaged, therapists need to work on themselves with the goal of developing their potential for staying grounded and engaged in this work.

Therapists require that their trainers and supervisors have the skills and sufficient internal security to help therapists safely explore their own issues and work on increasing their capacity to stay open and engaged as they work with people who aren't. In many ways, the supervisor needs to be a PACEful mentor for the therapist, where the therapist is safe to explore all aspects of her treatment cases. "All aspects" includes mistakes and successful interventions, along with confusion, doubts, and clear insights. It also includes the therapist's own personal life and attachment history to the extent that her own relationships, past and present, are influencing her presence with children (and parents) who may not trust her presence.

DDP has a certification program that involves training in the treatment model and supervision in the initial efforts to use the model in treatment. There is time in the training when the applicants are supported in exploring the impact of their attachment histories on their therapy, "for better or for worse." The trainer stresses that since we all have attachment histories that continue to influence our important relationships, we need to reflect on these influences on a regular basis if we are to ensure they do not have a detrimental impact on our treatment. In the practicum, where the applicants are receiving supervision around their treatment cases, the supervisor is sensitive to possible influences on the treatment emerging from the applicant's history and addresses them with PACE. The supervisor also evaluates the applicant's abilities in using this treatment model and does so in a way to build openness and safety. The principles of DDP, designed for building or renewing trust and care, are applied in all areas of interaction—professional and personal—within the DDP community.

Our recommendations for parents who are raising mistrustful children need to be important aspects of our own lives. These would include safe, open, and engaged relationships with a partner, friends, family, professional colleagues, including a supervisor and possibly a therapist. We need to be able to share the important aspects of our lives in some of these relationships whenever it is in our interest to do so. These relationships need to include a full range of experiences, from serious and intimate to light, playful, and casual.

Brain-Based Learning for Therapists

Helping therapists gain a good working knowledge of the neurobiology of blocked trust, blocked care, and attachment-based treatment processes is an essential component of preparation for this work, in our view. The knowledge that the brain-based approach provides underpins the ability to do attachment-based treatment well. Therapists need this knowledge as a guide to the therapy and also as a fund of information to use, in a timely, user-friendly way, with parents and children to help both generations get their minds around what they have experienced and are experiencing. Working with attachment problems without the benefit of this new knowledge is bound to be less effective than working with this knowledge. The neuroscience perspective provides the rationale for taking an integrative approach and helps therapists think deeply about the processes they are working with and how change happens.

Having a Life

If it is to have a real impact on children who mistrust and caregivers who are in blocked care, DDP therapy needs to be more than a job for the therapist. It needs to bring deep meaning and engagement; it needs to matter to the therapist whether the therapy is able to create safety and renewed trust and care. At the same time, the therapist needs a life that is more than being a DDP therapist. The therapist needs to have other passions and interests, other ways to be deeply engaged and experience meaning. The therapist needs experiences of rebooting, re-creation, and renewal. The therapist needs a range of experiences and skills that will enable him or her to regulate the full range of affective states, reflect on all aspects of life, and manage stress that occurs in life and in therapy. Training exercises in the following may be of value for many therapists in being able to consistently maintain a high level of therapeutic presence and skills.

- Mindfulness
- Relaxation
- Attention to diet and exercise

Summary

The DDP therapist helps children move from mistrust to trust while also assisting their parents in being able to care for them. This process involves using brain-based attachment interventions within the context of providing a safe relationship that is affectively and reflectively rich, varied, coherent, and integrated. We tell the therapists who develop their practice in this way that providing this treatment is easy. But the preparation for it begins at birth and requires ongoing personal updates and repairs, along with a comprehensive knowledge about how our brains are designed for trust and care. From there the therapist needs to know the history and struggles of the family and then relate with them in a spontaneous, open, and engaged manner, and trust the process. The process involves utilizing the principles of the affective-reflective dialogue, PACE, and maintaining a storytelling stance. There is a lot to hold in mind while relating spontaneously, so mistakes will happen and repair will be needed—with as little defensiveness as possible. Not so easy after all! But worth it, we think, each and every time a child moves from mistrust to trust and discovers the meaning of family.

CHAPTER 11

Expanding the Model:
Mindfulness, EMDR, Neurofeedback, and More

While we have focused on relational processes that facilitate the shift from mistrust to trust in attachment-focused therapy, other processes have a place in a comprehensive, integrated approach to attachment-based interventions. Ultimately, helping children with blocked trust learn to trust requires changing the way their brains react to sensory experiences. At the core, the limbic reactivity and fast triggering of the stress response system and self-defense system keep driving habitual mistrust toward caregivers. Processes that help decrease this negative limbic hyperreactivity to social cues, to the sensory experiences of social engagement, are potentially a welcome addition to the dyadic developmental psychotherapy (DDP) model of attachment-focused treatment. We emphasize, though, that none of these are a substitute for the enriched relational experiences at the heart of attachment-focused treatment.

In general, any process that safely helps people make the internal shift from defensive states to an open, engaged state could have a place in attachment-focused treatment. For example, research shows that four of the most powerful ways to disarm the stress/defense

**Figure 11.1 Relational and nonrelational processes
that calm the mid-brain defense system**

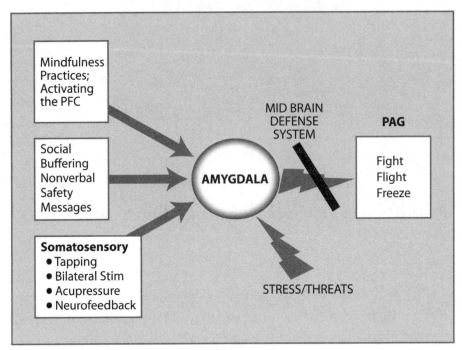

systems are laughing, singing, dancing, and receiving and giving good touch, including massage. This is why playfulness, the musical use of the therapist's voice, rhythmic movements, and the restoration of safe, soothing touch in parent–child dyads are powerful facilitators of change in this attachment work. All of the processes that have been shown to have a calming effect probably work by suppressing hyperarousal in the limbic system, specifically by quieting the mid-brain defense system (see Figure 11.1).

Let's look at some of the processes that may play a role in an integrated model of attachment-focused treatment, in conjunction with the core relational processes of DDP.

Processes Currently Used in Attachment-Focused Therapy
EMDR and Other Forms of Bilateral Rhythmic Stimulation

Eye movement desensitization and reprocessing (EMDR) uses bilateral stimulation, from eye movements to oscillating tactile and auditory stimulation, to calm hyperarousal during traumatic memory processing. Although no one knows for sure just how bilateral stimulation works, knowledge of how visual, tactile, and auditory inputs are processed in the brain strongly suggests that these types of stimulation quickly modify patterns of neuronal activity in the amygdala. In general, the amygdala seems to detect rhythmic input, including tapping on the skin (Vogt, 2009) and even the act of walking, as signaling safety. It is likely that EMDR, once a degree of relational safety is in place, reaches the amygdala fairly quickly, while keeping the superior colliculus from getting stuck in a "deer in the headlights" kind of orienting response, keeping this mid-brain circuit from hyperfocusing on one part of a memory. The amygdala has back projections to the sensory regions that were activated by the original frightening experience, and when it reactivates the alarm system, it uses these projections to make all of the sensory aspects of the memory much more intense and vivid. By quieting the amygdala, EMDR suppresses this process and helps make the memory seem more faded, older, further away in time and place. This in turn enables the person to tolerate the recall and reprocessing of traumatic material without dissociating or feeling overwhelmed. A number of DDP therapists incorporate some use of bilateral stimulation in their work with maltreated children and report that this helps these kids stay more open and engaged during treatment sessions.

Drumming, dancing, and other forms of bilateral movement have been shown to be helpful for calming the limbic system and helping people be more engaged socially. These forms of movement probably engage the limbic system in ways similar to what is described regarding EMDR, ultimately sending safety messages to the amygdala to promote a shift from defensiveness to openness. Finally, we might easily postulate that the storytelling dialogues of DDP also involve bilateral activity with the blend of the nonverbal and verbal components of the conversation.

Music: Promoting Openness and Social Engagement

Nigel Osborne, a neuroscientist who studies music on the brain, calls music a hotline to the subcortical brain, the limbic and deep motor systems, that moves people without having to pass through higher brain regions first (Osborne, 2010). Recently, dramatic videos show the use of music with elderly patients with dementia and chronic psychiatric illnesses. In these videos, we see people seemingly brought to life, reengaged by listening to favorite songs from their youth, or coming out of an angry state to start dancing. We suggest you search for these videos online (search for "iPod project") and watch them, because they are dramatic examples of the potential for reviving engagement in people for whom this potential appears to have been lost. One of the authors has seen adolescents with trauma histories put their narratives to song in the form of rapping to take the sting out of these stories and indeed to help these kids actually take pride in their stories and enjoy the process of sharing their musical versions with peers and others. Clearly music has a place in an integrative approach to treating children and teens with attachment-based problems. Music is definitely a powerful activator of the brain, usually in positive ways that enhance the sense of safety and engagement with life. Certainly many adolescents credit their music with getting them through hard times and even, sometimes, saving their lives.

Good Touch: The Power of Massage

For many years, Tiffany Field and her colleagues studied and demonstrated the power of massage, good touch, to suppress the stress response system and trigger oxytocin, serotonin, and other chemicals with soothing effects in the limbic system. Teaching depressed mothers to massage their babies was shown to be a powerful intervention that helped the babies recover from a lack of engagement and vitality. Furthermore, massaging the depressed mothers had an even more robust effect on the quality of mother–child interaction (Field,

Diego, and Hernandez-Reif, 2010). There is no doubt that good touch is one of the most powerful ways to promote safe social engagement. With touch having become such a controversial issue for psycho-therapists, it is an underused route for promoting social engagement in disengaged clients. Much of the therapeutic hesitation regarding touch focuses on how individual therapy allows little opportunity for safe touch for the client and therapist. When the child is with both caregivers and the therapist, there is likely a greater opportunity for safe touch during a treatment session. Although touch between the caregiver and child is likely to be the most indicated, a child's spontaneous expression of gratitude or affection toward the therapist after a trust-enhancing experience (in the presence of the caregiver) is likely to be therapeutic for the child as well. The child is never told that he should touch or hug his caregiver or therapist. However, when he seeks safe touch while learning to trust, it should probably not be discouraged.

One of the authors worked closely with a massage therapist on a case involving a very disengaged child and her adoptive mother. The use of light massage for the child and the parent was the single most effective intervention out of all the processes used in this case. (The therapist was not familiar with DDP at the time.) The massage rapidly appeared to disarm the defense system in these highly defended people, making it possible for a while for the two of them to engage openly and safely in a way they had never been able to before. If the therapist had known more about how to use the kind of relational processes included in DDP, perhaps the opening provided by the massage work could have been exploited to greater effect. The experience certainly provided a powerful anecdotal example of the power of good touch to augment attachment-focused treatment.

Sensory Integration Work and Occupational Therapy

Most children with developmental trauma and significant attachment problems exhibit poor sensory integration, and this probably plays an important role in their chronic problems with social engagement. In brain research, one of the regions most implicated in developmental trauma is the cerebellum, a structure at the base of the brain that was long thought to only be important for motor coordination. Now the cerebellum is known to be involved in all aspects of coordination, from walking to talking to emoting and thinking. Studies of adults who experienced childhood adversity consistently show apparent suppression of the cerebellum, particularly the cerebellar vermis, which has strong connections with the limbic system. This region tends to be smaller in these subjects and is known to be important for self-regulation, including emotion regulation (Teicher et al., 2003). The cerebellum is probably a target for the various kinds of occupational therapy work with children who have sensory integration problems, and this suggests a brain-based rationale for using sensory integration processes as an adjunct to relational processes to calm a chronically hyperaroused limbic system. The authors have found that such collaborative work between DDP and sensory integration therapy enabled many mistrusting children to develop much greater self-regulation ability without the need for medication.

Pets as Transitional Attachment Figures

Undoubtedly many maltreated children find it easier to feel safe in the presence of a pet or a stuffed animal toy than in the presence of other people. It makes great sense to include the use of pets in an integrated approach to attachment treatment for some children. As we discussed earlier, communicating with humans is a very complex process that can easily engender mistrust, whereas interactions with dogs and other animals are typically more straightforward and less prone to misreading intentions. Dogs especially (at least some breeds) are clearly unconditionally accepting and nonjudgmental, and they can be extremely helpful as transitional attachment figures for maltreated, mistrustful children. Training children to care for and ride horses has also helped some move toward greater trust of their caregivers. The possible use of pets should be explored in many cases as a stepping stone in relational treatment moving toward safety with trustworthy people.

In general, we can think about the processes described here as ways of enhancing the effects on the limbic system of the basic processes involved in social engagement: visual, auditory, and somatosensory stimulation. While relational therapy uses the power of these forms of stimulation to promote safe social engagement, these modalities of stimulation can also be used nonrelationally to target the limbic system of hyperaroused kids and caregivers to help calm the brain system that is central to reopening the capacity for safe engagement in children with blocked trust and caregivers with blocked care.

Mindfulness Practices

We should highlight the power of various mindfulness practices to enhance the ability to get above the deep limbic system and reflect on ourselves and our relationships in a slower, deeper, less reactive way (Wu, and Lo, 2008; Brewer et al., 2011). Recent brain imaging studies of people before and after engaging for some time in meditative practices have consistently shown apparent growth in the middle prefrontal region of the brain, an area extending from the most frontal part of the anterior cingulate cortex into the middle region of the prefrontal lobe (Cahn, and Polich, 2006; Tang et al., 2010). This is the middle prefrontal cortex, the region we described earlier as the thinking part of the default mode network and a crucial region to activate for reflecting on relational experiences to deepen one's capacity for compassion. What could be more useful in an integrated approach to attachment-focused treatment than practices that are being shown to strengthen the default mode network and the potential for compassion and reflective functioning in adults who care for kids with blocked trust? There are also many approaches to teaching mindfulness to children. Dan recently wrote a book chapter involving "intersubjective mindfulness," in which a case is made that the approach of playfulness, acceptance, curiosity, and empathy (PACE) is an effective way to facilitate mindfulness in children, as long as the adult is in a mindful state herself when she is engaged and attuned with the child (Hughes, 2013).

Medication and Attachment-Focused Treatment

The use of medication in the treatment of children is a complex issue, especially with children with developmental trauma and blocked trust. In the authors' experience, medications are sometimes helpful in attachment-focused treatment and can help facilitate a shift from chronic mutual defensiveness toward a more open, safer relationship between a caregiver and a child. We would never recommend that a child with blocked trust be given medication without providing attachment-focused treatment. Medication alone will not help a deeply mistrustful child learn to trust.

In our experience, it is essential to have a close collaborative relationship with a prescriber who is well informed about attachment and the neurobiology of developmental trauma or complex posttraumatic stress disorder. It is vitally important that any psychotropic medications be used to further the goals of attachment-focused treatment, including helping caregivers embrace the challenge of being trust builders for mistrusting children. This could include medication to address a caregiver's depression or anxiety disorder to help that person be more capable of providing the kind of enriched care children with blocked trust need.

Michael De Bellis at Duke University has written extensively on the subject of medication considerations with maltreated children, and his work provides a valuable resource for therapists and prescribers (De Bellis, 2005a, 2005b). De Bellis stressed that "the traumatic stress model can help physicians utilize a rational approach for prescribing medications" for maltreated children (2005a, p. 424). "In theory," he went on to say, "the appropriate use of medications aimed at desensitizing the maltreated child's hyperaroused biological stress response systems and thus attenuating their PTSD symptoms can help foster" the therapeutic alliance with deeply mistrustful children (2005a, p. 425). (A good model of collaboration between therapists and a prescriber can be found at the Kids TLC program in Olath, Kansas, led by psychiatrist George Thompson.)

Neurofeedback for Patients with Developmental Trauma

Recently Sebern Fisher, a therapist and practitioner of neurofeedback, wrote a book describing her use of neurofeedback in conjunction with relational therapy to treat primarily adults with histories of early life adversity (Fisher, 2014). She advocates the addition of neurofeedback, at least on a trial basis, in cases of developmental trauma because she has seen positive results using a neurofeedback protocol that indirectly targets the limbic system, specifically the chronic hyperarousal in the amygdala that she cites as the epicenter of developmental trauma. Although it isn't possible to work directly with electrical activity from the amygdala because this structure is too deep in the brain to monitor its electrical activity on the scalp, Fisher reported that she uses a protocol to reach a site higher in the brain that targets electrical patterns in the dorsal anterior cingulate cortex (DACC), a region that research shows is part of the "social pain" circuit (Eisenberger et al., 2006; Eisenberger, 2011). The DACC has two-way connections to the amygdala and can modulate the amygdala–periaqueductal gray (PAG) defense system from above in a way that decreases the tendency to shift into the midbrain defense system, losing top-down modulation (Mobbs et al., 2009). Based on this anatomy, it makes sense that neurofeedback affecting this DACC–amygdala–PAG circuitry could be beneficial in helping calm the self-defense system. Further research looking into the efficacy of neurofeedback as an adjunct to relational work in the treatment of developmental trauma and blocked trust would be very helpful. It is worth noting that a Boston treatment program headed by Bessel van der Kolk (2014) reported helpful results from the use of Fisher's neurofeedback protocol.

Newer Processes Showing Promise

Auditory Stimulation: Targeting the Smart Vagal System

Stephen Porges (2011), whose work on the polyvagal system has been so helpful to our development of a brain-based model of blocked trust and attachment-focused treatment, spent many years experimenting with an intervention using music. His goal is to activate the social engagement system by enhancing vagal tone, based on the knowledge that the upper vagal system is tied to the use of the smile muscles in the face, the listening "muscle" in the inner ear, and the vocal apparatus used to produce prosody. Most of Porges's research with this method has been with children on the autism spectrum, but he speculates that a similar process might be helpful for children with developmental trauma and environmentally induced disengagement. With some children with autism, Porges found that the engineered sound that exaggerates certain aspects of the auditory properties of a singer's vocalizations triggered the social engagement system and enabled the children to be more socially engaged for a while. Videos of some of these sessions show remarkable "awakenings" of the social engagement process in children who moments before were disengaged and self-stimulating. As Porges explains, this line of research has not led yet to an appropriate clinical use of this form of auditory stimulation but is rife with possible applications to attachment-based treatment. Other approaches using auditory processing to promote affective shifts are in clinical use; therapists using some of these systems report anecdotal improvements in social engagement.

Oxytocin Priming

Research looking at the neurobiology of parenting shows that oxytocin functions primarily to prime the bonding process between parents and children, and this priming effect is followed by a more dopamine-based learning process that strengthens the parent–child relationship in an ongoing way (Fleming et al., 2008; Feldman, Gordon, and Zagoory-Sharon, 2011). An international body of research on the experimental use of inhaled oxytocin to prime social engagement and promote trust now includes studies with parents as well as adults on the autism spectrum and adult partners involved in couple therapy (Bartz, and Hollander, 2006; Ditzen et al., 2009; Bartz et al., 2011). Most of these studies showed that this oxytocin priming, though short-lasting, enhances trust, improves mentalizing or mindsight abilities, and increases empathy (Domes et al., 2007). In terms of the mechanism in the brain for these effects, neuroimaging studies have shown that inhaling oxytocin can decrease activity in the amygdala and increase activity in brain regions known to be involved in social engagement. While the research on oxytocin priming has not yet led to the development of a method for promoting sustained oxytocin production in people like maltreated children, who are likely to have suppressed oxytocin functioning, this fast-growing body of research is tantalizing in its implications for use in attachment-focused treatment.

Recent studies include giving oxytocin to fathers, who then show more sensitive interactions with their young children than did the control group of dads. It is especially intriguing that inhaled oxytocin shifts brain activity in the very regions we have highlighted in this book as needing intervention in attachment-focused treatment. At the very least, it behooves mental health professionals and caregivers to stay abreast of this line of research to see if it leads to a safe method for boosting this key chemical system in caregivers and children as a way to strengthen the impact of relational processes in attachment-focused treatment.

Brainspotting

Another process that appears to be useful for helping people process troubling memories is called brainspotting, a process developed by David Grand (2013) that involves using light to target different areas of the retina at the back of the eye while the person keeps the troubling memory or thought "in mind." Since retinal cells are brain cells and send their output directly to the superior colliculus, the thalamus, and then the amygdala, brainspotting may be a way to rapidly change firing patterns in the amygdala, the target region for trauma-focused treatment. By gaining such rapid access via the retinal cell output, it makes sense that extremely rapid, "poof-like" changes in arousal and subjective distress could occur, as clinicians familiar with the use of this process report. Here again, then, is a process that seemingly can reach the amygdala very quickly, bypassing the slower, higher routes to this region, to bring about very rapid downshifting of the hyperarousal that is often the bane of most top-down approaches to psychotherapy with traumatized clients.

Opioid Antagonists as Adjunctive Medication

In trauma-focused treatment with adults, there is currently a line of experimental clinical research involving the use of opioid blockers such as naltrexone and naloxone, prior to adult therapy sessions, to help reduce dissociation and enable the client to have more access to feelings when processing traumatic material (see Lanius, Paulsen, and Corrigan, 2014, for an excellent review). Although this adjunctive use of these medicines to facilitate the therapeutic process is strictly experimental, the potential for using low doses of opioid blockers in the treatment of developmental trauma is intriguing given the large body of evidence that opioids play a key role in dissociation and emotional numbing. As we explained earlier, one of the core processes of attachment-focused therapy and DDP is to help the child with blocked trust regain the ability to feel his feelings—both feelings of separation pain and feelings of joyful connection with others. Knowing that opioids are involved in the neurobiology of comfort and joy makes the experimental research on the use of low dose opioid antagonists such as Naltrexone very much worth following.

We see attachment-focused treatment as a set of brain-based processes aimed at changing the minds of mistrusting children in ways that enable them to feel safe in the care of trustworthy caregivers. Whereas we see relational and emotion-focused processes (primarily involving right brain–to–right brain interactions between adults and children) as the core of treatment, there is clearly a need for an integrative approach to a brain-informed model of treatment that can include all processes that target the brains of children and caregivers in ways that help promote safe engagement and the strengthening of bonds between caregivers and their children. Ultimately, a robust combination of interpersonal (attachment-based) and intrapersonal (affective/emotional, somatosensory, and reflective/cognitive) processes will empower our efforts to treat these complicated children who so need and deserve all the help we can learn to give them.

References

Akaro, A., Huber, R., & Panksepp, J. (2007). Behavioral functions of the mesolimbic dopaminergic system: An affective neuroethological perspective. *Brain Research Reviews, 56*(2), 283–321.

Allman, J. M., Tetreault, N. A., Hakeem, A. Y., & Park, S. (2011). The von Economo neurons in apes and humans. *American Journal of Human Biology, 23*, 5–21.

Alper, J., & Howe, D. (2015). *Assessing adoptive and foster parents.* London: JP Kingsley.

Atkinson, L., Goldberg, S., Raval, V., Pederson, D., Benoit, D., Gleason, K., . . . Leung, E. (2005). On the relation between maternal state of mind and sensitivity in the prediction of infant attachment security. *Developmental Psychology, 41*, 42–53.

Barr, C. S., Schwandt, M. L., Lindell, S. G., Higley, J. D., Maestripieri, D., Goldman, D., . . . Heilig, M. (2008). Variation at the mu-opioid receptor gene (OPRM) influences attachment behavior in infant primates. *Proceedings of the National Academy of Sciences, USA, 105*, 5277–5281.

Barr, G. A., Moriceau, S., Shionoya, K., Muzny, K., Gao, P.,

Wang, S., & Sullivan, R. M. (2009). Transitions in infant learning are modulated by dopamine in the amygdala. *Nature Neuroscience, 12*, 1367–1369.

Bartz, J. A., & Hollander, E. (2006). The neuroscience of affiliation: Forging links between basic and clinical research on neuropeptides and social behavior. *Hormones and Behavior, 50*, 518–528.

Bartz, J. A., Zaki, J., Bolger, N., & Ochsner, N. (2011). Social effects of oxytocin in humans: Context and person matter. *Trends in Cognitive Sciences, 15*(7), 301–309. doi:10.1016/j.tics.2011.05.002

Baylin, S. B., & Ohm, J. E. (2006). Epigenetic gene silencing in cancer—A mechanism for early oncogenic pathway addiction? *Nature Reviews Cancer, 6*, 107–116.

Beach, S. R. H., Brody, G. H., Todorov, A. A., Gunter, T. D., & Philibert, R. A. (2010). Methylation at SLC6A4 is linked to family history of child abuse: An examination of the Iowa adoptee sample. *American Journal of Medical Genetics Part B, 153B*, 710–713.

Beebe, B., Jaffe, J., Markese, S., Buck, K., Chen, H., Cohen, P., . . . Feldstein, S. (2010). The origins of 12-month attachment: A microanalysis of 4-month mother-infant interaction. *Attachment and Human Development, 12*(1–2), 3–141. doi:10.1080/1461673090 3338985

Belsky, J. (2005). Differential susceptibility to rearing influence. In B. J. Ellis & D. F. Bjorklund (Eds.), *Origins of the social mind: Evolutionary psychology and child development* (pp. 139–163). New York, NY: Guilford Press.

Belsky, J. (2013). Perspective 1: Why would natural selection craft an organism whose future functioning is influenced by its earlier experience? In D. Narvaez, J. Panksepp, A. N. Schore, & T. R. Gleason (Eds.), *Evolution, early experience, and human development: From research to practice and policy* (pp. 397–403). New York, NY: Oxford University Press.

Benes, F. M. (1998). Brain development, VII. Human brain growth spans decades. *American Journal of Psychiatry, 155*(11), 1489.

Bernard, K., Dozier, M., Bick, J., Lewis-Morrarty, E., Lindhiem,

O., & Carlson, E. (2012). Enhancing attachment organization among maltreated children: results of a randomized trial. *Child Development, 83*, 623–636.

Berridge, K. C., & Kringelbach, M. L. (2008). Affective neuroscience of pleasure: Reward in humans and animals. *Psychopharmacology, 199*, 457–480. doi:10.1007/s00213-008-1099-6

Bowlby, J. (1982). *Attachment and loss* (2nd ed., Vol. 1). New York, NY: Basic Books. (Original work published 1969)

Branchi, I., Francia, N., & Alleva, E. (2004). Epigenetic control of neurobehavioral plasticity: The role of neurotrophins. *Behavioural Pharmacology, 15*, 353–362.

Braun, K., Lange, E., Metzger, M., & Poeggel, G. (2000). Maternal separation followed by early social deprivation affects the development of monoaminergic fiber systems in the medial prefrontal cortex of Octodon degus. *Neuroscience, 95*, 309–318.

Braver, T. S., Barch, D. M., Gray, J. R., Molfese, D. L., & Snyder, A. (2001). Anterior cingulate cortex and response conflict: Effects of frequency, inhibition and errors. *Cerebral Cortex, 11*, 825–836.

Brewer, J. A., Worhunsky, P. D., Gray, J. R., Tang, Y. Y., Weber, J., & Kober, H. (2011). Meditation experience is associated with differences in default mode network activity and connectivity. *Proceedings of the National Academy of Sciences, USA, 108*, 20254–20259.

Bridges, R. (Ed.). (2008). *Neurobiology of the parental brain*. San Diego, CA: Academic Press.

Broyd, S. J., Demanuele, C., Debener, S., Helps, S. K., James, C. J., & Sonuga-Barke, E. J. S. (2009). Default-mode brain dysfunction in mental disorders: A systematic review. *Neuroscience Biobehavioral Review, 33*, 279–296. doi: 10.1016/j.neubiorev.2008.09.002

Bush, G., Luu, P., & Posner, M. I. (2000). Cognitive and emotional influences in anterior cingulate cortex. *Trends in Cognitive Sciences, 4*, 215–222.

Cahn, B., & Polich, J. (2006). Meditation states and traits: EEG, ERP, and neuroimaging studies. *Psychological Bulletin, 132*(2), 180–211.

Caldji, C., Diorio, J., & Meaney, M. J. (2003). Variations in maternal care alter GABA-A receptor subunit expression in brain regions associated with fear. *Neuropsychopharmacology, 28,* 150–159.

Callaghan, B. L., Sullivan, R. M., Howell, B., & Tottenham, N. (2014). The international society for developmental psychobiology sackler symposium: Early adversity and the maturation of emotion circuits—a cross-species analysis. *Developmental Psychobiology, 56*(8), 1635–1650. doi:10.1002/dev.21260

Carter, C. S., & Porges, S. W. (2013). Neurobiology of the evolution of mammalian social behavior. In D. Narvaez, J. Panksepp, A. N. Schore, & T. R. Gleason (Eds.), *Evolution, early experience, and human development: From research to practice and policy* (pp. 132–151). New York, NY: Oxford University Press.

Cassidy, J., & Shaver, P.R. (Eds.). (2008). *Handbook of attachment: Theory, research, and clinical applications* (2nd ed.). New York, NY: Guilford Press.

Champagne, F. A., & Curley, J. P. (2011). Epigenetic influence of the social environment. In A. Petronis & J. Mill (Eds.), *Brain, behavior and epigenetics (Epigenetics and human health)* (pp. 185–208). Berlin: Springer.

Chen, E., & Miller, G. E. (2012). "Shift-and-Persist" strategies: why being low in socioeconomic status isn't always bad for health. *Perspectives in Psychological Science, 7,* 135–158.

Chen, E., Miller, G. E., Lachman, M. E., Gruenewald, T. L., & Seeman, T. E. (2012). Protective factors for adults from low-childhood socioeconomic circumstances: The benefits of shift-and-persist for allostatic load. *Psychosomatic Medicine, 74,* 178–186.

Chiron, C., Jambaque, I., Nabbout, R., Lounes, R., Syrota, A., & Dulac, O. (1997). The right brain hemisphere is dominant in human infants. *Brain, 120,* 1057–1065. doi:10.1093/brain/120.6.1057

Christianson, J. P., Benison, A. M., Jennings, J., Sandsmark, E. K., Amat, J., Kaufman, R. D., . . . Maier, S. F. (2008). The sensory insular cortex mediates the stress-buffering effects of safety signals but not behavioral control. *Journal of Neuroscience, 28,* 13703–13711.

Chugani, H., Behen, M., Muziko, O., Juhasz, C., Nagy, F., & Chugani, D. (2001). Local brain functional activity following deprivation: A study of post-institutionalized Romanian orphans. *NeuroImage, 14,* 1290–1301.

Cicchetti, D., Rogosch, F. A., & Toth, S. L. (2006). Fostering secure attachments in infants in maltreating families through preventive interventions. *Development and Psychopathology, 18,* 623–649. doi:10.1017/S09545794060329

Coan, J. A., Schaefer, H. S., & Davidson, R. J. (2006). Lending a hand: social regulation of the neural response to threat. *Psychological Science, 17,* 1032–1039.

Conrad, C. (Ed.). (2011). *The handbook of stress: Neuropsychological effects on the brain.* Oxford, UK: Wiley-Blackwell.

Corrigan, F. M. (2014). Threat and safety: the neurobiology of active and passive defense responses. In U. F. Lanius, S. L. Paulsen, & F. M. Corrigan (Eds.), *Neurobiology and treatment of traumatic dissociation* (pp. 29–50). New York, NY: Springer.

Cozolino, L. (2016). *Why therapy works: Using our minds to change our brains.* New York, NY: Norton.

Craig, A. D. (2009). How do you feel now? The anterior insula and human awareness. *Nature Reviews Neuroscience, 10,* 59–70.

Craig, A.D. (2003). A new view of pain as a homeostatic emotion. Trends in Neurosciences, 26(6), 303–307.

Craig, A. D. (2011). Significance of the insula for the evolution of human awareness of feelings from the body. *Annals of the New York Academy of Sciences, 1225,* 72–82. doi:10.1111/j.1749- 6632.2011.05 990.x

Curley, J. P., Davidson, S., Bateson, P. and Champagne, F.A., (2009). Social enrichment during postnatal development induces transgenerational effects on emotional and reproductive behavior in mice. *Frontiers in Behavioral Neuroscience,* 3: 25. doi:10.3389/ neuro.08.025.2009.

Curley, J. P. (2011). The mu-opioid receptor and the evolution of mother-infant attachment: Theoretical comment on Higham et al. (2011). *Behavioral Neuroscience, 125,* 273–278. doi:10.1037/a0022939

Cushing, B. S., & Kramer, K. M. (2005). Mechanisms underlying epigenetic effects of early social experience: The role of neuropeptides and steroids. *Neuroscience and Biobehavioral Reviews, 29,* 1089–1105.

Daniels, J. K, McFarlane, A. C., Bluhm, R. L., Moores, K. A., Clark, R., Shaw, M. E., . . . Lanius, R. A. (2010). Switching between executive and default mode networks in posttraumatic stress disorder: Alterations in functional connectivity. *Journal of Psychiatry and Neuroscience, 35*(4), 258–266.

Davidson, R. J., & McEwen, B. (2013). Social influences on neuroplasticity: Stress and interventions to promote well-being. *Nature Neuroscience, 15*(5), 689–695. doi:10.1038/nn.3093

De Bellis, M. D. (2005a). Medication considerations with maltreated children. In P. F. Talley (Ed.), *Handbook for the treatment of abused and neglected children* (pp. 423–463). New York, NY: Haworth Press.

De Bellis, M. D. (2005b). The psychobiology of neglect. *Child Maltreatment, 10,* 150–172.

Decety, J., Michalska, K. J., & Kinzler, K. D. (2012). The contribution of emotion and cognition to moral sensitivity: A neurodevelopmental study. *Cerebral Cortex, 22,* 209–220.

deHaan, M., & Gunnar, M. (Eds.). (2009). *Handbook of developmental social neuroscience.* New York, NY: Guilford Press.

deHaan, M., & Matheson, A. (2009). The development and neural basis of processing emotion in faces and voices. In M. deHaan & M. Gunnar (Eds.), *Handbook of Developmental Social Neuroscience* (pp. 107–121). New York, NY: Guilford Press.

Ditzen, B., Schaer, M., Gabriel, B., Bodenmann, G., Ulrike, E., & Markus, H. (2009). Intranasal oxytocin increases positive communication and reduces cortisol levels during couple conflict. *Biological Psychiatry, 65,* 728–731.

Domes, G., Heinrichs, M., Berger, C., & Herpertz, S. C. (2007).

Oxytocin improves "mind-reading" in humans. *Biological Psychiatry, 61*, 731–733.

Domes, G., Heinrichs, M., Glascher, J., Buchel, C., Braus, D. F., & Herpetz, S. C. (2007). Oxytocin attenuates amygdala responses to emotional faces regardless of valence. *Biological Psychiatry, 10*, 1187–1190.

Dozier, M., Meade, E., & Bernard, K. (2014). Attachment and biobehavioral catch-up: An intervention for parents at risk of mal-treating their infants and toddlers. In S. Timmer & A. Urquiza (Eds.), *Evidence-based approaches for the treatment of maltreated children* (pp. 43–60). New York, NY: Springer.

Dumas, G., Nadel, J., Soussignan, R., Martinerie, J., & Garnero, L. (2010). Inter-brain synchronization during social interaction. *Plos One, 5*(8), e12166. doi:10.1371/journal.pone.0012166

Eisenberger, N. I. (2011). Why rejection hurts: What social neuroscience has revealed about the brain's response to social rejection. In J. Decety & J. Cacioppo (Eds.), *The handbook of social neuroscience* (pp. 586–598). New York, NY: Oxford University Press.

Eisenberger, N. I. (2012). Broken hearts and broken bones: A neural perspective on the similarities between social and physical pain. *Current Directions in Psychological Science, 21*(1), 42–47.

Eisenberger, N. I., Jarcho, J. M., Lieberman, M. D., & Naliboff, B. D. (2006). An experimental study of shared sensitivity to physical pain and social rejection. *Pain, 126*, 132–138.

Eisenberger, N. I., & Lieberman, M. D. (2004). Why rejection hurts: The neurocognitive overlap between physical and social pain. *Trends in Cognitive Sciences, 8*, 294–300.

Eisenberger, N. I., Lieberman, M. D., & Williams, K. D. (2003). Does rejection hurt: An fMRI study of social exclusion. *Science, 302*, 290–292.

Eisenberger, N. I., Master, S. L., Inagaki, T. I., Taylor, S. E., Shirinyan, D., Lieberman, M. D., & Naliboff, B. (2011). Attachment figures activate a safety signal-related neural region and reduce pain experience. *Proceedings of the National Academy of Sciences, USA, 108*, 11721–11726.

Eluvathingal, T., Chugani, H., Behen, M., Juhasz, C., Muzik, O., Maqbool, M., . . . Makki, M. (2006). Abnormal brain connectivity in children after severe socioemotional deprivation: A diffusion tensor imaging study. *Pediatrics, 117*(6), 2093–2100.

Feldman, R., Gordon, I., Schneiderman, I., Weisman, O., & Zagoory-Sharon, O. (2010). Natural variations in maternal and paternal care are associated with systematic changes in oxytocin following parent–infant contact. *Psychoneuroendocrinology, 35*, 1133–1141.

Feldman, R., Gordon, I., & Zagoory-Sharon, O. (2011). Maternal and paternal plasma, salivary, and urinary oxytocin and parent-infant synchrony: Considering stress and affiliation components of human bonding. *Developmental Science, 14*, 752–761.

Feldman, R., Greenbaum, C., & Yirmiya, N. (1999). Mother–infant affect synchrony as an antecedent of the emergence of self-control. *Developmental Psychology, 35*, 223–231.

Field, C. B., Johnston, K., Gati, J. S., Menon, R. S., & Everling, S. (2008). Connectivity of the primate superior colliculus mapped by concurrent microstimulation and event-related FMRI. *Plos One, 3*(12), e3928.

Field, T., Diego, M., & Hernandez-Reif, M. (2010). Preterm infant massage therapy research: a review. *Infant Behavioral Development, 33*(2), 115–124. doi:10.10/j.infbeh.2009.12.004

Fisher, S. (2014). *Neurofeedback in the treatment of developmental trauma: Calming the fear-driven brain.* New York, NY: Norton.

Fleming, A. S., Gonazalez, A., Afonso, V., & Lovic, V. (2008). Plasticity in the maternal neural circuit: Experience, dopamine and mothering. In R. Bridges (Ed.), *Neurobiology of the parental brain* (pp. 519–536). San Diego, CA: Academic Press.

Fleming, A.S., & Li, M. (2002). Psychobiology of maternal behavior and its early determinants in nonhuman mammals. In M. Bornstein (Ed.), *Handbook of parenting* (Vol. 2, pp. 61–97). Mahwah, NJ: Erlbaum.

Fosha, D. (2000). *The transforming power of affect.* New York, NY: Basic Books.

Gee, D. G., Gabard-Durnam, L. J., Flannery, J., Goff, B., Humphreys, K. L., Telzer, E. H., . . . Tottenham, N. (2013). Early developmental emergence of human amygdala-prefrontal connectivity after maternal deprivation. *Proceedings of the National Academy of Sciences, USA, 110,* 15638–15643. doi:10.1073/pnas.1307893110

Gee, D. G., Gabard-Durnam, L., Telzer, E. H., Humphreys, L., Goff, B., Shapiro, M., . . . Tottenham, N. (2014). Maternal buffering of human amygdala-prefrontal circuitry during childhood but not during adolescence. *Psychological Science, 25*(11), 2067–2078. doi:10.1177/0956797614550878

Gimpl, G., & Fahrenholz, F. (2001). The oxytocin receptor system: Structure, function, and regulation. *Physiological Reviews, 81,* 629–683.

Golding, K., & Hughes, D. (2012). *Creating loving attachments: Parenting with PACE to nurture confidence and security in the troubled child.* London: Jessica Kingsley.

Grand, D. (2013). *Brainspotting: the revolutionary new therapy for rapid and effective change.* Boulder, CO: Sounds True.

Graves, F. C., Wallen, K., & Maestripieri, D. (2002). Opioids and attachment in rhesus macaque abusive mothers. *Behavioral Neuroscience, 116,* 489–493.

Guastella, A. J., Mitchell, P. B., & Dadds, M. R. (2008). Oxytocin increases gaze to the eye region of human faces. *Biological Psychiatry, 63,* 3–5.

Guastella, A. J., Mitchell, P. B., & Matthews, F. (2008). Oxytocin enhances the encoding of positive social memories in humans. *Biological Psychiatry, 64,* 256–258.

Hofer, M. A. (1994). Early relationships as regulators of infant physiology and behavior. *Acta Paediatrica, 83,* 9–18. doi:10.1111/j.1651-2227.1994.tb13260.x

Hofer, M. A. (1995). Hidden regulators: Implications for a new understanding of attachment, separation, and loss. In S. Goldberg, R. Muir, & J. Kerr (Eds.), *Attachment theory: Social, developmental, and clinical perspectives* (pp. 203–230). Hillsdale, NJ: Analytic Press.

Hostinar, C. E., Sullivan, R. M., & Gunnar, M. R. (2014). Psychobiological mechanisms underlying the social buffering of the hypothalamic-pituitary-adrenocortical axis: A review of animal models and human studies across development. *Psychological Bulletin, 140,* 256–282. doi:10.1037/a003267

Hughes, D. (2006). *Building the bonds of attachment* (2nd ed.). Lanham, MD: Jason Aronson.

Hughes, D. (2007). *Attachment-focused family therapy.* New York, NY: Norton.

Hughes, D. (2011). *Attachment-focused family therapy workbook.* New York, NY: Norton.

Hughes, D. (2013). Intersubjective mindfulness: Facilitating mindfulness in the abused and neglected child through the mindfulness of the therapist and parent. In D. Siegel & M. Solomon (Eds.), *Healing moments in psychotherapy* (pp. 17–34). New York, NY: Norton.

Hughes, D., & Baylin, J. (2012). *Brain-based parenting: The neuroscience of caregiving for healthy attachment.* New York, NY: Norton.

Humphreys, K. L., McGoran, L., Sheridan, M. A., McLaughlin, K. A., Fox, N. A., Nelson, C. A., & Zeanah, C. H. (2015). High-quality foster care mitigates callous-unemotional traits following early deprivation in boys: A randomized controlled trial. *Journal of the American Academy of Child and Adolescent Psychiatry, 54,* 977–983.

Hurley, C. M. (2012). Do you see what I see? Learning to detect micro expressions of emotion. *Motivation and Emotion, 26,* 371–381.

Insel, T. R., & Young, L. J. (2001). The neurobiology of attachment. *Nature Reviews Neuroscience, 2*(2), 129–136.

Johnson, S. (2004). *The practice of emotionally focused couple therapy.* New York, NY: Brunner-Rutledge.

Johnston, K., Levin, H. M., Koval, M. J., & Everling, S. (2006). Top-down control-signal dynamics in anterior cingulate and prefrontal cortex neurons following task switching. *Neuron, 53,* 453–462.

Kagan, J. (1994). *Galen's prophecy: Temperament in human nature.* New York, NY: Basic Books.

Kalin, N. H., Shelton, S. E., & Lynn, D. E. (1995). Opiate systems in mother and infant primates coordinate intimate contact during reunion. *Psychoneuroendocrinology, 20,* 735–742.

Kanneman, D. (2011). *Thinking, fast and slow*. New York, NY: Farrar, Strauss, and Giroux.

Kim, J.H., Hamlin, A.S., Richardson, R. (2009). Fear extinction across development: the involvement of the medial prefrontal cortex as assessed by temporary inactivation and immunohistochemistry. *Journal of Neuroscience, 29,* 10802–10808.

Lanius, U. F. (2014). Attachment, neuropeptides, and autonomic regulation: A vagal shift hypothesis. In U. F. Lanius, S. L. Paulsen, & F. M. Corrigan (Eds.). *Neurobiology and treatment of traumatic dissociation* (pp. 105–130). New York, NY: Springer.

Lanius, U. F., Paulsen, S. L., & Corrigan, F. M. (Eds.). (2014). *Neurobiology and treatment of traumatic dissociation*. New York, NY: Springer.

LaPrarie, J. L., & Murphy, A. Z. (2009). Neonatal injury alters adult pain sensitivity by increasing opioid tone in the periaqueductal gray. *Frontiers in Behavioral Neuroscience, 3,* 1–11. doi:10.3389/neuro.08.031.2009

Liddell, B. J., Brown, K. L., Kemp, A. H., Barton, M. J., Das, P., Peduto, A. S., . . . Williams, L. M. (2005). A direct brainstem-amygdala-cortical "alarm" system for subliminal signals of fear. *NeuroImage, 24,* 235–243.

Lieberman, M. D. (2013). *Social: Why our brains are wired to connect*. New York, NY: Crown.

Lillas, C. & Turnbull, J. (2009). *Infant/child mental health, early intervention, and relationship-based therapies: a neurorelational framework for interdisciplinary practice*. New York, NY: Norton.

Linehan, M. (1993). *Cognitive-behavioral treatment of borderline personality disorder*. New York, NY: Guilford Press.

Masten, C. L., Morelli, S. A., & Eisenberger, N. I. (2011). An fMRI investigation of empathy for "social pain" and subsequent prosocial behavior. *NeuroImage, 55,* 381–388.

Mayes, L., Magidson, J., Lejuez, C., & Nicholls, S. (2009). Social relationships as primary rewards: The neurobiology of attachment. In M. deHaan & M. Gunnar (Eds.), *Handbook of developmental social neuroscience* (pp. 342–376). New York, NY: Guilford Press.

McEwen, B., & Morrison, J. (2013). Brain on stress: Vulnerability and plasticity of the prefrontal cortex over the life course. *Neuron, 79*, 16–29. doi:10.1016/j.neuron.2013.06.028

Meaney, M. J. (2013). Epigenetics and the environmental regulation of the genome and its function. In D. Narvaez, J. Panksepp, A. N. Schore, & T. R. Gleason (Eds.), *Evolution, early experience, and human development: From research to practice and policy* (pp. 99–128). New York, NY: Oxford University Press.

Mills, D., & Conboy, B. T. (2009). Early communicative development and the social brain. In M. De Haan & M. R. Gunnar (Eds.), *Handbook of developmental social neuroscience* (pp. 175–206). New York, NY: Guilford Press.

Mitchell, J. P., Banaji, M. R., & Macrae, C. N., 2005. The link between social cognition and self-referential thought in the medial prefrontal cortex. *Journal of Cognitive Neuroscience, 17*, 1306–1315.

Mobbs, D., Petrovic, P., Marchant, J. L., Hassabis, D., Weiskopf, N., Seymour, B., . . . Frith, C. D. (2009). When fear is near: Threat imminence elicits prefrontal-periaquaductal gray shifts in humans. *Science, 317*, 1079–1083.

Moretti, M. M., Obsuth, I., Craig, S. G., & Bartolo, T. (2015). An attachment-based intervention for parents of adolescents at risk: Mechanisms of change. *Attachment & Human Development, 17*(2), 119–135. doi:10.1080/14616734.2015.1006383

Moriceau, S., Shionoya, K., Jakubs, K., & Sullivan, R. M. (2009). Early-life stress disrupts attachment learning: The role of amygdala corticosterone, locus ceruleus corticotropin releasing hormone, and olfactory bulb norepinephrine. *Journal of Neuroscience, 29*, 15745–15755.

Morris, R. (2007). Theories of hippocampal function. In P. Andersen, R. Morris, D. Amaral, T. Bliss, & J. O'Keefe (Eds.), *The hippocampus book* (pp. 581–714). New York, NY: Oxford University Press.

Nader, K., Schafe, G. E., & LeDoux, J. (2000). Fear memories require protein synthesis in the amygdala for reconsolidation after retrieval. *Nature, 406*, 722–726.

National Scientific Council on the Developing Child. (2009). *Excessive stress disrupts the architecture of the developing brain* (Working Paper No. 3). Cambridge, MA: Center on the Developing Child, Harvard University.

Neuman, I. D. (2008). Brain oxytocin: A key regulator of emotional and social behaviors in both females and males. *Journal of Neuroendocrinology, 20*, 858–865.

Noriuchi, M., KiKuchi, Y., & Senoo, A. (2008). The functional neuroanatomy of maternal love: Mother's response to attachment behaviors. *Biological Psychiatry, 63*, 415–423.

Ochsner, K. N., Knierim, K., Ludlow, D. H., Hanelin, J., Ramachanran, T., Glover, G., & Mackey, S. C. (2004). Reflecting upon feelings: An fMRI study of neural systems supporting the attribution of emotion to self and other. *Journal of Cognitive Neuroscience, 16*, 1746–1772.

Öhman, A. (2009). Human fear conditioning and the amygdala. In P. J. Whalen & E. A. Phelps (Eds.), *The human amygdala* (pp. 118–154). New York, NY: Guilford Press.

Oler, J. A., Quirk, G. J., & Whalen, P. J. (2009). CinguloAmygdala interactions in surprise and extinction: Interpreting associative ambiguity. In B. A. Vogt (Ed.), *Cingulate neurobiology and disease* (pp. 207–218). New York, NY: Oxford University Press.

Osborne, N. (2010). Music for children in zones of conflict and post-conflict: A psychobiological approach. In S. Malloch & C. Trevarthen (Eds.), *Communicative musicality: Exploring the basis of human companionship* (pp. 329–356). Oxford, UK: Oxford University Press.

Panksepp, J. (1998). *Affective neuroscience.* New York, NY: Oxford University Press.

Panksepp, J. (2003). Feeling the pain of social loss. *Science, 302*, 237–239.

Panksepp, J. (2013). How primary-process emotional systems guide child development: Ancestral regulators of human happiness, thriving, and suffering. In D. Narvaez, J. Panksepp, A. N. Schore, & T. R. Gleason (Eds.), *Evolution, early experience, and human development: From research to practice and policy* (pp. 74–94). New York, NY: Oxford University Press.

Panksepp, J., Herman, B., Conner, R., Bishop, P., & Scott, J. P.

(1978). The biology of social attachments: Opiates alleviate separation distress. *Biological Psychiatry, 13*, 607–618.

Panksepp, J. & Trevarthen, C. (2009). The neuroscience of emotion in music. In S. Malloch and C. Trevarthen (Eds.), *Communicative Musicality: Exploring the basis of human companionship*, pp. 105–146. Oxford, UK: Oxford University Press.

Perry, B. D. (1997). Incubated in terror: Neurodevelopmental factors in the "cycle of violence." In J. Osofsky (Ed.), *Children in a violent society* (pp. 124–148). New York, NY: Guilford Press.

Perry, B. D., Pollard, R., Blakely, T., Baker, W., & Vigilante, D. (1995). Childhood trauma, the neurobiology of adaptation and "use-dependent" development of the brain: How "states" become "traits." *Infant Mental Health Journal, 16*, 271–291.

Phelps, E. (2009). The human amygdala and the control of fear. In P. J. Whalen & E. A. Phelps (Eds.), *The human amygdala* (pp. 204–219). New York, NY: Guilford Press.

Pollak, S. D. (2003). Experience-dependent affective learning and risk for psychopathology in children. *Annals of the New York Academy of Sciences, 1008*, 102–111.

Porges, S. (2011). *The polyvagal theory: Neurophysiological foundations of emotions, attachment, communication, and self-regulation.* New York, NY: Norton.

Porges, S. & Lewis, G. F. (2009). The polyvagal hypothesis: Common mechanisms mediating autonomic regulation, vocalizations and listening. In S. M. Brudzynski (Ed.), *Handbook of mammalian vocalization: an integrative neuroscience approach* (pp. 255–264). New York, NY: Elsevier.

Posner, M. I., Rothbart, M. K., Sheese, B. E., & Tang, Y. (2007). The anterior cingulate gyrus and the mechanism of self-regulation. *Cognitive, Affective, and Behavioral Neuroscience, 7*(4), 391–395.

Pourtois, G., Vocat, R., N'Diaye, K., Spinelli, L., Seeck, M., & Vuilleumier, P. (2010). Errors recruit both cognitive and emotional monitoring systems: Simultaneous intracranial recordings in the dorsal anterior cingulate gyrus and amygdala combined with fMRI. *Neuropsychologia, 48*, 1144–1159.

Quirk, G. J., Pare, D., Richardson, R., Herry, C., Monfils, M. H., Schiller,D., & Vicentic, A. (2010). Erasing fear memories with extinction training. *Journal of Neuroscience, 30,* 14993–14997. doi:10.1523/JNEUROSCI.4268-10.2010

Raichle, M. E., & Snyder, A. Z. (2007). A default mode of brain function: A brief history of an evolving idea. *NeuroImage, 37,* 1083–1090.

Rizzolatti, G., & Craighero, L. (2004). The mirror-neuron system. *Annual Review of Neuroscience, 27,* 169–192.

Roth, T. L., Levenson, J. M., Sullivan, R. M., & Sweatt, J. D. (2006). Epigenetic marking of the genome by early experiences: Implications for long-lasting effects of early maltreatment on adult cognitive and emotional health. In S. M. Sturt (Ed.), *Child abuse: New research* (pp. 79–114). New York, NY: Nova Science.

Sabatini, M., Ebert, P., Lewis, D., Levitt, P., Cameron, J., & Mirnics, K. (2007). Amygdala gene expression correlates of social behavior in monkeys experiencing maternal separation. *Journal of Neuroscience, 27*(12), 3295–3304.

Sachs, O. (1990). *Awakenings.* New York, NY: Vintage.

Schoenbaum, G., Saddoris, M. P., & Stalnaker, T. A. (2007). Reconciling the roles of orbitofrontal cortex in reversal learning and the encoding of outcome expectancies. *Annals of the New York Academy of Sciences, 1121,* 320–335.

Schore, A. N. (1994). *Affect regulation and the origin of the self: The neurobiology of emotional development.* Hillsdale, NJ: Erlbaum.

Schore, A. N. (2003). *Affect regulation and the repair of the self.* New York, NY: Norton.

Schore, A. N. (2013). Bowlby's "environment of evolutionary adaptedness": Recent studies on the interpersonal neurobiology of attachment and emotional development. In D. Narvaez, J. Panksepp, A. N. Schore, & T. R. Gleason (Eds.), *Evolution, early experience, and human development: From research to practice and policy* (pp. 31–67). New York, NY: Oxford University Press.

Siegel, D. (2012). *The developing mind, second edition: How relationships and the brain interact to shape who we are.* New York, NY: Guilford Press.

Siegel, D. (2013). *Brainstorm: The power and purpose of the teenage brain*. New York, NY: Penguin.

Siegel, D. & Bryson,T. (2011). *The whole-brain child: 12 revolutionary strategies to nurture your child's developing brain*. New York, NY: Delacorte Press.

Siegel, D. J., & Hartzell, M. (2003). *Parenting from the inside out*. New York, NY: Tarcher/Putnam.

Sripada, R. K, Swain, J. E., Evans, G. W., Welsh, R. C., & Liberzon, I. (2014). Childhood poverty and stress reactivity are associated with aberrant functional connectivity in default mode network. *Neuorpsychopharmacology, 39*, 2244–2251.

Steinberg, E. E., Keiflin, R., Boivin, J. R., Witten, I. B., Deisseroth, K., & Janak, P. H. (2013). A causal link between prediction errors, dopamine neurons and learning. *Nature Neuroscience, 16*, 966–973.

Stern, D. (1985). *The interpersonal world of the infant: A view from psychoanalysis and developmental psychology*. New York, NY: Basic Books.

Tang, Y. Y., Lu, Q., Geng, X., Stein, F. A., Yang, Y., & Posner, M. I. (2010). Short-term meditation induces white matter changes in the anterior cingulate. *Proceedings of the National Academy of Sciences, 107*, 15649–15652.

Teicher, M. H., Andersen, S. L., Polcari, A., Anderson, C. M., Navalta, C. P., & Kim, D. M. (2003). The neurobiological consequences of early stress and childhood maltreatment. *Neuroscience Biobehavioral Review, 27*(1-2), 33–44.

Teicher, M. H., Samson, J. A., Polcari, A., & McGreenery, C. E. (2006). Sticks, stones, and hurtful words: relative effects of various forms of childhood maltreatment. *American Journal of Psychiatry, 163*(6), 993–1000.

Timmer, S., & Urquiza, A. (Eds.). (2014). Why we think we can make things better with evidence-based practice: theoretical and developmental context. In S. Timmer and A. Urquiza, (Eds.), *Evidence-based approaches for the treatment of maltreated children: Considering core components of treatment effectiveness* (pp. 19–42). New York, NY: Springer.

Tobler, P. N. (2010). Behavioral functions of dopamine neurons.

In L. Iversen, S. Iversen, S. Dunnett, & A. Bjorklund (Eds.), *Dopamine handbook* (pp. 316–330). Oxford, UK: Oxford University Press.

Tottenham, N. (2012). Human amygdala development in the absence of species-expected caregiving. *Developmental Psychobiology, 54,* 598–611. doi:10.1002/dev.20531

Tottenham, N. (2014). The importance of early experiences for neuro-affective development. *Current Topics in Behavioral Neuroscience, 16,* 109–129. doi:10.1007/7854_2013_254

Tottenham, N., Hare, T. A., & Casey, B. J. (2009). A developmental perspective on human amygdala function. In P. J. Whalen & E. A. Phelps (Eds.), *The human amygdala* (pp. 107–117). New York, NY: Guilford Press.

Tottenham, N., Shapiro, M., Telzer, E. H., & Humphreys, K. L. (2012). Amygdala response to mother. *Developmental Science, 15,* 307–319. doi:10.1111/j1467.2011.01128.x

Trevarthen, C. (2001). Intrinsic motives for companionship in understanding: Their origin, development, and significance for infant mental health. *Infant Mental Health, 22,* 95–131.

Trevarthen, C. (2013). Born for art and the joyful companionship of fiction. In D. Narvaez, J. Panksepp, A. N. Schore, & T. R. Gleason (Eds.), *Evolution, early experience, and human development* (pp. 202–220). New York, NY: Oxford Press.

Tronick, E. (2007). *The neurobehavioral and social–emotional development of infants and children.* New York, NY: Norton.

van der Kolk, B. A. (2014). *The body keeps the score: Brain, mind, and body in the healing of trauma.* New York, NY: Viking.

van IJzendorn, M. (1995). Adult attachment representations, parental responsiveness, and infant attachment. *Psychological Bulletin, 117*(3), 387–403.

Vogt, B. A. (Ed.). (2009). *Cingulate neurobiology and disease.* New York, NY: Oxford University Press.

Vogt, B. A., & Lane, R. D. (2009). Altered processing of valence and significance-coded information in the psychopathic cingulate gyrus. In B. A. Vogt (Ed.), *Cingulate neurobiology and disease* (pp. 571–585). New York, NY: Oxford University Press.

Vogt, B. A., & Sikes, R. W. (2009). Cingulate nociceptive circuitry and roles in pain processing: The cingulate premotor pain model. In B. A. Vogt (Ed.), *Cingulate neurobiology and disease* (pp. 311–338). New York, NY: Oxford University Press.

Vogt, B. A. & Vogt, L. J. (2009). Mu-opioid receptors, placebo map, descending systems, and cingulate-mediated control of vocalization and pain. In B. A. Vogt (Ed.), *Cingulate neurobiology and disease* (pp. 339–364). New York, NY: Oxford University Press.

Way, B. M., Taylor, S. E., & Eisenberger, N. I. (2009). Variation in the mu-opioid receptor gene (OPRM1) is associated with dispositional and neural sensitivity to social rejection. *Proceedings of the National Academy of Sciences, USA, 106,* 15079–15084.

Weaver, I. C. G., Meaney, M. J., & Szyf, M. (2006). Maternal care effects on the hippocampal transcriptome and anxiety-mediated behaviors in the offspring that are reversible in adulthood. *Proceedings of the National Academy of Sciences, USA, 103,* 3480–3485.

Whalen, P. & Phelps, E. (Eds.). (2009). *The human amygdala.* New York, NY: Guilford Press.

Wu, S. D., & Lo, P. C. (2008). Inward-attention meditation increases parasympathetic activity: A study based on heart rate variability. *Biomedical Research, 29,* 245–250.

Yehuda, R. & McEwen, B. (Eds.). (2004). Biobehavioral stress response: protective and damaging effects [Special issue]. *Annals of the New York Academy of Sciences, 1032.*

Zak, P. J. (2012). *The moral molecule: How trust works.* New York, NY: Penguin.

Index

Also available from

THE NORTON SERIES ON INTERPERSONAL NEUROBIOLOGY

The Birth of Intersubjectivity: Psychodynamics, Neurobiology, and the Self
MASSIMO AMMANITI, VITTORIO GALLESE

Neurobiology for Clinical Social Work: Theory and Practice (Second Edition)
JEFFREY S. APPLEGATE, JANET R. SHAPIRO

Mind–Brain–Gene
JOHN B. ARDEN

The Heart of Trauma: Healing the Embodied Brain in the Context of Relationships
BONNIE BADENOCH

Being a Brain-Wise Therapist: A Practical Guide to Interpersonal Neurobiology
BONNIE BADENOCH

The Brain-Savvy Therapist's Workbook
BONNIE BADENOCH

The Neurobiology of Attachment-Focused Therapy
JONATHAN BAYLIN, DANIEL A. HUGHES

Coping with Trauma-Related Dissociation: Skills Training for Patients and Therapists
SUZETTE BOON, KATHY STEELE, AND ONNO VAN DER HART

Neurobiologically Informed Trauma Therapy with Children and Adolescents: Understanding Mechanisms of Change
LINDA CHAPMAN

Intensive Psychotherapy for Persistent Dissociative Processes: The Fear of Feeling Real
RICHARD A. CHEFETZ

Timeless: Nature's Formula for Health and Longevity
LOUIS COZOLINO

The Neuroscience of Human Relationships: Attachment and the Developing Social Brain (Second Edition)
LOUIS COZOLINO

Sex Addiction as Affect Dysregulation: A Neurobiologically Informed
Holistic Treatment
ALEXANDRA KATEHAKIS

The Interpersonal Neurobiology of Play: Brain-Building
Interventions for Emotional Well-Being
THERESA A. KESTLY

Self-Agency in Psychotherapy: Attachment, Autonomy, and Intimacy
JEAN KNOX

Infant/Child Mental Health, Early Intervention, and Relationship-Based
Therapies: A Neurorelational Framework for Interdisciplinary Practice
CONNIE LILLAS, JANIECE TURNBULL

Play and Creativity in Psychotherapy
TERRY MARKS-TARLOW, MARION SOLOMON, DANIEL J. SIEGEL

Clinical Intuition in Psychotherapy: The Neurobiology of Embodied Response
TERRY MARKS-TARLOW

Awakening Clinical Intuition: An Experiential Workbook for Psychotherapists
TERRY MARKS-TARLOW

A Dissociation Model of Borderline Personality Disorder
RUSSELL MEARES

Borderline Personality Disorder and the Conversational Model:
A Clinician's Manual
RUSSELL MEARES

Neurobiology Essentials for Clinicians: What Every Therapist Needs to Know
ARLENE MONTGOMERY

Addiction, Attachment, Trauma, and Recovery
OLIVER J. MORGAN

Borderline Bodies: Affect Regulation Therapy for Personality Disorders
CLARA MUCCI

Neurobiology and the Development of Human Morality:
Evolution, Culture, and Wisdom
DARCIA NARVAEZ

Brain Model & Puzzle: Anatomy & Functional Areas of the Brain
Norton Professional Books

Sensorimotor Psychotherapy: Interventions for Trauma and Attachment
Pat Ogden, Janina Fisher

Trauma and the Body: A Sensorimotor Approach to Psychotherapy
Pat Ogden, Kekuni Minton, Clare Pain

The Archaeology of Mind: Neuroevolutionary Origins of Human Emotions
Jaak Panksepp, Lucy Biven

The Polyvagal Theory: Neurophysiological Foundations of Emotions, Attachment, Communication, and Self-regulation
Stephen W. Porges

The Pocket Guide to Polyvagal Theory: The Transformative Power of Feeling Safe
Stephen W. Porges

Foundational Concepts in Neuroscience: A Brain-Mind Odyssey
David E. Presti

Right Brain Psychotherapy
Allan N. Schore

The Development of the Unconscious Mind
Allan N. Schore

Affect Dysregulation and Disorders of the Self
Allan N. Schore

Affect Regulation and the Repair of the Self
Allan N. Schore

The Science of the Art of Psychotherapy
Allan N. Schore

Mind: A Journey to the Heart of Being Human
Daniel J. Siegel

The Mindful Brain: Reflection and Attunement in the Cultivation of Well-Being
Daniel J. Siegel

The Mindful Therapist: A Clinician's Guide to Mindsight and Neural Integration
DANIEL J. SIEGEL

Pocket Guide to Interpersonal Neurobiology: An Integrative Handbook of the Mind
DANIEL J. SIEGEL

Healing Moments in Psychotherapy
DANIEL J. SIEGEL, MARION SOLOMON

Healing Trauma: Attachment, Mind, Body and Brain
DANIEL J. SIEGEL, MARION SOLOMON

Love and War in Intimate Relationships: Connection, Disconnection, and Mutual Regulation in Couple Therapy
MARION SOLOMON, STAN TATKIN

How People Change: Relationships and Neuroplasticity in Psychotherapy
MARION SOLOMON AND DANIEL J. SIEGEL

The Present Moment in Psychotherapy and Everyday Life
DANIEL N. STERN

The Neurobehavioral and Social-Emotional Development of Infants and Children
ED TRONICK

The Haunted Self: Structural Dissociation and the Treatment of Chronic Traumatization
ONNO VAN DER HART, ELLERT R. S. NIJENHUIS, KATHY STEELE

Prenatal Development and Parents' Lived Experiences: How Early Events Shape Our Psychophysiology and Relationships
ANN DIAMOND WEINSTEIN

Changing Minds in Therapy: Emotion, Attachment, Trauma, and Neurobiology
MARGARET WILKINSON

For all the latest books in the series, book details (including sample chapters), and to order online, please visit the Series webpage at wwnorton.com/Psych/IPNB Series